THE CENSOR MARCHES ON

A Da Capo Press Reprint Series

CIVIL LIBERTIES IN AMERICAN HISTORY

GENERAL EDITOR: LEONARD W. LEVY

Claremont Graduate School

THE CENSOR
MARCHES ON

Recent Milestones in the Administration
of the Obscenity Law in the United States

By Morris L. Ernst and Alexander Lindey

DA CAPO PRESS • NEW YORK • 1971

Library of Congress Cataloging in Publication Data

Ernst, Morris Leopold, 1888-
    The censor marches on; recent.   >Reprint of the 1940 ed
    (Civil liberties in American history)   published by ...
    1. Censorship.   2. Censorship—U.S.
3. Obscenity (Law)   4. Sex in literature.
I. Lindey, Alexander, 1896-   joint author.
II. Title.   III. Series.
KF9444.E75 1971   344'.73'0531   73-164512
ISBN 0-306-70295-9

Published by Da Capo Press, Inc.
A Subsidiary of Plenum Publishing Corporation
227 West 17th Street, New York, New York 10011
                All rights reserved

Printed in the United States of America

THE CENSOR MARCHES ON

THE CENSOR MARCHES ON

Recent Milestones in the Administration of the Obscenity Law in the United States ☆ By MORRIS L. ERNST & ALEXANDER LINDEY

NEW YORK 1940

DOUBLEDAY, DORAN & COMPANY, INC.

PRINTED AT THE *Country Life Press*, GARDEN CITY, N. Y., U. S. A.

". . . *unless warinesse be used, as good almost kill a man as Kill a good Book; who kills a man kills a reasonable creature, God's Image, but he . . . who destroyes a good Booke, kills reason itselfe, kills the Image of God as it were in the eye.*"

MILTON, *Areopagitica* (1644)

Foreword

CENSORSHIP has been a social phenomenon since the dawn of civilization. We shall not attempt to trace its history here. All we propose to do is to give a bird's-eye view of its manifestations during the last few decades. We shall concern ourselves mainly with telling the story of efforts to save society from sex. Taking up in turn literature, sex instruction, birth control, the stage, the movies, the radio, the graphic and plastic arts and nudism, we shall indicate how successful or unsuccessful these efforts have been, and where they have led or are leading us. Although we shall discuss court cases we shall avoid technicalities and speak the layman's language.

It has been our good fortune to have argued many of the important sex censorship cases during the last fifteen years. The victories in these cases and others we shall tell about have been significant not only because they have served to erase the stigma of obscenity from sex education, forthright literature and birth control, but because they have set enlightened precedents and have laid bare the functioning of the censorship process.

It will be noted, however, that in the main the victories have sprung from court decisions, not from the eradication of obsolete, repressive and often vicious laws. The Comstock laws are still on our statute books. The new frontiers of decency which now prevail were set by judicial interpretation, not by legislation. Some of our judges have been wise enough to reject the letter of the law and to carry out its spirit in a way consistent with our ever-changing morality. Their task has been a difficult one. They have been handicapped by dead-letter statutes, their good work has in some instances been nullified by obstructionist tactics on the part of official-dom and more than once they have drawn upon themselves the denunciations of the uplifters.

Freedom of expression, like every human liberty, is never permanently secured but must be rewon each day. The liberalization of the sex code which attended the turn of the century was a revolt against Victorian prudery. The obscenity drives that followed were in effect a counterrevolt, a futile attempt to embalm the conventions of a dead age. But the evolution of morals went forward inexorably, and the liberalization became an accomplished fact. Whether they acknowledge it or not, the Pecksniffs and the Grundys know this; they know, too, that the force behind the anti-sex drive, in the sense of the 1920's, is all but spent.

Yet it would be rash to suppose that sex censorship is dead. It is a menace to be reckoned with because it is one of the first expedients seized upon by an authoritarian government to enslave its citizens, and because it carries with itself the germs of other repressions. The earliest manifestations of censorship under Hitler concerned sex no less than politics. Women were ordered to become breeders of the legions of tomorrow; they were to forswear paint and powder; the doors of the Reich-stag were closed to them. No one familiar with recent attempts in this country to suppress certain kinds of films and plays can doubt that the censors of the future will use sex as a pretext to crush hostile political views, nor that the full battery of tricks and expedients devised to combat obscenity will be wheeled into action anew to smash another target.

Dictatorships of the right and left live by censorship. The United States is the last citadel of democracy capable of defying the rising tide of totalitarianism. So long as its foundations rest on the Bill of Rights, the citadel will stand.

MORRIS L. ERNST
ALEXANDER LINDEY

Contents

THE CENSOR MARCHES ON

CHAPTER I

Sex and Literature

Of the many awful and pathetic cases brought to our attention, perhaps the saddest and most pathetic of all was when a lady in deep mourning called and told of the death-bed confession made by her sister, eighteen years of age, who just before she died told of having received from the mails certain foul matters which had been sent by a procuress in this city for her to read, and which was followed up by her downfall, ruin and death. She told of other girls who had first received similar matters by mail and then had been ruined in the same manner. This mourning sister in speaking of those who had been the cause of the ruin of her younger sister said: "They have diamonds and money but may the curse be upon them!"

ANTHONY COMSTOCK, Vice Society Report (1898)

THERE IS A STORY about a publisher who received the manuscript of a sex novel and was rather worried about it. He decided to play safe and went to his lawyer. The lawyer shook his head. "Give me a set of facts," he said, "and I'll tell you with a fair degree of certainty whether the facts constitute a run-of-the-mill crime. The law of embezzlement, of forgery, of assault, is clear; I can define each offense and give you the elements. But the law of obscenity is something else again. It uses such weasel words as obscene, lewd, lascivious and indecent; it affords no realistic yardstick to measure the illegality of material."

The publisher snorted. "That's a lot of comfort," he said. "Do you mean to say there's no way I can make sure?" The attorney thought awhile, and then said: "Let's go down to the district attorney and put it up to him. He's the prosecuting officer of the county; if the book violates the law, he's the one that 'll have to get after you. Maybe he'll give us an opinion." So they went down to see the district attorney, told their story. The district attorney listened without interest. His job, he said, was to prosecute, not to review books. They somehow persuaded him to take the manuscript, and told him they'd be back in a week. When the week was up, they were in his office again.

The publisher rejoiced to think that his problem was about to be solved. He tapped the manuscript that lay on the district attorney's desk. "It isn't obscene, is it?" he asked cheerily. The district attorney handed him the manuscript. "You go ahead and publish it," he said. "We'll indict you and try you. If the jury convicts you, it's obscene. If it acquits you, it's not obscene."

The Legal Test of Decency

The legal test of obscenity was first laid down in 1868, in the famous English case of *Regina* v. *Hicklin*. There it was said that an obscene book was one which had the tendency "to deprave and corrupt those whose minds were open to immoral influences, and into whose hands the publication might fall."

One does not have to examine hundreds of obscenity cases to realize what a web of generalities is woven into this definition, and how susceptible it is of misapplication and abuse. How is a person depraved? How is he corrupted? Just what is the nature of the morally corrosive process which is intended to be banned? How is it to be ascertained? When is a mind open to immoral influences? What constitutes a non-receptive mind, and who may be presumed to possess one? What if a book is fit for a normal adult, but may conceivably harm a child or a moron? Is it the intent and purport of the law to reduce the reading matter of mature persons to the level of adolescents or idiots?

Let's take a look at some of the cases that have come up in the courts during the last generation, and see if they throw any light on these questions.

MADEMOISELLE DE MAUPIN

Théophile Gautier's *Mademoiselle de Maupin,* back in 1916, gave the first impetus to the drive for the liberalization of the obscenity law as applied to books. Despite its sensuous imagery and erotic episodes, despite the cynical and derisive foreword which made light of virtue, the novel was not an apology for libertinism; it was an indictment of the sterile aestheticism of Gautier's day. It urged the worship of beauty and the rejection of taboos that stood between man and the enjoyment of life. To the moralists of a generation ago, as to the censor of Gautier's time (Gautier lost the wreath of the Academy for writing the book), *Mademoiselle de Maupin* was heresy. Mr Sumner, secretary of the New York Society for the Suppression of Vice, and successor to the mantle of Anthony Comstock, haled bookseller Halsey into court for selling a copy. One magistrate dismissed the complaint, but Mr Sumner found another who was willing to hold Halsey for trial in the Court of Special Sessions. Halsey was acquitted. He then sued the Vice Society for malicious prosecution, and recovered substantial damages. The case was carried to the highest court of the state of New York in 1922, and Halsey's judgment was upheld by a divided court. Judge Andrews wrote the prevailing opinion, in which Judges Cardozo (later Supreme Court Justice), Pound and McLaughlin concurred. Judges Crane and Hogan dissented; Judge Crane blasted the book in a lengthy opinion in the course of which he said: "Oscar Wilde had a great reputation for style, but went to jail just the same. Literary ability is no excuse for degeneracy." At any rate the Vice Society paid Halsey $2500 and interest.

The *Mademoiselle de Maupin* case was important for several reasons. It established the precedent that classics were not to be judged by standards applicable to ordinary works. For generations judges had insisted that the question of obscenity was one for the average man (who was presumed to know what was decent), and that expert testimony was therefore not admissible. While the New York Court of Appeals did not avowedly override this ancient and vulnerable rule in the *Mademoiselle de Maupin* case, by quoting generously from authorities concerning Gautier and his literary reputation the Court, at least by implication, emasculated the long-established interdict. Furthermore, the prosecution had urged that Gautier's book should be condemned because it made light of chastity. The Court made it clear that there was nothing in the law which required literary works to be moral tracts.

The groundwork was laid for the cases that were to follow.

MADELEINE

It is a mystery how the sober house of Harper's ever came to publish *Madeleine,* the anonymous autobiography of a lady of joy. The consequences were curious.

The book was a detailed account of a career of prostitution. It described the workings of brothels, the methods of enticement used, the perversities and extortions practiced. There were passages dealing with drunken orgies, venereal diseases, pregnancies and abortions. At the instance of Mr Sumner, both Harper's and Clinton T. Brainard, its president, were charged with violation of the obscenity law.

The naming of Mr Brainard as a defendant was puzzling. For one thing, it was not the policy of the Vice Society to get after the officers of publishing firms or even the firms themselves; as a rule complaints were filed only against booksellers. For another, Mr Brainard had had nothing to do with *Madeleine*. In accordance with the usual practice at Harper's, the manuscript had been referred to and accepted by a literary conference composed of certain officers and employees of the firm. Mr Brainard had not been a member of the conference; he had had no knowledge of the submission or the approval; indeed, he had been out of the country at the time. And yet he now found himself faced with a criminal charge.

The source of the animus behind the prosecution was soon revealed. It seems that Mr Brainard had been a member of a grand jury that had been investigating Mayor Hylan's administration on charges of political corruption. The action of the grand jury had aroused the displeasure of Mr Hearst, who happened to be championing the mayor just then. The appearance of *Madeleine* was, for reprisal purposes, manna from heaven. The Hearst papers were instructed to make a *cause célèbre* of the case.

Let it be said in justice to Mr Sumner that when he found himself an unwitting party in a private grudge fight, he tried to get out. He said in open court that he would drop the case if Harper's agreed to withdraw the book. The Hearst papers rose up in arms. There were, they said, apparently two obscenity laws: one for the rich and one for the poor. If a poor man sold a dirty book he went to jail; if a rich man did it, he was let off. Mr Sumner was in a quandary. In the face of such righteous clamor he had to go ahead.

Both Harper's and Mr Brainard were convicted in Special Sessions in January 1920. On appeal the convictions were reversed by a divided bench of the Appellate Court. Speaking for the majority, Judge Smith said:

Section 1141 of the Penal Law makes it criminal for a person to have in his possession with intent to sell, lend, or give away, or to show "any obscene, lewd, lascivious, filthy, indecent or disgusting book," and such is the information upon which these defendants have been convicted.

He pointed out that Section 1141 was similar to Section 317 of the Penal Code, of which the Court of Appeals had said that it was "directed against lewd, lascivious and salacious or obscene publications, the tendency of which is to excite lustful or lecherous desire." He went on:

It (i.e., the book) contains the autobiography of a prostitute, but without the recital of any facts which come within the condemnation of the section as thus interpreted. I can see no useful purpose in the publication of the book. I cannot agree that it has any moral lesson to teach.

But the absence of moral content was not enough, the Court ruled, to condemn a publication. The legal test did not concern itself with sermons. Judge Smith concluded:

I venture that no one can read this book and truthfully say that it contains a single word or picture which tends to excite lustful or lecherous desire. Upon an examination of the book I am satisfied that neither defendant has been guilty of the offense charged in the information . . .

There can be little doubt that the Appellate Division was influenced in its decision by the *Mademoiselle de Maupin* case. The old definition of obscenity was dead. The legal frontiers of decency were expanding.

WORDS VERSUS THEME

About eleven years ago Radclyffe Hall's *The Well of Loneliness* appeared inconspicuously in England. It was a long and somewhat tedious novel. Although its theme was Lesbianism, it was not a pioneer in the field. It seemed destined to slip into oblivion. The editor of an obscure English periodical took it upon himself to denounce it. The authorities stepped in; the novel was declared obscene, and all copies were ordered destroyed. When Covici-Friede undertook to publish it in this country, Mr Sumner took the case into court.

The case was significant because the prosecution sought to inject a new principle into the obscenity law. Up to that time only offensive words and expressions had been held criminal; no theme, as such, had been proscribed. Now an attempt was being made to suppress a book simply because it dealt with a questionable subject. An adverse adjudication meant that it would be impossible to discuss a grave social problem in print.

Magistrate Bushel, before whom the hearing was held, was convinced that it tended "to debauch public morals," and that the subject matter of sexual inversion was "offensive to decency." For some inexplicable reason, hypersensitive Boston had made no move against the novel, so at this point it was taboo at one end of the Boston Post Road and legal at the other. The Court of Special Sessions eventually disagreed with Magistrate Bushel, and exonerated the book.

Boston "Cleans Up"

When D. H. Lawrence died, Heywood Broun said: "A first-class writing man is dead, and I can't help feeling that the yapping of the censors had something to do with driving a flaming spirit out of a frail body."

The yapping had been mainly the British censor's doing, but Lawrence's works had found no haven in this country either. Both *The Rainbow* and *Women in Love* had run into trouble; *Lady Chatterley's Lover* met the full fury of the protectors of New England morals.

The general censorship wave that swept Boston in the latter part of 1929 resulted in the memorable wholesale book holocaust. When the wave subsided it was found that something like sixty-eight books by prominent authors had been swept away, among them the following:

Dark Laughter, by Sherwood Anderson
The Wayward Man, by St John Ervine
Blue Voyage, by Conrad Aiken
What I Believe, by Bertrand Russell
Circus Parade, by Jim Tully
Oil, by Upton Sinclair
From Man to Man, by Olive Schreiner
Nigger Heaven, by Carl Van Vechten
Power, by Lion Feuchtwanger
Twilight, by Count Keyserling
Black April, by Julia Peterkin
An American Tragedy, by Theodore Dreiser
The World of William Clissold, by H. G. Wells
Ariane, by Claude Anet
The Hard-Boiled Virgin, by Frances Newman
Elmer Gantry, by Sinclair Lewis
Doomsday, by Warwick Deeping
The Sun also Rises, by Ernest Hemingway

The Allinghams, by May Sinclair
Bad Girl, by Vina Delmar
Antic Hay, by Aldous Huxley

Which prompted an irreverent versifier to indite:

Your honor, this book is a bucket of swill:
It portrays a young couple alone on a hill,
And a woman who lived in a shoe as a house
With her brood, but not once does it mention her spouse.
I submit that this volume's obscene, vile and loose,
And demand its suppression. Its name? Mother Goose.

In May 1930 the full bench of the Massachusetts Supreme Court upheld the conviction of Donald S. Friede, New York publisher, for the sale of Theodore Dreiser's *An American Tragedy.* (It was not a novel experience for Dreiser. *Sister Carrie* had been suppressed in 1900, *The Genius* in 1916.) In the course of the trial the lower court had permitted the prosecution, over the objections of the defense, to read to the jury only such portions of the book as were claimed to violate the statute. As a result the jury had not had an opportunity to judge the work as a whole. This formed the main basis of the appeal, but was rejected by the Supreme Court. At the same time the Court overruled the appeal of James A. DeLacey, the Boston bookseller who had been entrapped into and convicted for selling a copy of D. H. Lawrence's *Lady Chatterley's Lover* to an *agent provocateur* of the New England Watch and Ward Society.

These convictions served to focus public attention on the Massachusetts obscenity law. The statute forbade the public sale of any book "*containing* obscene, indecent language . . ." Accordingly the presence of a single objectionable paragraph in a novel was enough, in the eye of the law, to infect the entire work. An attempt was made to liberalize the law so that a book would have to be considered as a whole. The attempt was only partly successful. In 1930 the law was changed to read: "A book which *is* obscene, indecent . . ." Presumably the new law requires a book to be read in its entirety, but until the highest court of the Commonwealth says so, the question remains open.

SCHNITZLER CONDEMNED

In 1929 a New York bookseller was convicted for selling a copy of Schnitzler's *Reigen* (*Hands Around*). The book consisted of a series of related dialogues. Written with delicacy and restraint, it was a psychological study of the effect of sexual satiety on the two sexes. Dr Otto P. Schinnerer, professor of German literature at Columbia University, summarized it as follows:

In *Reigen* Schnitzler is exclusively interested in analyzing the psychological reactions of his characters before and after the gratification of their desires, and never in their physiological experiences. The *Reigen* scenes are a ruthless unmasking of the animal instincts in man which often parade under the guise of friendship and love. *Reigen* is on every count superior to *Anatol* (another work of Schnitzler's which is universally considered inoffensive and which has been published in the Modern Library in this country without interference), both as a work of art and in its unerring observation and its almost uncanny dissection of human motives. In writing the work Schnitzler simply obeyed the dictates of his artistic conscience, without ulterior motives.

Since it emphasized the futility of carnal passion, the book was, in essence, a moral tract. Mr Sumner did not think so, and the Court of Special Sessions of the City of New York agreed with him.

The Appellate Division upheld the conviction, basing its decision not so much on the contents of the book

as on the lush exaggerations in the introduction, which
spoke, among other things, of the "exquisite handling
of the licentious." Schnitzler had had no part in the
composition of this introduction, had not even heard of
it. The book had been pirated and privately printed;
the anonymous publishers had indulged in an orgy of
extravagant verbiage in order to stimulate sales. The
Appellate Court picked random excerpts from the unfortunate introduction to damn the work itself.

It is very clear [said the Court] that the author of the book
now before us for consideration was not thinking of the spiritual,
but devoted the whole book to the animal instincts of the human
race. His efforts were not a lesson in morality nor an attempt to
uplift the mind of the reader, but an attempt to depict in a
manner that might possibly be called clever, adulterous relations
vulgar and disgusting in the extreme. While some people may
think this quite smart, a book of this kind which has nothing
to recommend it and dealing wholly with such details is properly
held to be disgusting, indecent and obscene . . . No better
appraisal of its value is needed than that given by the introduction.

The Court ignored the enlightened principles laid
down by the Court of Appeals in the *Mademoiselle de
Maupin* case. It gave no consideration to the fact that
Schnitzler had for many years been recognized throughout the civilized world as a distinguished man of letters,
and that his novels had been translated into every
major language and were being studied in every college
and university giving a course in twentieth-century German literature.

The case was carried to the highest state court.
Schnitzler, nearing the end of a long and honorable
literary career, learned of the prosecution and was
deeply grieved. A separate memorandum was filed in
court on his behalf; the entire history of *Reigen* was
told in detail.

What followed was one of those incomprehensible things that reduce to futility any attempt to extract order, sanity or consistency from the welter of obscenity cases. The Court that had weighed Gautier's work with such clear-eyed detachment became unaccountably apathetic. It turned a deaf ear and permitted the conviction to stand.

The *Reigen* case, unlike some of the prosecutions above described, was handled from the outset like an ordinary criminal case. The defense apparently failed to realize that literary decency cases were *sui generis,* and called for special technique. Had the defense emphasized the free-press issue and forced the prosecution to fight on broad general grounds, the result might have been otherwise.

The courts had had their say, but—as often occurs when legislative mandates or court decisions are at variance with popular feelings—society rejected the result. A short time later *Reigen* was published by the Modern Library, and was widely sold. No attempt was made to suppress it; it may be found on the shelves of reputable bookstores today.

SCHNITZLER ABSOLVED

There is good reason to believe that *Reigen* would not have engaged the censor's attention had it not been for the tribulations, six years before, of another Schnitzler book. *Casanova's Homecoming* first appeared in this country in 1923. It was attacked by Mr Sumner, who failed to obtain a conviction. The magistrate before whom the case came up wrote a decisive opinion in exoneration. Not satisfied, Mr Sumner secured an indictment. The publisher moved for a dismissal before Judge (now Senator) Wagner. The judge refused to grant the motion, handing down an opinion more than a little flavored with chauvinistic self-righteousness.

I am asked [he said] to consider, as evidence of current opinion that the book in question is a distinct contribution to our literature and as not savoring of obscenity, that it has been accepted in other countries. And I am asked to consider also a number of comments made by literary critics that the work has distinct literary merit. Acceptance in other places than our own of a publication is of no importance to us unless the moral standard of these other countries is a replica of our own . . . We, therefore, cannot accept a book's adoption by another land or the approval of critics as conclusive of non-obscenity under the statute, for we may assert with pride—though not boastfully— that we are essentially an idealistic and spiritual nation and exact a higher standard than some others.

The novel was withdrawn from circulation, the case never went to trial and the indictment was ultimately dismissed. This was in 1923. In 1930 the book was reprinted, and was once more assailed by Mr Sumner.

This persistent molestation was difficult to comprehend. The book was in truth a tract on the vanity of human desires. The Casanova of Schnitzler was not the Casanova of the *Memoirs*. He was not the young and dashing duelist, wit, gamester, master of intrigue, destroyer of virtue and despair of cuckolds. He was a shabby old man who, because he would not acknowledge he was senile and no longer attractive to women, knew frustration and shame.

What Mr Sumner specifically objected to was two brief episodes. The question the court had to decide, therefore, was whether a few paragraphs which constituted integral parts of a full-length novel could so contaminate it as to warrant its condemnation.

Kindly old Judge Gottlieb (now dead) sat on the case. Following the lead of the Court of Appeals in the *Mademoiselle de Maupin* case, the defense attorneys presented to the judge a sheaf of letters from prominent persons in various walks of life, all testifying to the literary reputation of Schnitzler and the artistic integrity of the book. The judge wanted to know what Heywood Broun thought of it. The lawyers, a little puzzled, got a testimonial from Broun and submitted it.

After due consideration Judge Gottlieb dismissed the complaint. He couldn't find anything offensive in the novel.

Mr Sumner made no secret of his chagrin. The defense attorneys asked Judge Gottlieb to return the letters. "What do you want them for?" asked the judge. "We'd like to use them if Mr Sumner tries to get a grand jury indictment," they said. "Well," said the judge, "you can't have them back. Why do you suppose I asked for Broun's opinion?" "Because," ventured the lawyers, "he's a sound critic, brilliant journalist and man of common sense." The judge smiled. "Not at all. My son is an autograph collector, and he wanted Broun's autograph."

And so in the brief space of seven years a book which had drawn severe judicial censure at the outset emerged with a clean bill of health.

Censorship at the Customs

Prior to 1930 customs inspectors exercised complete and unquestioned sway over the moral content of books and pictures sent here from abroad. Some idea of the soundness of their judgment may be gleaned from the fact that they seized as obscene such works as Aristophanes' *Lysistrata*, Defoe's *Moll Flanders and Roxana*, Pierre Louys' *The Songs of Bilitis* and *The Twilight of the Nymphs*, the *Arabian Nights* (both in the Burton and the Mardrus-Mathers editions), the *Satyri-*

con of Petronius, Ovid's *Art of Love,* the *Golden Ass* of Apuleius, the *Letters of Abélard and Héloïse,* the complete works of Rabelais, Boccaccio's *Decameron,* Balzac's *Droll Stories,* Rousseau's *Confessions,* Casanova's *Memoirs,* Gauguin's *Journals,* E. E. Cummings' *The Enormous Room,* March's *The Wild Party,* and Krafft-Ebing's *Psychopathia Sexualis*—despite the fact that most of these titles were readily available in this country.

Before 1929 there seemed to be little disposition to challenge the wisdom of the customs censors. Then the tide began to turn.

Huntington Cairns, an able young Baltimore attorney, protested the seizure of *Daphnis and Chloë* by Longus, *Satyrs and Sunlight* by Hugh McCrea, and *The London Aphrodite.* He carried the case into court, argued it brilliantly, and won.

Shortly thereafter Judge Kirkpatrick of the federal court in Philadelphia ruled that the *Decameron* was not obscene and should be admitted into the country.

The collector of the Port of Boston detained a copy of Voltaire's *Candide* sent here for use in a Harvard classroom. A month later a copy of Rabelais' *Pantagruel* imported by A. Edward Newton, the eminent bibliophile, suffered the same fate at the Port of New York.

These seizures attracted public attention. The unwholesome situation which had long existed was exposed. Because it operated by means of bureaucratic fiat, customs censorship was shown to be particularly vicious. If a collector deemed a book salacious he simply confiscated it; he was not legally required to submit his conclusion to a court for approval or rejection. The person to whom the book was addressed could, if he wished, go into the Customs Court for a review, but as a practical matter, this was a scant safeguard. The burden of going forward was on the addressee, not on the collector as it should have been; the Customs Court, disinclined to take on the work of supervising the material that came to our shores, laid down the principle that it would not disturb a collector's decision unless a substantial abuse of discretion was shown. A seizure in most cases meant confiscation.

The late Senator Cutting investigated the situation and was shocked by the extent of ignorance, high-handedness and red tape in customs matters of this kind. As a result of his efforts the Tariff Act was amended in 1930 in two important respects:

(1) The new law assured a jury trial in the federal court whenever a seizure was contested, and required the government, not the addressee, to press the proceedings.

(2) The secretary of the treasury was permitted, in his discretion, to admit the classics or books of recognized literary or scientific merit, even if obscene.

The new law had a wholesome effect. The customs people were brought to their senses. They lifted the ban on Voltaire, Rabelais, Boccaccio and hundreds of others without judicial compulsion.

The court cases which have arisen since 1930 are persuasive proof of the sound social philosophy implicit in the law. As long as we have obscenity statutes, full court review of administrative rulings is an essential safeguard against bureaucratic blundering and bigotry.

PICTURING LIFE IN THE SOUTH

There had been a time when the censor had found New York magistrates receptive, when it had been a simple matter to have defendants held for trial in Special Sessions and convicted there. Many a defendant, short of money or courage, had been persuaded to plead guilty without further ado. Now Mr Sumner was encountering increasingly stiffer opposition.

In 1933 he brought criminal proceedings against Erskine Caldwell's *God's Little Acre*. An authentic study of the poor whites of Georgia, it was an important piece of literature. It was dragged into court because here and there on its pages references were made to certain sexual practices. After an extended trial the complaint was dismissed. The case was ably handled by Wolf Schwabacher.

This is not a book [said Magistrate Greenspan who heard the case] where vice and lewdness are treated as virtues, or which would tend to incite lustful desires in the normal mind. There is no way of anticipating its effect upon a disordered or diseased mind, and if the courts were to exclude books from sale merely because they might incite lust in disordered minds, our entire literature would very likely be reduced to a relatively small number of uninteresting and barren books. The greater part of the classics would certainly be excluded. Those who see the ugliness and not the beauty in a piece of work are unable to see the forest for the trees.

BOOKS AND MORALS

The forward march was not without setbacks. Donald Henderson Clarke's *Female* furnished a serious one.

It was the story of Margy Kane, a child of the slums, whose vitality and beauty carried her by successive steps from the squalor of a New England mill town to New York's Park Avenue. One reviewer found it to be "a strong indictment of the present social system with its bootleg gin, free love and laxity of morals"; another compared it to Defoe's *Moll Flanders;* a third described it as "a plain book about honest-to-goodness, breathing people. It seems impossible to

imagine any ordinary mortal not reading and enjoying its reality." Lewis Gannett of the New York
Herald Tribune, always a discerning critic, said that it
was "essentially a Sunday-school lesson for this gin-
soaked age."

There can be no doubt that *Female* was a frank and
unreticent record. It may have been offensive to the sensibilities of some persons, but in this respect it was no
better or worse than thousands of other novels which
were published at the same time. For some obscure
reason Mr Sumner singled it out for attack. He proceeded against the publisher in Manhattan. Magistrate Van Amringe considered the case carefully for
more than two months and finally handed down an oral
opinion dismissing the complaint. He said: "I have
read this work with a great deal of care, and I have
reached the conclusion that it does not violate any of
the laws laid down with reference to obscene books."

Prior to the *Female* case it had been the uniform
practice, whenever a book was assailed for obscenity, to
submit the issue to *one* tribunal for determination. In
connection with *Female,* however, two prosecutions
were instituted: one in Manhattan and the other in
Astoria almost immediately afterward. When the case
came up in Astoria before Magistrate Haukstra, it
was pointed out to him that *Female* was already under
judicial consideration in New York, and it was urged
that the Astoria case be held in abeyance pending decision in New York. Magistrate Haukstra refused to
do this and held the defendant for trial in the Court of
Special Sessions. The favorable decision in New York
then followed. At this point, therefore, *Female* was
legal in Manhattan and *prima facie* illegal just across
the Queensboro Bridge.

We need not dwell on the viciousness of a practice
which permits the censor, by bringing wholesale com-

plaints on the same book, to go shopping for a conviction. That such a practice is bound to yield preposterous results goes without saying.

The Court of Special Sessions held the book was obscene. It was "neither humorous, entertaining nor instructive," the court found, nor did it "attempt to guide the footsteps of the unwary from the pitfalls of life." The case was carried to the Appellate Division, and there too *Female* was subjected to excoriation. And then the Court of Appeals, which in the *Mademoiselle de Maupin* case had stated explicitly that a book did not have to be a moral preachment to be lawful, doubled back on its tracks and upheld the conviction.

THE PENDULUM KEEPS SWINGING

Flaubert may have been the father of the modern novel, but Mr Sumner had no use for him. In 1927 he prosecuted *The Temptation of St Anthony* without success. He then attacked *November*, but Magistrate Goldstein cleared it, saying that the obscenity law was aimed against "dirt for dirt's sake." The same judge held Jim Tully's *Ladies in the Parlor* for Special Sessions, where it was adjudged obscene. André Gide's *If It Die* was absolved by Magistrate Perlman, but a bookseller paid a two-hundred-and-fifty-dollar fine for having a copy of Pierre Louys' *Aphrodite* in his possession, and Special Sessions condemned the *Kama Sutra,* an Indian classic.

Despite the setbacks, the trend of court decisions was unmistakably liberal. The stage was set for *Ulysses.*

CHAPTER II

Sex and Literature (*Cont'd*)

After all it was not the novelists, not even the modern ones, who invented sex. Both the fundamentalists and the evolutionists agree that the scheme has at least the merit of antiquity. Anthony Comstock may have been entirely correct in his assumption that the division of living creatures into male and female was a vulgar mistake, but a conspiracy of silence about the matter will hardly alter the facts.

HEYWOOD BROUN and MARGARET LEECH,
Anthony Comstock (1927)

WALTER HINES PAGE, back in the days when he was a member of the publishing firm of Doubleday, Page & Company, had refused to print a book containing the "suggestive" word "chaste." It was a long cry from "chaste" to some of the words in Molly Bloom's soliloquy in James Joyce's *Ulysses.*

THE VICISSITUDES OF ULYSSES

For a decade and a half the censor pursued *Ulysses.* Issues of *The Little Review* containing early chapters were confiscated by the post office in 1918. Margaret Anderson and Jane Heap, the editors, were convicted in General Sessions, and fined. Copies of the book were burned in 1922 in England, Ireland, Canada and the United States.

There were those who felt that the virulence of the attack was scarcely warranted by the nature of the work. Molly Bloom's erotic thought wanderings constituted a negligible portion of the book; there were long dull stretches in the seven-hundred-page labyrinth; full comprehension of it required almost encyclopedic knowledge. And since immature and susceptible persons —the only ones conceivably subject to "corruption"— would never be attracted to the book, it was hard to see how it could harm anyone. But the censor thought otherwise, and his judgment was directly responsible for the bootlegging of the work on a large scale.

In 1928 a Customs Court judge found "only a casual glance" enough to convince him that *Ulysses* was "filled with obscenity of the rottenest and vilest character."

In 1933 an imported copy of *Ulysses* was barred at the customs. This time the addressee (it was Random House) decided to put up a fight, and there was a showdown in the Federal Court. The authorities relied rather heavily on the virulent condemnation in the Customs Court, and also on prior convictions. Judge Woolsey, before whom the case came up, was determined to arrive at an independent conclusion. After a full hearing he cleared the book of the charge of literary turpitude.

With his opinion, which has already become a classic, the law took a great stride forward, possibly a greater stride than in any previous single case. Certain four-letter Anglo-Saxon words, long banned from polite conversation and literature, were no longer necessarily taboo. It cannot be doubted that Judge Woolsey's decision directly paved the way for the degree of forthrightness to be found in John Steinbeck's masterly *The Grapes of Wrath*. The common-sense principle that the effect of a book must be appraised with reference to a person of average sex instincts (*l'homme moyen sen-*

suel), and not with reference to adolescents or de-
ranged or subnormal people, was explicitly laid down.
The importance of creative honesty was judicially recognized; an author's loyalty to his technique and to the
rationale of his story became major considerations in
the process of court appraisal. Since judges could be unconsciously influenced by their prejudices, no matter
how fair they tried to be, Judge Woolsey counseled
them to check their judgments with other people in the
community whose views on literature and life might be
of value.

Mr Sumner of the Vice Society promptly branded
Judge Woolsey's opinion as "a literary review trying to
explain away the appearance of admitted obscenity and
filth," and paused to wonder whether the judge was
serving society or playing into the hands of "a rather
reprehensible type of author and publisher." The prosecution shared Mr Sumner's feelings. The case was appealed.

It was at this point that the authorities let the cat out
of the bag. Until then the case had been argued on the
usual grounds: that *Ulysses* was obscene, lewd, lascivious, indecent and so on. On the argument of the appeal
United States Attorney Martin Conboy abruptly took
a different tack. He read to the court portions of the
book which he claimed to be blasphemous, contending
that whatever constituted a reflection on the Church
was "indecent." And so a law primarily aimed to suppress *sexually* impure matter was sought to be used
to silence supposedly *irreligious* utterances.

Judge Woolsey was upheld by a vote of two to one.
Judge Augustus N. Hand wrote the prevailing opinion
in which Judge Learned Hand concurred. Judge Manton, dissenting, declared his adherence to the sixty-six-
year-old rule in *Regina* v. *Hicklin,* repeatedly rejected
by his court. The majority opinion made clear that "the

dominant effect" of a given book was the test of its obscenity, and that "in applying this test, relevancy of the objectionable parts to the theme, the established reputation of the work in the estimation of approved critics if the book is modern, and the verdict of the past if it is ancient, are persuasive pieces of evidence."

Judge Woolsey's opinion and that of the Circuit Court signalized the emergence of common-sense doctrine in the obscenity field.

THE LAW IS FURTHER CLARIFIED

The seed thus planted bore fruit, in part at least, in the Levine case, which was decided by the same Circuit Court in 1936. Though expertly defended by George Wolf, a gifted and experienced lawyer, Levine had been found guilty of mailing obscene circulars advertising five obscene books. Three of the five books were specifically adverted to by the court—*Secret Museum of Anthropology,* a reproduction of photographs predominantly of nude female savages; *Crossways of Sex,* an anonymous treatise on sexual pathology; and *Black Lust,* a novel describing the adventures of an English girl captured by dervishes. Trial Judge Kennamer had told the jury that there was a group of people "found in every community, the young and immature, the ignorant and those who are sensually inclined," and that it was this group that the federal obscenity statute was designed to protect. The Circuit Court held that he was wrong, saying:

This . . . doctrine necessarily presupposed that the evil against which the statute is directed so much outweighs all interests of art, letters or science, that they must yield to the mere possibility that some prurient person may get a sensual gratification from reading or seeing what to most people is innocent and may be delightful or enlightening. No civilized community not fanatically puritanical would tolerate such an imposition. . . .

The court then proceeded to paraphrase its holding in the *Ulysses* case, concluding that "what counts is its [a book's] effect, not upon any particular class, but upon all those whom it is likely to reach." Because Judge Kennamer had erroneously instructed the jury as to this, and because he had incorrectly charged them that a single passage might condemn a work regardless of its merits as a whole, Levine's conviction was reversed.

Thus three highly salutary rules emerged from the *Levine* case: that a book said to be obscene must be judged as a whole; that its obscenity must be measured by the effect it is likely to have, not on the diseased or the immature, but on readers generally; and that the opinions of critics are admissible in evidence to show a book's significance as a work of art, and its importance to the community.

THE BOOKSELLER'S DILEMMA

It may not be amiss to pause here a moment and reflect on some of the implications of the cases we have discussed.

Halsey, the man who bore the brunt of Mr Sumner's stubborn fight against *Mademoiselle de Maupin,* was a bookseller. The defendant in the *Reigen* case was Pesky, a clerk in a bookshop; in the *Female* case, the owner of a circulating library; and in the *November* case, a small distributor of books; in the *If It Die* case, a bookseller. All these people were trying, earnestly enough, to earn a living. Their livelihood depended on selling books not on reading them; and even if they had done nothing but read twenty-four hours a day, they couldn't possibly have read all the volumes on their shelves. The law nevertheless placed them in the same category with the willful author and publisher of obscene material; and if they innocently happened to sell an indecent publication (sometimes by entrapment to a decoy of Mr Sumner's), they ran the risk of a criminal conviction resulting in a fine or a jail sentence. In other words, the obscenity statute made them guarantors of the moral integrity of their wares.

THE "BAD BOOK" BILL

The so-called Bad Book Bill, sponsored by the National Council for Freedom from Censorship a number of years ago, was designed to remedy this situation. It placed the primary responsibility for selling obscene publications, not on the retailer, but where it belonged: on the publisher or the distributor. It provided a common-sense procedure in the prosecution of alleged pornography. Upon being accused of selling a salacious book, a bookseller was permitted to show that he had no knowledge of any previous court decision holding the book obscene, and that he himself was not the publisher. If he then furnished an affidavit disclosing his source of supply, together with an undertaking to assure his appearance in court as a witness, he would be let go, and the prosecution could be launched against the responsible parties. The underlying purpose of the bill was: (1) to protect the innocent bookseller, (2) to fix criminal responsibility on the real offender, and (3) to stem the flow of pornography at the source.

The Bad Book Bill was no novelty in the field of law. There was legislative precedent for it in the New York Code of Criminal Procedure. The code provides that if a jeweler unwittingly sells a falsely stamped article of gold or silver, he may escape the penalty of the law by bringing in and testifying against the person who manufactured the article and sold it to him. This section has been in the code since 1909 and has always operated salutarily. The Bad Book Bill expresses the same essential philosophy.

When the bill was first put forward its sponsors believed—naïvely, perhaps—that it would instantly enlist the approval of the Vice Society. Was it not Mr Sumner's primary aim to root out pornography? Wasn't it best to strike at the source?

Well, the bill has gone down to defeat year after year in the New York State Legislature, and each time the Vice Society has been the most vociferous opponent of it. The sanguine sponsors should have known better. When the Society goes after a book, it wants a victory in the form of a prompt conviction. It is not interested in a long court fight in which the issue of legality may be fully and fairly tested out. That is why the Society has repeatedly proceeded against small booksellers instead of large distributors or publishers. A small bookseller can be easily persuaded to plead guilty on the promise of a suspended sentence; a large distributor or a publisher is apt to furnish tougher opposition.

The Bad Book Bill would not—as has been repeatedly urged—provide an easy loophole for the corrupt bookseller. It would afford a decent opportunity for an honest dealer to bring into court the people whose product got him in trouble. For it must be borne in mind that nothing in the present law requires the prosecution to bring the publisher into court or even to make an effort to find him.

THE CAN OF SOUP

In opposing the bill Mr Sumner and some others resort to the "can-of-soup" argument. They point out that if a customer is made ill by the contents of a can sold to him by a retail grocer, he may sue and recover from the grocer even though the grocer had no way of knowing that the soup was contaminated. The analogy will not stand close scrutiny. For one thing, foodstuffs directly affect the public health; their inspection and supervision have been always deemed to be within the scope of governmental control. Not so with books. We have a Food and Drug Act and a Food and Drug Administration; fortunately, we have no equivalent statute for books.

The analogy is false because it relates to two fundamentally different things. A new soup will tempt palates; a new idea is apt to shock people and make them suspicious. Besides, whether a can of soup is edible or spoiled is a question on which neither laymen nor experts are likely to differ, but no one can say with any degree of certainty whether a publication is lawful or unlawful until a court of last resort has spoken the apocalyptic word. The soup liability of the grocer is predicated upon two theories: first, that he is at liberty to take the can down from his shelves, open it and ascertain its quality before selling it (an absurd argument); and second, the grocer may safeguard himself by dealing only with reliable manufacturers and wholesalers.

These theories, tenuous enough when applied to the grocer, disappear into thin air when applied to books. Even if a bookseller could physically read every book on his shelves, and every law case ever decided on the subject, he would not know for certain whether a book violated the law. The criteria of the crime are much too vague and uncertain, and depend upon too many variable factors. Nor can a bookseller protect himself by dealing only with responsible publishers. The publication of a reputable house (witness *Jurgen,* published by Robert McBride; *Casanova's Homecoming,* published by Simon and Schuster; *Married Love,* published by Putnam's; and *Ulysses,* published by Random House) is just as likely to precipitate prosecution as that of a lesser-known firm. Nor is the reputation of the author a talisman of immunity, as James Branch Cabell, Theodore Dreiser, Dr Marie Stopes and James Joyce can testify. D. H. Lawrence and Dr Arthur Schnitzler, both of whom were hounded by the censor during their lives, would probably nod assent in their graves.

TURNING BACK THE CLOCK

When pressed for a solution other than the Bad Book Bill, some of its opponents shrug their shoulders and say that the present law, while not perfect, is good enough. Others are not quite as resourceless. They propose that each state set up an official board to which a publisher or bookseller might submit a book for examination prior to publication and distribution. If the board found the book unobjectionable, its decision would be conclusive proof of its legality. If the board held otherwise, the book could still be published and sold, but anyone dealing with it would be acting at his peril.

It is hard to believe that this indefensible scheme, hostile to the Bill of Rights and shot through with endless possibilities of bureaucratic intermeddling, corruption, political reprisal and bigotry, can be seriously urged.

Shortly after Caxton set up his press in Westminster in 1476, the Crown forbade all printing except by royal permission. That was the beginning of pre-licensing. It continued for about a hundred years, eventually calling forth Milton's *Areopagitica.* Pre-censorship of the press was abolished in 1695, and has not been in force since then either in England or in America.

Yet what many well-intentioned reformers—it will

be remembered that Mr Walter Lippmann suggested a similar plan for plays back in the days of *Sex* and *Pleasure Man*—propose to do is to set up a machinery for the pre-licensing of books; they would make book censorship duplicate all the stupidity and indefensible bungling of motion-picture censorship.

Fortunately books are still free from previous restraint. But the expedient of licensing has been indirectly applied to magazines in a manner which deserves analysis.

OBSCENITY IN THE COURTS

The authorities claim that ninety per cent of the questionable material which floods the country comes from New York. There can be no doubt that New York is the publishing center of the United States. Half of the country's population is more than thirty miles from a library or a bookstore.

In New York, as in other states, there are criminal statutes against the dissemination of offensive matter. If a vice hunter happens upon a book which he considers obscene, he either files a complaint in the Magistrate's Court, or presents the matter to the district attorney for indictment. He prefers the former method. Public prosecutors are often dilatory and sometimes unsympathetic; grand juries occasionally refuse to indict. The proceeding in the Magistrate's Court has many features to recommend it. It is direct, in that the censor can act as complainant himself; it is intimidating, because the censor can resort to arrest as well as the service of the summons; it is speedy, since the hearing can be forced on in a few days; it is likely to be successful because most magistrates are reluctant to take upon themselves the responsibility of dismissal and prefer to hold for Special Sessions; it promises victory, since it is easier as a rule to get a conviction in Special Sessions than in

General Sessions, where the case would be tried if an indictment was returned.

But there is a fly in the ointment of the Magistrate's Court, too. The onus of the first positive legal move is on the censor. He has to shoulder the burden of proof. The accused is obliged merely to defend; he doesn't have to go into court in the first instance to vindicate his rights.

Now the vice crusader has a strange view of justice. If he secures a conviction he praises the judge. But if he's thrown out the front door, he'll come in through the back.

WITHOUT JUDGE OR JURY

In 1931 a clergyman was scandalized by what he deemed a "flood of lewd, lascivious and obscene magazines" on the newsstands. Rallying some support, he called on the Commissioner of Licenses of New York City to do something. The Commissioner was obliging. He sent out a circular letter to the owners of newsstands throughout the city, threatening them with the revocation of their licenses if they sold magazines and papers which might be "classified as lewd and obscene literature." No mention was made of the person who was to do the classifying.

The scheme worked like a charm. The Interborough News Company withdrew three magazines at once from its fourteen hundred newsstands. Newsdealers were not disposed to kick up a row; they wanted to earn a living, not to fight court battles.

From the censor's point of view the result was perfect. The whole thing had been so simple and easy. No delay, no going into court, no proof—just a little pressure on a city official, and it was done.

There were repercussions. Public-spirited elements

in the community, including the National Council for Freedom from Censorship, and such well-known people as B. W. Huebsch, Maxwell Perkins, Robert E. Sherwood, Thatcher Hughes, Bruce Bliven, Henry Seidel Canby and Barrett H. Clark, raised their voices in condemnation. They did not defend the magazines which had precipitated the situation, but denounced the abuse of administrative power. The National Council wrote to District Attorney Crain:

We call your attention to the fact that none of these alleged indecent magazines have been barred from the mails or taken from the express companies, though the federal laws concerning such matter are strictly enforced. Whether any of these publications violate the law is, therefore, obviously a matter open to debate—to be decided fairly only by juries.

The protest had the effect of making the Commissioner watch his step. He had sent out his "warning," and that had been enough. He did not have to revoke or suspend a single license; he scored a bloodless victory.

From the point of view of the social desirability of keeping alive magazines involved, the episode was unimportant. But it had gravely disturbing implications. The point was not that a handful of questionable periodicals had been summarily wiped out, but that a weapon had been forged which could be easily turned against other matter.

Since it is fairly clear that the censorship of the future will resort to this technique, it may be worth while to analyze it.

The method substitutes the arbitrary act of an official for the orderly processes of law. Since licensing officials are usually political appointees, censorship over a vast portion of our reading matter is thus removed from the courts into the arena of politics. Juries and judges are for all practical purposes ousted. Bad as judicial censorship may be, political censorship is infinitely worse.

It makes little difference whether or not, once the method is adopted, licenses are actually revoked. Intimidation is an effective bludgeon; a great deal can be done by duress. The licensing authorities in Boston succeeded in barring a production of O'Neill's *Strange Interlude* there by the mere threat of revoking the license of any theater which housed the play.

If the method is used the licensing authorities lay themselves open to domination by pressure groups. These groups have far-reaching influence: influence derived from fear, not sympathy. There seems to be a conviction prevalent among public officials that failure on their part to do the bidding of a vice society will bring them into disrepute as allies of corruption.

The method enables the censor to shift the onus from himself to the person he attacks. More than that, the scope of his activities is overwhelmingly enlarged. Instead of proceeding against each purported offender individually, he is able to keep under his thumb, by means of ukases of his for which the authorities are the mouthpiece, thousands of newsdealers.

If a license is actually revoked, the newsdealer has to go into court to test out the legality of the revocation. In such a proceeding he has to bear the expense as well as the burden of proof. His chances of success are substantially slimmer than in a criminal prosecution wherein he would be a defendant.

The method is especially insidious because of the nature of the immediate target. If the customs bureau places a ban on the importation of the works of Rabelais or Voltaire, public sentiment is likely to be aroused because of the reputation of the books. The campaign in New York was directed against six or seven periodicals of ribald humor. Many liberal-minded persons who would have been scandalized by the suppression, let us say, of Havelock Ellis, were unmoved. The magazines may have been intrinsically unworthy of solicitude. That was beside the point. The question was, did they contravene the law? If they did, the machinery of our criminal courts was available to punish the offenders. If they did not, they were legally entitled to distribution.

The method is susceptible of drastic extension. Newsstands sell other things besides magazines of dubious wit: newspapers, pamphlets and, in some cases, books. Once the censor wins, through public indifference, sanction for his procedure as against the scatological school of humor, what is there to prevent him from extending it for other purposes and along other lines? It may well outstrip the bounds intended for it by the censor. It may, for example, become a handy means for a corrupt city administration to ban from newsstands all matter tending to expose its activities.

We may well be apprehensive about this situation. The method is already in operation in many places throughout the country. Boston is an example. There is a censorship committee there composed of a police commissioner, two police captains and a clerk. The committee requires that all magazines that "may be said to be questionable" be submitted to it for consideration. The committee then determines for itself whether or not a magazine is offensive, and proceeds to prevent distribution.

The Anatomy of an Obscenity Case

Francis Bertram Elgas, president of the Vice Society, said in the society's 1935 report:

Tastes necessarily differ, and with books that simply offend good taste and are hopelessly vulgar (and not flagrantly pornographic, obscene or immoral), we cannot in this age, when former notions of propriety and decency have so radically changed, attempt to take restraining steps which might not meet with the broader views now taken by our courts. To do so would impair our usefulness. Always we strive to be sane and sensible, broad, not narrow. Times have changed and we must change with them.

Mr Sumner, executive secretary of the society, did not share Mr Elgas' mood of sweet reason. The balm of the *Female* victory had not been enough to assuage the smart of numerous defeats. So while Mr Elgas may have been willing to read the signs of the times, Mr Sumner wasn't. After the *Female* case he rested on his laurels for a while. Then he instigated proceedings against James T. Farrell's *A World I Never Made,* a five-hundred-page novel depicting slum life in Chicago's South Side twenty-five years ago. He deemed eighty-one of the pages offensive.

The case came up in the Magistrate's Court in New York City in 1937. Mr Rubens, an able and resourceful attorney, now dead, appeared for the defense. Before the trial opened, an enterprising reporter passed around a copy of the book for autographs. Mr Sumner signed his name with the notation: "I thoroughly disapprove of this book." Mr Carl Van Doren affixed his signature and wrote: "I thoroughly disapprove of John S. Sumner and his works."

Bernard de Voto, editor of *The Saturday Review of Literature,* was the first witness for the defense. He described the book as realistic. "Just what do you mean by realistic?" asked Magistrate Curran. "I mean," said De Voto, "an attempt to describe the essence of human experience without heightening it in the direction of romance or fantasy." He gave his opinion that Farrell's novel was of exceptional merit and likely to be a permanent addition to literature.

The question of profanity came up. De Voto insisted that since profanity had been part of the life depicted in the novel it was essential to the presentation of a truthful picture. The magistrate remarked: "In 1908 I tried to describe a ball game at the Polo Grounds in a book. Perhaps I didn't use enough profanity. The book has never been heard of since."

Carl Van Doren, author and critic, was the next witness. He said that Farrell's novel was not as outspoken as the people it depicted. Magistrate Curran grew reminiscent again. "Do you remember," he asked, "the horse-drawn drays on West Street in the old days? And the language the drivers used?" Having been brought up on a farm, Van Doren didn't remember, but he admitted that the Van Doren hired man hadn't been any too restrained in his speech. Mr Sumner broke in to say that the draymen on West Street used to get arrested for obscenity. The magistrate said: "They should have let them go. They were beautiful. No taxi driver of today could approach them."

Columnist Heywood Broun also testified. He observed that Farrell "went back to good old Anglo-Saxon words; he didn't invent them." Then he proceeded to deliver a disquisition on changing fashions in the use of words. He told the story of Bill Orr, an old-time reporter, who was assigned to cover the campaign against prostitution in 1910. His editors refused to let him use the word "prostitute," so he invented the phrase "members of the scarlet army."

Mr Broun's quips moved the courtroom to laughter and Mr Sumner didn't like it. "He's entertaining his audience," he said with some heat. "I'd like to point out that we furnish the material."

This did not dampen Mr Broun's spirits. Proceeding with his discussion of changing fashions in morality, he pointed out that though Shaw's *Mrs Warren's Profes-*

sion was now considered innocuous, it had been raided in the days of Mr Sumner's predecessor. "The heroine," said Mr Broun, "was the keeper of a disorderly house —no, maybe I'm getting a little bit too fancy myself— I'll say brothel."

The magistrate shared Mr Broun's dislike of circumlocution. He said that he had encountered with dismay a word in the novel with the first and last letters joined with a dash. "That's my pet abomination," he declared. "It should be either spelled out or left out. It makes the printed page look like a rail fence." He ventured to guess that Mr Sumner had looked over Mr Farrell's shoulder when he wrote it.

After hearing the evidence Magistrate Curran came to the conclusion that the book was not "dirt for dirt's sake," and dismissed the complaint. He observed that "the short Anglo-Saxon words" which Mr Sumner found offensive were "known by practically everybody."

It seems to me [he said] that if this book is to be found lewd, lascivious, libidinous, lustful, lecherous or licentious—it appears that all such words begin with an "l" in our language—purely on the basis of certain detached words or episodes, we'll have to start in by banning Homer, parts of the Bible, a good deal of Chaucer and certainly some of Shakespeare. Also quite a little of Fielding would have to go. By the way, Fielding was a justice of the peace in England, and that corresponds to a magistrate in New York City. Also we would have to omit Wagner's Venus music, and there are certain paintings of the Flemish school which would not pass.

Having thus touched upon literature, music and painting, the judge felt he ought to say something about the stage. He recalled his visit to the Folies-Bergères, saying: "I saw a beautiful scene in this show. It was a nude scene. Absolutely beautiful. Done in the best Parisian taste. I was sitting there looking at it and enjoying it, when a man behind me tapped my shoulder.

He said: 'Are you an American?' I said that was right. He said: 'Are we going to sit here and let this thing go on?' I told him that I certainly was and that I was enjoying it immensely."

At the conclusion of the case Mr Farrell said: "There are few enough countries left where a writer can strive to write seriously and frankly. I am glad that America still remains one of them."

CHAPTER III

Sex Instruction Books

The professed end is never attained. The subject is not suppressed. On the contrary, everyone talks of it. The common prejudices are repeated: the unsavoury jokes are retailed. The effect is indeed to advertise the existence and exaggerate the importance of this abnormal relationship. But something, if the appeal against police censorship should fail, is in a measure achieved. The effort to think seriously and humanely about questions of sex is discouraged and postponed. The taboos are reinforced which have perpetuated every social evil. We can advance in morals only by free discussion.

H. N. BRAILSFORD, *The Immorality of Censors* (1928)

A FATHER, anxious to apprise his twelve-year-old son of the facts of life, decided to dispense with the birds-and-flowers approach, and gave his son a printed manual of sex information instead. The booklet was explicit. It described in detail the sexual urge, the male and female sex organs, the act of intercourse, conception and birth. There were references to the reproductive habits of animals in order to afford a complete biologic picture. The father told his son that the subject was complicated, and urged him to read the book carefully and then ask questions about anything he didn't understand. A week passed without questions. The father became a little uneasy. He spoke to the boy. Had he read the book? Yes, he had, but—this with a measure of disdain —it was all old stuff. Old stuff? Had he known it before? Of course! Every bit of it? Wasn't there *anything* in the book that was new to him? The boy reflected a while. "Yes," he said, "one thing. I never knew that the period of gestation in elephants was two years."

THE BACKGROUND

There is no more hazardous enterprise, Macaulay observed in his essay on Milton, than bearing the torch of truth into those dark recesses in which no light has ever shone.

Twenty years ago the legal status of sex education, for adults as well as for adolescents, was in a precarious state. Books dealing with sex were few, and their career uncertain. Dr Robie's *Art of Love* had been adjudged obscene; Dr Stopes' *Married Love* was being circulated surreptitiously. There was no appeal for sexual ethics based on decency and good taste. The age-old deterrents were still being resorted to: threat of disease, public disgrace, damnation. Children, animated by a natural curiosity, were driven for the most part to the streets, pornographic literature and corrupt companions for information. Even those who believed that sex education for the young was necessary clung to the view that the process should take place in the home. They ignored the results of repeated surveys which showed that most parents were derelict in this duty, and that many of them weren't sufficiently versed in the subject to give intelligent instruction.

Dr Joseph Collins wrote at about that time: "The truth about sex is a large order. Church, convention and commerce do not want it and will not have it. Were I to tell as much of the truth as I know about sex, society would frown at me, the postal authorities would forbid its circulation, some self-constituted censor would hale me before a tribunal."

The Dennett case marked the turning point. It involved the mails.

The record of the post office up to that time was one of successful suppressions. In 1911 the report of the Chicago Vice Commission, headed by Dean Sumner of the Episcopal Church, had been excluded from the mails. Melchow's *The Sexual Life,* Butler's *Love and Its Affinities,* and Sanger's *History of Prostitution* had been similarly dealt with.

The Sex Side of Life

Shortly after Comstock drove Madame Restell to suicide (she was the target of one of his innumerable morality drives), he made a speech in Boston urging the organization of a society like the New York Society for the Suppression of Vice. A clergyman asked him: "Did you ever use decoy letters or false signatures? Did you ever sign a woman's name when writing a letter? Did you ever try to make a person sell you forbidden wares and then, when you had succeeded, use the evidence thus obtained to convict him?" Comstock answered yes to all three questions.

The technique of entrapment developed by him was used many years later to "get" Mrs Dennett.

In 1918 Mary Ware Dennett, long an active worker for reform, made a short compilation of elementary sex information for her two adolescent sons. The material was subsequently published in the *Medical Review of Reviews.* It was so well received that the editor persuaded Mrs Dennett to reprint it in pamphlet form for general use. The pamphlet was called *The Sex Side of Life: An Explanation for Young People,* and contained detailed charts of male and female sex organs. Widely and continuously circulated for years, it won

the approval of many educational, religious and welfare organizations. It was sold at twenty-five cents a
copy, which barely covered its costs.

In 1922 the postal authorities ruled that the pamphlet
was unmailable. Mrs Dennett wrote several times to
the postmaster, asking him to specify what portions in
his opinion contravened the postal law. She received
no explanation. Six years later, in 1928, she received a
request for a copy from a "Mrs Miles" in Grottoes,
Virginia. She mailed the copy. It later turned out that
"Mrs Miles" was a postal inspector who had been
instructed to entrap Mrs Dennett. She was indicted for
sending obscene matter through the mails. Grottoes,
the home of caverns of darkness, had been well chosen.

A motion was made to quash the indictment. It came
on for hearing before Federal Judge Moscowitz. He
resorted to an unusual procedure. He invited three
clergymen—a Catholic priest, a Jewish rabbi and a
Protestant minister—to share the bench with him when
the motion was argued. He said he wished them to "aid
the conscience of the court." The publicity that attended
the case disturbed him. He declared that there would
be no further public hearings. He never disclosed the
recommendations of his religious advisers, but refused
to quash the indictment.

Mrs Dennett was placed on trial in April 1929. She
was the accused in a criminal case. She faced a jury of
stolid Brooklyn elders whose ideas of sex—as one
commentator remarked—must have been gleaned solely
from studying the growth of rubber plants. She heard
herself denounced by Prosecutor Wilkinson as a woman
who was trying to drag society into the sewer. No wonder the New York *World* wrote that "the ghost of
Anthony Comstock rose like a palpable presence from
the grave, exulting to see his work go marching on."

In the course of the trial the defense attempted to show that Mrs Dennett had never profited by distributing her pamphlet; that she had received large orders from such institutions as Y.M.C.A.'s, the Child Study Association, and the Union Theological Seminary; that the government itself, through its Federal Health Service, had for many years distributed millions of sex booklets practically identical in content with Mrs Dennett's. All these efforts were blocked by Judge Burrows at the instance of the prosecution. The jury was out forty minutes and brought in a verdict of guilty.

Technically, Mrs Dennett was convicted of sending obscene matter through the mails. In effect, however, she was adjudged guilty of being a sex heretic. She had advocated the dissemination of basic biologic facts, and had dared to assert that physical love might be not only noble and beautiful but pleasurable. She had expressed the hope that birth control would some day be legally recognized. She had suggested that venereal diseases were curable, and that masturbation would not necessarily consign an adolescent to eternal damnation.

The verdict raised a storm of public protest. The comment of the Detroit *Free Press* was typical of the attitude of the press:

The atrociousness of this conviction is less surprising than the fact that an intelligent and earnest mother can be exposed to such a sentence for no greater a crime than attempting to give boys and girls the benefit of mature experience on the most important subject in life. The mentality of those responsible for the prosecution of Mrs Dennett is that of the first fifteen centuries of the Christian Era. Neither the doctors nor enlightened laymen have been able to break down the barriers that keep from youth the truth about marriage and parenthood. The process of racial reproduction is still regarded as a divine mystery, which it is impertinence on the part of man to penetrate.

A less sober commentator wrote:

"You are fourteen, my son," said the elegant dame,
  "And of sex you're beginning to mutter.
There are facts you should know, but remember your name,
  And learn in the very best gutter."

The victory for comstockery—George Bernard Shaw coined the word "comstockery" back in the days when *Mrs Warren's Profession* was hounded by the Vice Society—was short lived. In March 1930, the Circuit Court of Appeals, consisting of Judges Swan, Augustus N. Hand and Chase, unanimously reversed the conviction and freed Mrs Dennett. The opinion, written by Judge Hand, constituted the first outspoken judicial recognition of the social need for sexual enlightenment.

It may be assumed [said the Court] that any article dealing with the sex side of life and explaining the functions of the sex organs is capable in some circumstances of arousing lust . . . But it can hardly be said that because of the risk of arousing sex impulses there should be no instruction of the young in sex matters, and that the risk of imparting instruction outweighs the disadvantages of leaving them to grope about in mystery and morbid curiosity, and of requiring them to secure such information as they may be able to obtain from ill-informed, and often foul-minded companions, rather than from intelligent and high-minded sources . . .

The old theory that sex information should be left to chance, observed the Court, had changed. While there was still a difference of opinion as to just what kind of instruction should be given, people were generally agreed that mystery and reticence were no solution.

The statute we have to construe [the Court went on] was never thought to bar from the mails everything which might stimulate sex impulses. If so, much chaste poetry and fiction, as well as many useful medical works, would be under the ban. Like everything else this law must be construed reasonably with a view to the general objects aimed at . . . The defendant's discussion of the phenomena of sex is written with sincerity of feeling and with an idealization of the marriage relation and sex emotions. We think it tends to rationalize and dignify such emotions rather than to arouse lust . . . Accurate information, rather than mystery and curiosity, is better in the long run and is less likely to occasion lascivious thoughts than ignorant anxiety.

The good work had begun.

THE CUSTOMS AGAIN

The Dennett case gave the authorities something to think about. They saw that, considering the temper of the courts, convictions would be hard to sustain on appeal. They concluded, very probably, that it would be wise to restrict their suppressions to books coming in at the customs. An indicted defendant had no recourse but to fight; in a customs case the "defendant" was the thing imported, not the importer himself, and expense and trouble were likely to deter the importer from contesting a seizure.

So, shortly after the Tariff Act of 1930 went into effect, the customs officials seized as immoral 120 copies of Dr Johannes Rutgers' book, *The Sexual Life in Its Biological Significance*, consigned to C. E. Midgard in Seattle. They were somewhat nettled to find that Mr Midgard, encouraged by help from the American Civil Liberties Union, was bent on litigating the issue.

The case came up for trial in the Seattle Federal Court before Judge Bourquin and a jury. The prosecutor read to the jury the sections of the book marked obscene by the customs. As he did so he "blushed to the roots of his hair," so the press said, but the jury was unperturbed.

Then the government made a surprise move. In cases

of this kind it was customary for the defense to offer expert testimony as to the scientific soundness and social worth of the material under attack, and for the prosecution to object on the ground that such evidence was incompetent, irrelevant and immaterial, since under the law the question of obscenity was reserved for the jury. In this case, however, the government placed a Dr Beeler on the stand to show that the volume was not a standard medical work. Midgard's attorney objected on the ground that the issue was whether the book was obscene, not whether it was a scientific text. "The doctor is not here," said Judge Bourquin, "to pass on the book one way or another. The jury will do that. Thousands of medical authorities may testify that the book is technical and thousands more might not." Judge Bourquin accepted a simple expression of opinion from Dr Beeler regarding its possible benefit to society, and stopped there. Dr Peterkin gave similar testimony for the defense.

There was some wrangling between counsel as to whether the witnesses were testifying as general practitioners or as specialists. In charging the jury, the judge said:

Gentlemen, you have heard the testimony of experts in the medical profession. Doctor Beeler thinks the volume would be harmful if placed before the young or abnormal person. Doctor Peterkin thinks it will be beneficial to the human race in general. Well, a general practitioner is a doctor who knows a little bit about everything, while a specialist knows a whole lot about very little.

There was a ripple in the courtroom. Judge Bourquin went on:

It is my belief that the author intended this work to be a serious biological study. He has written plainly on certain delicate subjects . . . The matter of sex has bothered the human race ever since Adam ate the apple. It is a fact that children have been left to satisfy their curiosity about this important phase of life as best they can, often learning of it from unscrupulous sources. If there were not some happiness in the love relation between men and women the human race would soon die out. I doubt if parents would go to all the trouble to bring children into the world, support and educate them, care for them when they are ill, if there weren't some attraction in their union together.

Observing that only excerpts had been read by the prosecution, the Court pointed out that "isolated passages even from the sacred writings might not read well alone," and directed the jury to pass upon the book as a whole.

After short deliberation the jury gave the volume a clean bill of health.

UNITED STATES AGAINST MARRIED LOVE

Prior to 1931 Dr Stopes' *Married Love,* a dignified discussion of the physical and psychological obstacles to conjugal happiness, had met with considerable trouble in the United States. Although the *Medical Review of Reviews* had said that it represented the most notable recent advance in the knowledge of women's psycho-physiological life, and although it had sold hundreds of thousands of copies in England and elsewhere, for many years it was branded by the customs people as obscene, and denied entry into this country. In New York State a physician was convicted of selling a copy in 1921. The case went to the Court of Appeals, and the conviction was upheld. A treatise of real social usefulness was thus branded as pornography and compelled to circulate through devious channels.

The book came up in court once more in 1931. This time it was fully exonerated by Judge Woolsey of the federal court. His opinion was as lucid, well-reasoned and scholarly as his utterance in the *Ulysses* case. He referred first to the thesis of the work:

It makes some apparently justified criticisms of the inopportune exercise by the man in the marriage relation of what are often referred to as his conjugal or marital rights, and it pleads with seriousness, and not without some eloquence, for a better understanding by husbands of the physical and emotional side of the sex life of their wives. I do not find anything exceptional anywhere in the book, and I cannot imagine a normal mind to which this book would seem to be obscene or immoral within the proper definition of those words, or whose sex impulses would be stirred by reading it.

Whether or not the book was scientific in some of its claims, he said, was unimportant. It was informative and instructive, and married people could not fail to be benefited by its counsels of perfection and its frank discussion of the difficulties which necessarily arise in the more intimate aspects of married life.

. . . as Professor William Sumner [he went on] aptly used to say in his lectures on the Science of Society at Yale, marriage in its essence is a status of antagonistic co-operation. In such a status, necessarily, centripetal and centrifugal forces are continuously at work, and the measure of its success obviously depends on the extent to which the centripetal forces are predominant. The book before me here has as its whole thesis the strengthening of the centripetal forces in marriage, and instead of being inhospitably received, it should, I think, be welcomed within our borders.

Thus, curiously enough, a book designed for the sex instruction of children was legalized *before* a similar book intended for adults.

At a later date the authorities threatened to suppress Dr Stopes' *Enduring Passion*, a book similar in theme to *Married Love*. An adverse decision had been handed down by the Customs Court years before, but the Woolsey decision served to deter further official action.

SEX TECHNIQUE

Helena Wright's *The Sex Factor in Marriage* was originally published in England, where it was well received by medical and scientific journals. A copy was sent to this country, seized at the customs, examined for obscenity and officially declared legal for admission in April 1931. Though accorded little publicity, this administrative ruling was of far-reaching importance. Neither of Dr Stopes' books had gone into the subject of the technique of sex relations with the degree of particularity to be found in *The Sex Factor in Marriage*. The Wright book was explicit on the subject of various bodily positions in intercourse. An American edition appeared shortly thereafter.

One arm of bureaucracy seldom knows what the other is doing. The American publishers were notified by the postal authorities that steps were about to be taken to declare the volume unmailable. The publishers retorted that the customs people had already placed the governmental seal of approval on the book; they wanted to know whether the government was going to take the position that a book legal for importation was illegal for mailing. The post office had been unaware of the customs ruling. There was considerable chagrin and irritation in official quarters, but the book was not molested.

NORMAL VERSUS ABNORMAL

Both the Dennett decision and the *Married Love* decision were predicated on the principle that any information which enabled a person to understand his own sex nature and thus to lead a healthier and happier life was of social benefit and should not be suppressed.

There is no cogent reason, however, why this principle should be restricted to books dealing solely with normal sex problems. The average man requires a knowledge of the pathological aspects of sex in order to enable him, as a responsible member of the community, to deal intelligently with the social problem of sexual deviations. There are many other works generally sold that treat of the abnormalities of sex. Among these are Krafft-Ebing's *Psychopathia Sexualis,* Symonds' *Sexual Inversion,* Stekel's *Bi-Sexual Love* and *Homosexual Neuroses,* Van de Velde's *Ideal Marriage,* Thesing's *Genealogy of Sex,* Havelock Ellis' *Studies in the Psychology of Sex,* Hirschfeld's *Sexual Pathology,* Stone's *Sexual Impotence in Man* and Forel's numerous studies. There can be no doubt that these works have become part of the general reading matter of the community and are legal for distribution, not only to qualified persons such as physicians, surgeons, psychiatrists, psychologists, pathologists, hospital officials, health officers, professors and students of medicine, but also to laymen. And it is well that this is so. It is not pleasant to recall that there was a time when Havelock Ellis' monumental work, now accepted as a classic, was barred from the library of the British Museum.

Sex in the Halls of Learning

Progress has not been entirely smooth, and some of the setbacks have been encountered in unexpected quarters.

Some time ago two members of the faculty at the University of Missouri—Dr H. O. de Graff, professor of zoology, and Dr Max F. Meyer, professor of experimental psychology—prepared a sex questionnaire to be circulated among the students in connection with a course in sociology. It was designed to elicit frank answers upon which a system of practical ethics might be predicated. There were two sets of questions, one for men and one for women. Some of the questions on the women's paper were as follows:

If you were engaged to marry a man and suddenly learned that he had at some time indulged in illicit sexual relations, would you break the engagement?

Would you break the engagement if you learned that he had so indulged frequently and indiscriminately?

And if, after marriage, you were to find that your husband was sexually unfaithful to you, would you terminate your relations with him?

Would you quit associating with an unmarried woman on learning that she had at some time engaged in sexual irregularities?

On learning that she had so engaged often and promiscuously?

On learning that she had accepted money in return for her sexual favors?

Would you quit associating with a married woman on learning that she engaged in extramarital sexual activities?

Are your own relations with men restrained most by religious convictions, fear of social disapproval, physical repugnance, fear of pregnancy, lack of opportunity, fear of venereal disease or pride in your own ability to resist temptation?

During your childhood did you ever engage in mutual sex play with another individual?

Since sexual maturity, have you ever engaged in specific sexual relations?

There were other questions dealing with trial marriage, divorce and companionate marriage. A corresponding paper was used for the men. No publicity attended the investigation. When the Board of Curators of the university learned about it, the two professors were suspended a year without pay.

Some years ago *Varsity*, Columbia University's literary magazine, directed a questionnaire to four hundred seniors, requesting information as to their personal views on modern trends in marriage, morals and religion. Mindful of the University of Missouri incident, the editors of *Varsity* requested opinions only, not reports based on actual experience. The questions were:

Do you agree that the present moral code is antiquated and should be reformed?

Do you believe in sex affairs outside of marriage?

Do you agree with the marriage reforms advocated in *Marriage and Morals* by Bertrand Russell?

Would you marry only a woman who had had no sex affairs?

Do you feel that any serious attachment for a woman should imply marriage?

Does religion have any appeal to you as part of a personal philosophy?

Just before the scheduled publication date, Dean Hawkes announced that the article setting forth the results of the questionnaire would not be published. He gave no reason. The student editors, when interviewed, refused to state why and by whom the article had been suppressed. It was found, however, that Dean Hawkes' announcement had come after a preliminary tabulation of the first seventy-five answers. In these the seniors had insisted that "the present moral code is antiquated and ought to be reformed"; had approved of extramarital sex relations; had indicated a willingness to marry women of previous sex experience; and had opposed the notion that serious attachment should imply marriage.

THE BIRTH OF A BABY

Early in its career the weekly news-picture magazine, *Life,* inaugurated a series of "photographic essays" on medical subjects touching on public health. From 1936 to 1938 it published essays on epilepsy, cancer, syphilis, nursing, socialized medicine, X rays, tuberculosis and pneumonia.

Of its article on cancer, Dr Clarence Cook Little, managing director of the American Society for the Control of Cancer, said: "It has advanced the cause of cancer educational work more successfully than any other influence during the past twenty years." The essay on tuberculosis elicited the following from Charles A. Frack, executive secretary of the Missouri Tuberculosis Association: "Your splendid presentation of our story is, I believe, one of the greatest single aids to our work that I have seen in years." Dr Herman N. Bundesen, president of the Chicago Board of Health, said of the article on pneumonia: "It was the largest single factor adding impetus to our pneumonia control drive here in Chicago."

In 1938 *Life* decided to run a picture story based on the film, *The Birth of a Baby.* (The suppression of this film by the New York censors is described in Chapter VI.) Advance proofs were shown to a wide group of representative persons, including Dr Thomas Parran, surgeon general of the United States Public Health Service, and Miss Katharine Lenroot, director of the Children's Bureau of the Department of Labor. The response was practically unanimously in favor of publication.

The picture story appeared in the April 11, 1938, issue of *Life*. It consisted of a series of stills taken from the motion picture and explanatory comment. There were two sets of anatomical diagrams. There was no nudity or unnecessary disclosure whatever. The presentation was factual and dignified.

Since the film itself had been the target of protectors of public morals it was to be expected that the picture story would not go unchallenged. Attacks were launched against it from numerous official quarters. Governor Earle of Pennsylvania banned the sale of the issue in his state under a statute dating back to the Civil War. The Canadian authorities were likewise hostile, as were the district attorneys and police chiefs in approximately thirty-three cities.

One of the cities was New Haven, Connecticut. There *Life* magazine decided to test the issue of obscenity. The case came up before Judge Thomas C. Sullivan in the City Court. Yale University medical professors, a prominent New Haven physician, a clergyman and the secretary of the Child Welfare Association testified for *Life*. The result was complete exoneration. The terse, common-sense remarks of the judge boded well.

Another case came up in the City Court of Buffalo and resulted in an acquittal. At about the same time the Post Office Department in Washington ruled that the issue containing the picture story was mailable under the federal laws. It began to look dark for the uplifters.

In New York State the official reaction was varied. In Mineola, the Nassau County grand jury decided that the pictures did not violate the law, and approximately one thousand seized copies of the magazine were returned to newsdealers. The Brooklyn grand jury likewise refused to act against *Life*.

Bronx County, however, was of a different mind. Four

newsdealers were arrested for selling copies. Roy E. Larsen, publisher of *Life,* voluntarily appeared in the county and sold a copy of the magazine to a detective; he wished the test case to involve him as the publisher, not some newsdealer who was in no way responsible for the picture story. He was arraigned, pleaded not guilty and was tried before Judges Kozicke, McDonald and Perlman in the Court of Special Sessions. In their brief the attorneys for *Life* stated:

The sole question involved in this case is whether it is unlawful to present in a serious and dignified manner, in a publication of general circulation, pictures dealing with the problems of motherhood, prenatal care and childbirth. That question in turn resolves itself into whether such pictures are likely to promote the corruption of morals or to lower the standards of right and wrong concerning sexual behavior.

The only witness for the prosecution was the detective who had purchased a copy of the magazine from Larsen. The defense called the following experts in the fields of medicine, social work and education:

Dr Frederick C. Holden, diplomate of the American Board of Obstetrics and Gynecology; consulting obstetrician at the New York and Brooklyn hospitals.

Dr Robert L. Dickinson, diplomate of the American Board of Obstetrics and Gynecology; consulting obstetrician at the Brooklyn Hospital.

Dr Ernest Osborne, assistant professor of education at Teachers College, Columbia University; advisory editor of *Parents' Magazine;* member of the Advisory Committee of the Girl Scouts of America; member of the Executive Committee of the Child Study Association.

Dr Lewis Doshay, psychiatrist of the New York City Children's Court; associate neurologist at the Neurological Institute, the College of Physicians and Surgeons, and the Bronx Hospital;

diplomate in psychiatry of the American Board of Psychiatry and Neurology.

Miss Hazel Corbin, executive secretary of the Maternity Centre Association; member of the National Committee on Maternal Health; consultant of the Children's Bureau.

C. E. Tobias, Jr, headmaster of the Perkiomen School for Boys; professor of zoology of LaSalle College; Quaker minister; lay reader of the Protestant Episcopal Church.

All these people testified that in their considered opinion *Life's* picture story was a valuable contribution to sex education, and that it could not possibly corrupt the morals even of susceptible minors. In addition the defense submitted hundreds of letters from distinguished persons in all walks of life—authors, critics, publishers, editors, educators, doctors, psychiatrists, clergymen—condemning the action taken against the picture story. Edna St Vincent Millay's letter deserves quotation:

If to be born is a pretty disgraceful business, a necessary evil; if to foster and nourish in one's body and expel into the world with pain a new human being is no phenomenon properly calling for keen interest and studious attention, but rather a thoroughly shocking incident to be hushed up as much as possible; then these discreet and dignified pictures are offensive, and human life is at its root obscene.

We have gone too far in our daintiness and prudery, holding the cup of life to our lips with a crooked little finger. Surely the giver of life could not be favorably impressed by such insolence; surely we should be punished for our ingratitude. The gift of life, so cherished, so guarded every moment of the day—surely it should be taken from us if we feel in our hearts that the very first moment of that life, the moment of our birth, was in reality a shameful affair, and the less said about it and the less known about it the better.

If only childbirth were a venereal disease! It might then be considered a fit subject to be dealt with in our popular periodicals.

The court dismissed the charge of obscenity, saying in its opinion:

Section 1141, which purports to define the material condemned by the law, exhausts practically all of the synonyms for the word "obscene." An analysis of the meaning of the adjectives appearing in this section will serve no useful purpose, and there is an inherent impossibility of verbal precision in matters of this kind.

At the trial the prosecution and the defense had clashed over the perennial question of the propriety of introducing expert testimony. The Court addressed itself to this issue:

Upon the trial of this action, the defense produced as witnesses responsible public health authorities, welfare workers and educators who testified to the sincerity, honesty and educational value of the picture story complained of. The prosecution objected to the admission of this testimony . . . Strictly speaking, the contention of the people is correct. In a case such as this the jury or the triers of the facts must declare what the standard shall be. Such evidence is, however, rationally helpful and in recent years courts have considered the opinions of qualified persons.

It is regrettable that the court's opinion tended to create the impression that the question of expert testimony in an obscenity case was pretty much up in the air. The judges had apparently ignored the clear-cut utterance of the Circuit Court of Appeals in the *Ulysses* case:

In applying this test (i.e., whether a book is obscene), the established reputation of the work in the assumption of approved critics . . . are persuasive pieces of evidence . . .

But the troubles of *Life* were by no means over. Massachusetts was not going to be left out of the parade. Two prosecutions were commenced against the picture story; one in Cambridge, and another in Boston. The former resulted in an acquittal. In the latter the court convicted the defendant, a newsdealer, and fined him five hundred dollars. The case was appealed to the Superior Court and was affirmed.

These cases shed a light on censorship in action. Geography, it seems, is a determinant of obscenity. Pictures may pollute newsstands and leave the mails undefiled. They may be decent in Queens and Brooklyn, and yet be indecent enough for the Bronx to prosecute criminally. They may offend in Boston to the extent of warranting a heavy fine, and yet pass uncensored in Cambridge.

It's a bad jigsaw puzzle. The pieces don't fit, and no sensible person will try to make them fit.

CHAPTER IV

The Theater and the Law

I might almost favor a censorship myself if I thought we could get one that would pass Aristophanes and suppress Earl Carroll; but what we would get under any political or ecclesiastical supervision would probably be a board that would pass Carroll and suppress Aristophanes.
ELMER DAVIS, *Theatre Guild Magazine* (1931)

THE APPEAL OF BOOKS is largely mental; the graphic and plastic arts have never fully entered into the lives of ordinary people; it is only within the past decade that the movies have ceased to be purely visual. The stage addresses itself to almost all the senses. Of all the arts, it affords the closest approximation of life.

Moreover, since the conflict of people and passions is the essence of drama, the stage concerns itself to a large extent with the varied manifestations of love.

For these reasons the stage has always been anathema to the censor. The Church frowned on it from the very beginning, calling it an arsenal of prostitution. Puritan England denounced it as a temple of pagan lusts.

THE CHANGING TIMES

In 1906 *Sappho* was suppressed because Olga Nethersole was carried upstairs in it by a man. Ibsen's *Ghosts* was taboo for years. In 1917 the New England Watch and Ward Society prevented Mary Garden from appearing in Strauss' *Salome*. Not so very long ago Lewis Carroll (the Reverend Mr Dodgson), author of *Alice's Adventures in Wonderland,* went to a performance of *Pinafore* given by children, and of the famous "Damme, it's too bad," of the captain and the chorus he wrote:

I cannot find words to convey to the reader the pain I felt in seeing those dear children taught to utter such words to amuse ears grown callous to their ghastly meaning. . . . How Mr Gilbert could have stooped to write, or Sir Arthur Sullivan could have prostituted his noble art to set to music such vile trash, it passes my skill to understand.

Reviewing a performance of *Salome* at the Metropolitan Opera House in 1938, Lawrence Gilman, music critic of the New York *Herald Tribune,* observed that the "once scandalous aberration of the Muse" had at last joined the roster of unimpeachables, along with *Mignon, Lohengrin* and *Aïda*. Recalling the time when such "malodorous vegetables of disesteem" as monstrous, pestilential, mephitic, abhorrent, diseased, polluted, bestial and loathsome had been flung at the work, he wrote:

In those days, tender-minded souls, contemplating the scene in which the exigent daughter of Herodias fondles the severed head of John, were filled with alarm for the safety of the moral order. They feared, as Mr Ernest Newman (safe in unregenerate London) remarked at the time, that "if women in general were suddenly to become abnormally morbid, conceive perverse passions for clergymen, have these holy men decapitated when their advances were rejected, and then start kissing the severed heads in a blind fury of love and revenge in the middle of the drawing room, the householder would feel the earth rocking beneath his feet." Thus does Time extenuate even the most formidable assaults upon the hearth and home.

Mrs Warren's Profession, The God of Vengeance, Frankie and Johnnie, the sex plays of the boom years, and the burlesque of the depression days are the milestones that mark the development of the obscenity law in the theater. The specters that stand beside the milestones are those of prostitution and sexual inversion, and the strip tease.

COMSTOCK VERSUS SHAW

Comstock—Ernest Sutherland Bates called him the Sinister Old Man, for Comstock boasted of having caused sixteen suicides—learned in 1905 of Arnold Daly's intention to produce *Mrs Warren's Profession* in this country. He wrote to Daly, pointing out that George Bernard Shaw's play had been suppressed in London. Daly replied that in his opinion the play was "a strong sermon and a great moral lesson," and he invited Comstock to a rehearsal. Comstock did not accept. He notified the police instead.

Hearing of this, Shaw said: "Comstockery is the world's standing joke at the expense of the United States. Europe likes to hear of such things. It confirms the deep-seated conviction of the Old World that America is a provincial place, a second-rate country-town civilization after all." Comstock retorted by calling Shaw an Irish smut dealer, and his play "reekings." "The English and the Irish," he warned, "have furnished their full quota of unfit books and pictures and plays." He declared that he would bring Shaw's works and the people who disseminate them to the test of the law. "This Shaw," he said, "is not outside our rules." Shaw gibed back: "Comstock has declared his intention of suppressing me. He had better, for if he does not I am afraid I shall end by shocking him out of his wits."

If Shaw, thousands of miles away, was no match for

the Old Man in influence, the Old Man was no match
for him in a verbal combat. The word "comstockery"
must have stung him more than a little. He was used
to diatribe; much of it had been leveled at him before;
he had made a practice of ignoring it. This time he felt
called upon to answer. With the devious psychology
characteristic of the censor, he twisted the invective into
an encomium. In his annual report to the Vice Society
he accepted the term as a "decoration," and offered his
own definition of it: "The applying of the noblest
principles of law . . . in the interest of public morals,
especially those of the young."

The surprising thing is that Comstock did not stand
alone in his disapproval of *Mrs Warren's Profession*.
The press sided with him. One newspaper referred to
the play as "tainted drama." Another, too squeamish to
mention prostitution, fearfully suggested that a theme
"hitherto unspeakable" would now become the subject
of discussion.

The play was finally carried into the Court of Special
Sessions. It was cleared of the charge of obscenity by
a divided vote. In its opinion the court turned dramatic
critic. It denounced the play as a "shock producer"
making use of "old and hackneyed materials," and containing "stereotyped railings against current social conditions." The Court ventured to predict that "its life on
the boards would be short."

The prediction proved true. In the end the Old Man
won anyway. The play collapsed, and Daly was through.
Bankrupt and embittered, he never fulfilled the brilliant promise of his early years.

THE GOD OF VENGEANCE

This play was produced in New York City in 1923.
Although several of the scenes were laid in a brothel the

play was harmless enough. Coals of retribution were ultimately heaped on the head of the brothel keeper, and this should have satisfied the moralists. It did not.

A criminal prosecution was started, and a number of participants were convicted. The case was carried from the Court of Special Sessions to the Appellate Division, where it was affirmed without opinion. The Court of Appeals reversed the convictions on a technicality, carefully avoiding the question of obscenity. The defendants were never tried again, but the play never reopened.

FRANKIE AND JOHNNIE

Eight years later *Frankie and Johnnie* appeared on the New York stage. It was a dramatization of the folk song, "Frankie and Johnnie," and was laid in a St Louis resort for drinking, gambling and prostitution in the 1850's.

Convictions were obtained but were ultimately reversed. The opinion of the court of last resort contained scant solace for the vice hunter.

First of all, the Court stated that it was not a censor of plays and that it did not attempt to regulate manners. One could call a spade a spade, the Court said, without offending decency, even though modesty might be shocked. The question was not whether the play depicted a low dive shunned by refined people, but whether the tendency of the production was to excite "lustful and lecherous desire." Coarse scenes and vulgar language, the Court insisted, did not in themselves create such desire. The argument of the prosecution that the play was indecent because it portrayed doings of prostitutes was rejected.

Prostitutes [the Court said] are not so rarely represented on the stage as to arouse the sexual propensities of the spectators whenever they appear. G. B. Shaw's play, *Mrs Warren's Pro-*

fession, deals, in the language of the polite dramatist, with what has been styled "the oldest profession in the world." The heroine of *Rain* was a seductive harlot. Scenes of *The Shanghai Gesture* are laid in a house of bad character. *Lysistrata* is frank in the discussion of sex relations but does not excite desire as might the lascivious display of female charms. The Bible talks bluntly of harlots and whores but it does not incite to immorality.

The presentation of such a play, the Court went on, might be "repulsive to puritanical ideas of propriety," as would *Camille,* and might be offensive even to the liberal-minded as lacking in taste, as would the morally unobjectionable *Abie's Irish Rose.* The play might be gross, and its characters wanting in moral sense. It might depict women who carried on a vicious trade.

It cannot [the Court ruled] be said to suggest, except "to a prurient imagination," unchaste or lustful ideas. It does not counsel or invite to vice or voluptuousness. It does not deride virtue. Unless we say that it is obscene to use the language of the street rather than that of the scholar, the play is not obscene under the Penal Law, although it might be so styled by the censorious.

Toward the end of its opinion the Court apparently became worried that its pronouncement might invite unbridled license. The conclusion carried a warning:

We do not purpose to sanction indecency on the stage by this decision or to let down the bars against immoral shows or to hold that the depiction of scenes of bawdry on the stage is to be tolerated. We hold merely that the fact that Frankie and Johnnie and their companions were not nice people does not in itself make the play obscene. A history of prostitution or of sexual life is not *per se* indecent, although such a book might easily be so written as to offend decency.

SEXUAL INVERSION

Early in 1927 the New York police stopped three plays: *The Captive, The Virgin Man* and *Sex. The*

Captive had been running without interruption for five months, and *Sex* for eleven months. The former was a sensitive study of sexual deviation in women. It would probably have continued to run unmolested if its success had not precipitated a succession of plays about abnormality. *The Hymn to Venus* and *The Drag,* dealing with Lesbianism and homosexuality, were about to open in New York. The authorities felt they had to stem the tide. The good had to go the way of the bad. It is said that one of the people responsible for closing *The Captive* was Walter Lippmann, who had for years, ostensibly at least, espoused the cause of free speech.

The defendants in *Virgin Man* were tried, and all but one were found guilty. *The Captive* was voluntarily withdrawn after the issuance of warrants. The defendants in *Sex* were tried and convicted. There were no appeals.

THE PADLOCK LAW

The stir caused by the sex plays furnished excellent ammunition for those who felt that the stage was living up to its historic reputation as a sink of iniquity, and that a drastic remedy was needed.

A high-powered crusade was begun in New York to tighten the provisions of the obscenity statute. The result was the Wales Law, the padlock provisions of which represent censorship at its worst. In addition to re-enacting the old law penalizing "obscene, indecent, immoral and impure" dramas, it prohibited the portrayal of sex degeneracy or sex perversion on the stage, and provided that if a conviction was obtained under the statute, the theater itself could be refused a new license for a year.

The Wales Law was nefarious because it was a weapon of intimidation. It could be used against theater owners even though never actually enforced. If it was

enforced an innocent theater owner might find his
property padlocked for a year because of a production
for which he was in no way responsible. He auto-
matically became the guarantor of the decency of the
shows which any tenant of his might choose to present.
Like the bookseller, he was made responsible for something he could not adequately guard against even with
the greatest prudence; unlike the bookseller, his property was subjected to temporary forfeiture.

Although the padlock provisions have never been
invoked repeated efforts to repeal the law have failed.
It stands on our statute books, a sword of Damocles
over theater owners.

PLEASURE MAN

Arguing, back in the old days when he was a public
figure, against too rigid an application of the obscenity
law to literature, Jimmy Walker once remarked that he
had never known a woman who had been ruined by a
book. Yet he was responsible, so it is said, for the closing of *Pleasure Man* in 1928.

The play ran for two weeks before the police descended on it. The raid was a carnival, with all the
trappings of clanging patrol wagons, brass buttons,
plain-clothes men and reporters. The cast was photographed in the police cars, at the bar of justice, in jail;
the newspapers whooped up the story for all it was
worth. The net result was that the police publicized the
very thing they were supposed to be suppressing.

THE FIGHT GOES ON

The agitation for "cleaning up" the stage continued
unabated. It survived the stock-market crash and
zoomed into the depression years. In 1930 Bishop

Manning issued a statement to the effect that most Broadway plays were "unfit." William A. Brady, a veteran of the theater, agreed with him; he declared that "what was filthy in Caesar's time is filthy in Jimmy Walker's." Channing Pollock, too, was shocked by "rampant indecency on the stage." Rev. James M. Gillis, editor of the *Catholic World,* denounced realism in the theater as "a hypocritical excuse for introducing lewdness."

We must guard [he said] against the sophisticated argument of those who say that moral standards change, and that what might have shocked our fathers or grandfathers is all right for us. This thesis is heretical. It is absolutely immoral. And we must guard against the argument of the realists who say: "We have grown up; we want the meat of life; we no longer want the lollipops." That is a damnable piece of hypocrisy.

Actors' Equity, panicky lest there be a stampede resulting in political censorship along the lines of the movies, proposed a plan of censorship within the theater. Under the plan a committee of nine, chosen by the industry, was to pass on all protested plays.

The Dramatists' Guild blocked action on the Actors' Equity proposal. Marc Connelly had a few things to say about the "snarling busybodies" who were clamoring for censorship. He pointed out that we had ample laws against immoral exhibitions, and that it was up to the authorities to apply them. Elmer Rice insisted that the dramatist must be guided solely by the dictates of his own taste and conscience. Lewis Mumford said: "I had rather banish the theater altogether, as Plato banished the poet, than see it put under censorship." "The artist knows," wrote Sheldon Cheney, "that art, and particularly the theater, dies of prohibitions and limitations."

Eventually the agitation died down. Somehow the

theater managed, without legal pre-censorship, to survive the doom prophesied for it by those who saw in the
new plays nothing more than—to use Mr Brady's
words—"a lot of lousy jokes and ideas."

But the zealots emerged from the fray with an idea.

THE STRIP TEASE

New York State has a specific statute covering immoral shows. No one contends that this statute is
deficient. Under it persons responsible for presenting
an obscene play may be prosecuted criminally. The
vice hunters never liked this law because it involves a
jury trial and all the incidents of judicial proceedings.
They found time and again that judges and juries did
not agree with them. So they cast about for a short
cut which would eliminate the courts and assure quick
success. They found an ally in the person of License
Commissioner Moss of New York City.

Every theater in New York must be licensed. It was
always assumed that a theater which had complied with
all the fire and health requirements was entitled to a
license, and to a renewal of the license upon its expira-
tion. In 1935, acting upon pressure from morality
groups, the License Commissioner—the same man that
had proved his friendship for vice crusaders before in
the matter of magazines—revoked the license of a
burlesque theater. The ground of the revocation was
the "offensive" nature of the exhibition. Nudity and
the strip tease were given as reasons.

The case was carried to the highest state court and
resulted in a defeat for the Commissioner. The court
held that he could not *revoke* a license on the ground
of immorality unless there was a prior conviction on
that score. Unfortunately the court made a distinction
between revocation and renewal, and intimated that the

Commissioner might refuse to *renew* a license at will. This meant that on renewals at least the Commissioner could exercise censorship powers. Since licenses had to be renewed yearly, the Commissioner's power was not really impaired. He was only temporarily stalemated. So he waited.

THE DUNNIGAN BILL

When the licenses of the burlesque theaters ran out in 1937, the Commissioner refused to renew them. At the same time a bill specifically giving him the power to *revoke* licenses was introduced in Albany and was passed by the state legislature. This bill, known as the Dunnigan Bill, provided that "upon proof *satisfactory to the licensing authority* of a violation of this section [i.e. the obscenity law] . . . the licensing authority . . . may revoke such license unless the person named as chargeable with the violation shall then have been prosecuted, tried and acquitted thereof." In other words, the Commissioner was to have sweeping censorship powers on revocations as well as on renewals.

This time the theatrical forces were stung to something more than mere vociferation. The Joint Committee of the Legitimate Theater Opposed to Censorship was formed, and a campaign was launched to defeat the bill. A mass meeting was held at the New Amsterdam Theater, and all the branches of the industry—producers, authors, directors, actors, critics, stagehands—participated. The support of liberal and progressive groups was enlisted. Publicity was freely given by the press.

The Joint Committee was largely instrumental in having the Dunnigan Bill vetoed by Governor Lehman. The excitement about the non-renewal of the licenses of the burlesque houses quieted down. A compromise was reached between the theater owners and the city authorities: the word "burlesque" was to be taboo; the houses were to reopen as "follies" of some kind; the producers were to set up self-regulation along the lines of the Hays office, with a czar and a voluntary code.

STAGE PURITY IN BOSTON

The Boston of book-burning notoriety evinced no greater tolerance in the theater. In 1929 Mayor Nichols forbade the production of Eugene O'Neill's *Strange Interlude*. Instead of putting up a fight, as it should have, the Theatre Guild moved the production to a suburb beyond the jurisdiction of the city authorities; thousands flocked to view it there. Decency on the stage had become a matter of miles.

Six years later Boston refused to permit Sean O'Casey's *Within the Gates* to open there. The authorities went further; they tabooed public readings of the play. It was not made clear whether they objected to it because a whore was one of the principal characters, or because the clergy was presented in an unfavorable light. Nor were the authorities more explicit when later in the same year they refused to let *The Children's Hour* open. But this time the producer, Herman Shumlin, was not supine; he contested the ban vigorously. It was largely due to this that the law applicable to plays was changed in 1936.

Under the statute previously existing, the city license commissioner had been a virtual dictator of stage morals, vested with power to prevent presentation. The new law requires at least one performance free of censorship and a public hearing before the authorities take any action through the revocation or suspension of a license.

Due to this legislative change, the situation has become much more wholesome. No play has been entirely suppressed, and comparatively few changes have been made in those licensed. Under the new regime a few profane expressions were eliminated from Ben Hecht's *To Quito and Back;* the words "bitch" and "bastard" were deleted from *Boy Meets Girl* ("bitch" being replaced by "dame," "bastard" by "son of a gun" and "buzzard"); "blasphemous" expressions were eliminated from Sidney Howard's *Ghost of Yankee Doodle;* "God damn" was dropped from George Kaufman's *You Can't Take It with You.*

The puzzling thing about Boston is that despite an extraordinary civic sensitiveness to indecency on the legitimate stage, burlesque has been allowed to flourish without hindrance. When, many years ago, the police closed Eugene Walter's *The Easiest Way,* a honky-tonk called *Moulin Rouge* was going full blast. *The Children's Hour* couldn't go on, but things hummed merrily at the Old Howard, the leading burlesque house.

The explanation that suggests itself is significant. While in most cases legitimate producers have shown no disposition to put up determined opposition, burlesque has. In 1933 the Watch and Ward Society had the license of Old Howard suspended for a month. The Old Howard promptly sued the society for damages. The case was settled, and since that time there has been no attempt to molest burlesque.

OTHER CITIES

When *Tobacco Road,* Jack Kirkland's dramatization of Erskine Caldwell's novel about Georgia white trash, moved to Chicago in 1935, Mayor Edward Kelly denounced it as "just a mess of filth and degeneracy, without any plot, rhyme or reason," and ordered the police to stop the show. The producers of the play obtained a temporary injunction in the federal court, but the Circuit Court of Appeals dissolved the injunction and upheld the mayor. In the meantime the Detroit authorities had followed Mayor Kelly's lead and had closed the show there.

Later Shostakovich's opera, *Lady Macbeth of Mzensk*, was "toned down" in Philadelphia at the instance of the censorship forces there; some of the music was deemed too suggestive. Claire Boothe's *Kiss the Boys Goodbye* was banned in Salt Lake City on the ground that it was "too off color" for the Mormon population. After several performances of Robert Sherwood's *Idiot's Delight* in Memphis, Tennessee, Lloyd B. Binford, chairman of the City Censor Board, charged Alfred Lunt and Lynn Fontanne with using objectionable language and ruled that if they ever came to Memphis again they would have to submit advance scripts of their shows. Benjamin P. Moulton, chairman of the Providence, Rhode Island, Bureau of Police and Fire, refused to issue licenses to John Steinbeck's *Of Mice and Men* and Claire Boothe's *The Women,* claiming that the underlying theme of both plays was "morbid and degrading in character," and that the former contained "a most unusual amount of blasphemy and unwholesome vulgarity."

It is interesting to note that all the productions which had trouble outside New York passed the New York bulldogs unscathed. Perhaps the latter were too busy disinfecting burlesque.

Previous Restraint?

Strictly speaking, there is no pre-censorship in the theater. Unlike the movies, plays need not be submitted for approval to a politically constituted review board before they may be presented. And yet the situation is far from being wholesome. It is honeycombed with possibilities of abuse of bureaucratic power, intimidation and duress.

The Wales Padlock Law remains a weapon that may be used for purposes of suppression at any time. Originally created to safeguard the public against risks of fire or faulty construction, licensing agencies have arrogated to themselves censorship powers that virtually oust judges and juries.

The stage looks to the screen. Barrett H. Clark, one of the best-informed people on the subject of plays, wrote in *Theatre Arts Monthly* some time ago:

Very few manuscripts are bought (by a commercial theater producer) before they have been read either officially or otherwise by someone in the office of the story editor of one or more of the motion-picture companies, or at least before the manager is reasonably sure that his manuscript will ultimately interest one of the picture companies. Nearly all . . . of the managers . . . submit scripts to persons affiliated with a picture company before they will think seriously of signing a contract. If you don't believe this try sending out a manuscript—a really good manuscript—and put a note on the cover saying, "Picture rights of this manuscript are not for sale." Most of the managers will refuse even to read the play.

As a result, the moral standards of the films are impressed, though to a lesser extent, on the theater. These moral standards are cumulative. They represent the edicts of the Hays office and the ideas of the six state review boards which the Hays office tries to evaluate and apply.

SEX VERSUS POLITICS

The stage censors—the License Commissioner in New York City, the elected officials of other municipalities, the morality groups that whip up "public" indignation, the courts that condemn plays—are all avowedly concerned with protecting the theater from "immorality." The pretext is an old one. Ibsen, Brieux, Maeterlinck and Shaw were all hounded in their day because their works were said to be offensive to decency. Today no one doubts the real reason. They were too outspoken about some sore of the existing social order.

In 1932 Sklar and Maltz wrote *Merry-Go-Round*, attacking the corruption of Jimmy Walker's city administration. The Tammany Hall regime bedeviled the production by placing a succession of violations on the theater where the production was housed.

The pattern was copied by other cities. In 1934 Los Angeles, varying the technique only in that a different excuse was used, arrested members of the workers' theater for "carrying concealed weapons" which turned out to be wooden props. In 1935 the authorities in Philadelphia jumped on Christopher Wood's *Too Late to Die*, a study of unemployment. Washington, D. C., followed suit in connection with a Negro group's production of *Stevedore*. Clifford Odets' *Waiting for Lefty*, charged with being "un-American," was suppressed in Boston, Philadelphia, Newark and New Haven; the police broke up a performance in Chelsea, Massachusetts; vigilantes tried to prevent its presentation at Laguna Beach, California.

Pins and Needles, the highly successful revue produced by the International Ladies' Garment Workers Union, met its troubles in Canada. When the show reached Montreal the authorities there insisted that two skits be cut entirely: *Mussolini Handicap*, a satire on the Italian crusade for larger families, and *Four Little Angels of Peace*, which lampooned Mussolini, Hitler, Chamberlain and a representative of Japan. It was only after changes were made in the skits that they could be shown.

These instances—a few of many—are worth pondering. The number of places where unpalatable truths may not be dramatized is growing. The work begun by bluenoses is being carried forward by vigilantes.

The problem was clearly stated by the Authors' League of America at the time *Waiting for Lefty* was running into difficulties: "The tactics employed are familiar and timeworn. Technicalities of the fire laws, obsolete statutes from the old 'blue laws' period, red tape in connection with licenses—all these are used to bar the play from theaters or to stop performances. But the real issue of freedom of opinion and the right to express it is clearly the crux of the matter. Not only those who are concerned with the theater but everyone who wants to preserve the American heritage of civil liberties will bitterly resent this arbitrary suppression of a play which has been widely acclaimed."

CHAPTER V

The Censor and the Movies

Motion pictures have ruined a lot more evenings than they have morals.

TED COOK, *Reader's Digest* (1939)

THERE IS A CURIOUS STORY connected with the birth of motion-picture censorship in New York State. When the bill was introduced in the legislature, some of the producers on the West Coast got together and decided to fight it. Counting on the co-operation of exhibitors, they sent a representative East to organize the opposition. The emissary called a meeting of the more important New York exhibitors, explained the gravity of the situation and asked for contributions to a war chest. He stressed the fact that unless the bill was strenuously resisted it would certainly pass.

He was in for a surprise. The exhibitors shook their heads. They had no intention of fighting censorship, they said. On the contrary, they'd welcome it. There was a criminal statute in New York against obscene shows. Without censorship, exhibitors ran the risk of prosecution if they played a salacious picture. Censorship would place an official stamp of approval on all films, and would insure theater owners against criminal charges for indecency.

The emissary of the producers threw up his hands. Opposition to the bill crumbled, and it became law.

FACTS AND FIGURES

The movies represent a relatively new art. They date back to the turn of the century. Yet with the exception of the radio, they are the most important single factor in the entertainment of the nation.

It is estimated by the Hays office that eighty-five million people attend the movies weekly in the United States.

There are over eighteen thousand motion-picture houses in this country, out of a world total of ninety thousand.

About two billion dollars is invested in the industry here, and over a quarter of a million people are employed.

Annual production costs run between one hundred and fifty and two hundred million dollars.

During the 1937–38 season 588 pictures were produced in Hollywood, constituting 70 per cent of the world output.

Americans spend well over half a billion dollars a year for amusement, and about 80 per cent of this goes to the movies.

The policing of the screen is the most completely organized and most far-reaching form of censorship existing today. Since it is pre-censorship by official censors as well as unofficial ones, it is also the most drastic. It directly prescribes the mental fare of the entire nation.

THE BIRTH OF AN ART

The first commercial movies were shown in Koster and Bial's Music Hall in Herald Square, New York, shortly before the turn of the century. They spread like wildfire. Nickelodeons sprung up everywhere. The penny arcades, which up to that time had furnished much of the amusement for impecunious millions in cities, found a new rival. People flocked to hastily built theaters, to vaudeville houses that included pictures in their programs, to ramshackle stores which, with the addition of a ticket booth, rows of wooden benches, a sheet and a broken-down piano, were metamorphosed overnight into cinemas.

The pictures were poor. They flickered badly; their contrastiness hurt the eyes; the film was brittle and needed frequent splicing. The emulsions were so slow that the producers could not use artificial light; even interiors had to be taken in broad sunlight.

Nor was the subject matter of the films any better. The aim was not to tell a story or convey an idea, but to depict motion. The first connected narrative appeared in *The Great Train Robbery*. For years afterward lurid Westerns and slapstick comedies held full sway.

Production was haphazard, distribution poorly organized, the industry chaotic. There was cutthroat competition; rival distributors didn't hesitate to use gangster tactics; so bitter was the struggle to survive that there was no opportunity to be concerned about the integrity of the product. In many ways the new art resembled in its infancy the early years of the West it portrayed with such gusto and frequency. It was unbridled, rowdy and ribald.

Excesses were inevitable. A questionable picture sprang up here and there. Good folk were shocked. Their apprehensions were compounded of several things: disapprobation of the vulgar pictures then shown, fear of what the screen might bring in the future, the distrust and hostility with which society always greets a new art form, and probably a recognition of the potentialities of the movies for molding the thoughts and actions of millions.

The screen continued uncurbed for about fifteen years. Then the vigilantes sprang into action.

THE SUPREME COURT SPEAKS

Several states passed laws requiring movies to be officially approved before exhibition. Similar laws as to newspapers had been declared unconstitutional. The Ohio censorship law was therefore attacked:

(1) On the ground that motion pictures, like the press, were vehicles for the expression of opinion, and that any *previous* restraint on their exhibition violated the constitutional right of free speech and free press; and

(2) On the further ground that the Ohio statute, in authorizing the showing only of films that were educational, moral, amusing or harmless, failed to provide a standard whereby these qualities could be judged, and thus permitted the approval of films to hinge on the "arbitrary judgment, whim and caprice" of the censors.

The case was carried to the United States Supreme Court in 1915. It was argued before Justices White, McKenna, Holmes, Day, Hughes, Van Devanter, Lamar, Pitney and McReynolds. The Court swept aside both objections and upheld the censorship law as constitutional.

The Court said that the motion-picture industry was a private enterprise, the primary purpose of which was to amuse and entertain, not to express opinion. It insisted that pictures of an educational character constituted merely one of the incidental branches of the industry, and not by any means its main branch.

It cannot be put out of view [said the Court] that the exhibition of moving pictures is a business, pure and simple, originated and conducted for profit, like other spectacles, not to be regarded or intended to be regarded by the Ohio Constitution, we think, as part of the press of the country, as organs of public opinion.

Nor did the Court find fault with the fact that the statute failed to furnish any precise criteria of propriety. The hope was expressed that in the long run the statute would derive "precision from the sense and experience of men, and become certain and useful guide in reasoning and conduct." And so movie censorship became firmly entrenched.

One rarely knows what actuates the judicial mind in arriving at a decision; a court opinion is often a carefully constructed piece of rationalization, not a frank disclosure. But it cannot be doubted that in ruling on the Ohio law the Supreme Court must have had in mind the movies as they then existed, and felt itself impelled, on *that* basis, to put them in the same category with circuses, prize fights, baseball and other mass exhibitions. The Court could not—or, at any rate, it did not—foresee the eventual evolution of the screen as a powerful medium for disseminating ideas.

Shortly after the Ohio case the Supreme Court upheld the Kansas censorship law, and that seemed to settle the question of constitutionality beyond dispute. The point has not been raised since. When talking pictures appeared it was generally assumed that they were amenable to the same restrictions as the silent films. The power of the motion-picture censor seems to be complete.

It's almost twenty-five years since the Supreme Court has spoken on this subject. Much water has since flowed over the dam. We are living in a vastly different world today; the movies have grown to gargantuan proportions in resources, technical advancement and influence; the court itself is a changed body.

What would happen if the question of constitutionality were raised anew and ably argued? It's a provocative question, even if somewhat on the academic side. For the likelihood of a new test case is slim. The industry doesn't want it.

THE STATES

Seven states have imposed previous restraints on motion pictures: New York, Kansas, Maryland, Ohio, Pennsylvania, Virginia and Massachusetts, the last named only as to Sunday shows. This does not mean that only a small portion of the country is affected. The film producers manufacture for national consumption and cannot afford to prepare separate versions of pictures. The censorship states are key states. The producers always work with the censors in mind.

It is heartening to note that since 1922, despite the unceasing efforts of the reformers, no state has passed a censorship law. In 1922 a censorship law was enacted by both houses of the Legislature in Massachusetts, but was defeated in the general referendum by a vote of almost three to one. Between 1922 and 1927, forty-eight different bills calling for censorship were introduced in the free states, and all of them failed.

NEW YORK STATE

Censorship in New York is fairly typical of the process elsewhere. The Education Department of the state has a Motion Picture Division. All films must be licensed for exhibition and must be submitted for review to the Division in advance of release. No license is issued for any picture if it is "obscene, indecent, immoral, inhuman, sacrilegious or is of such a character that its exhibition would tend to corrupt morals or incite to crime." No license is required for newsreels. An aggrieved applicant for a license has the right of review by the Board of Regents, and by the courts.

There have been comparatively few cases in which the rulings of the Motion Picture Division have been contested. From the cases that have been litigated it is clear that the regents and the courts are reluctant to reverse the findings of the reviewing officers. The rule is that no reversal·may be had unless it is shown that the censors acted arbitrarily, capriciously or in bad faith, or have abused their discretion. There is no protection against ineptness or stupidity. The reason for the rule is obvious. If appeals were encouraged the regents and the courts would be swamped. That's the last thing in the world that they want.

During the year ending June 30, 1938, the Motion Picture Division reviewed 1955 pictures. Of these 952 were feature pictures and 1003 were shorts. Twenty-three films were rejected in toto, and eliminations were made in 110 others. The pictures which were cut were classified as follows:

Dramas	61
Comedies	26
Comedy dramas	5
Serials	1
Educational	3
Cartoons	1
Scenic	8
Miscellaneous	5
	110

Here's a breakdown of the 772 separate cuts which were made in these 110 pictures:

Classification	Number of Cuts	Percentage of Total
Indecent	364	47.2%
Immoral	265	34.3%
Inciting to crime	60	7.7%
Sacrilegious	55	7.1%
Inhuman	28	3.7%

In New York and elsewhere, the forbidden categories are sex, crime, violence, government and religion. The first three must not be made too attractive or too gruesome; the last two must not be directly attacked or indirectly libeled. Sex is the chief bugaboo. In 1937–38 it was responsible for almost 80 per cent of the cuts ordered.

The percentages differ from year to year, depending on the current screen fad. If it's a year of gangster pictures the crime category will outweigh sex. Here's a tabulation, taken from *Censored: The Private Life of the Movies* (Ernst and Lorentz), of cuts made by all state censors in 1928:

Classification	Number of Cuts	Percentage of Total
Crime	1672	56.4%
Sex	872	29.5%
Impropriety	348	11.8%
Government	49	1.7%
Religion	16	.6%

It is illuminating to study the operations of the censors:

Such words as "bum," "bitch," "wop," "chippy," "mistress," "harlot," "naked" and "prostitute" are forbidden. So, too, are such phrases as "twin beds," "it wasn't love," "long, lonely nights," "you were with him all last night," "marriage needn't make any difference between us," and "there is a man who's a hound with women." The restrictions often result in clumsy and ridiculous circumlocutions. In a recent film "floozy" was changed to "parasite," "girls of the streets" became "women like that," and "on the make for" wound up as "chasing after."

Kisses may not last more than four feet of film. Passionate embraces are taboo.

Among acts or scenes that may not be shown are thumbing of the nose, slapping a woman's posterior, unmarried couples living together, partly clad men or women when the opposite sex is present, a lover making exit through a window, a wedding ring on the finger of an unmarried girl, and the key to a young lady's apartment in the possession of a man not her husband.

Nudity is decent or indecent, depending upon color.

Cockfights and bullfights are forbidden.

Profanity is frowned on. Until recent years the word "hell" couldn't be used.

Scenes of drinking and gambling must be brief. This is also true of maternity scenes.

Many themes of importance to society may not be discussed: pregnancy, venereal disease, eugenics, birth control, abortion, illegitimacy, prostitution, miscegenation, divorce.

The New York censors appear to be well intrenched. The studios won't defy them; the exhibitors feel safer with them; the uplifters stand solidly behind them. There's another reason, too. The state charges a license fee for passing on films that are submitted, and the fees exceed by far the cost of running the Motion Picture Division. Whether it's legal or not, New York State profits handsomely on censorship.

FEDERAL CENSORSHIP

The threat of federal censorship is an ever-present one. Films made in Hollywood or elsewhere must be shipped from state to state, and foreign pictures must come in through the customs. The national obscenity laws apply to interstate and foreign shipments. The federal power is rarely exercised, except as to foreign films. Notable on the list of barred entries was *Ecstasy*, starring Hedy Lamarr. It was a love story frankly and directly told. The late Pope Pius XI was said to have disapproved it when it was shown in Europe. The picture was sent to Washington and was privately shown to representatives of the Treasury Department. They voted against it, and an official order was issued barring it from entry. Subsequently, the order was confirmed by a federal court decision. An appeal was taken, but before it was argued the federal authorities destroyed the reels in question, and the Appellate Court refused to entertain the appeal for that reason. Since the subject matter of the suit was no longer in existence, the Court said that the question of its obscenity was no longer moot. The picture, considered by many to be a work of art, has remained banned. It is only one of a number that have been kept out of the country.

Despite the zealous scissor work of the state review boards, the uplifters have not been content. They have cast a jaundiced eye on the forty-one states in which pre-licensing has failed to gain a foothold, and have been distressed by the spectacle. They have launched repeated drives for a more rigid moral code on the screen, and stricter official surveillance. Their efforts have consisted of religious exhortation and agitation for federal censorship. In his encyclical *On Clean Motion Pictures,* July 2, 1936, and other encyclicals, the late Pope Pius XI condemned immorality in the films and urged prelates all over the world to get their parishioners to pledge themselves to shun pictures not approved by the Church. The New York Society for the Suppression of Vice has long fought for a national reviewing body "with a single standard applicable in all forty-eight states." Calvin Coolidge turned down such legislation in 1926.

The Patman Bill

In 1934 Representative Patman introduced the H. R. 6097, which sought to set up federal regulation of motion pictures.

The bill was nefarious for many reasons. Although its sponsor inferred that it was to supplant state censorship and thus dispense with having forty-eight different standards for motion pictures, it did not—and indeed could not—abolish the existing state boards, nor did it prevent the creation of additional boards in other states. It merely added federal supervision to the existing burden of state and municipal regulation. It widened the area of control in point of time: in addition to making *completed* films subject to review, it called for federal control from the preparation of the script onward. It established a governmental censorship analogous in principle to that exercised by totalitarian nations. It was more drastic than any state law, because it extended the forbidden categories and sought to dictate, in addition to the pictures themselves, all advertising. It put politics into the motion-picture industry and made the government the arbiter of the nation's screen morals and tastes.

The bill was fortunately defeated. But that does not mean that it is dead. Legislation of this kind has a curious persistence; it reappears time and again. And the danger is that it may someday slip through as part of a political deal or because its opponents are caught napping.

The demise of the Patman Bill raised a clamor. There were fulminations from rostrum and pulpit about the evils of sex and gangster films. The movies were corrupting people, it was charged, by inviting them to lust and crime. The Legion of Decency was organized. The screen was to be disinfected. The leaders of the movement said that since the industry had failed to "purge" itself, they would use moral pressure to bring about a boycott.

THE INDUSTRY DOES SOMETHING

Boycott was a threat to be reckoned with. To meet it, the motion-picture producers revived the Production Code.

The code, said to have been written by Mr Martin Quigley and Rev. Daniel A. Lord, S.J., had been promulgated in 1930 by the Hays organization, the Motion Picture Producers and Distributors of America. It had been devised as a means of "self-regulation" to effect prophylaxis from within. A Code Administration had been set up to enforce it.

During the first four years of its existence the code failed to make its impress on the Hollywood product. The principal reason for this—as given by Mr Quigley in his book, *Decency in Motion Pictures*—was "that there was not a sufficient pressure and support of public opinion to encourage or compel the industry at large to conform with the letter and spirit of its regulations."

With the boycott in the offing, the code became a force in the industry. All scripts had to be submitted in advance to the administration, and no picture was to be released without its seal of approval. Extremely severe penalties were prescribed. For the last five years the code has exerted a strict internal censorship over motion pictures.

WHAT THE CODE IS

The code is an elaborate sort of decalogue. The amended form, adopted in June 1934, consists of a preamble, a statement of general principles, specific rules and regulations and reasons for these.

The code is reprinted in full in Appendix C. A brief

summary of it (following its wording as much as possible) will reveal its structure and philosophy:

General Principles:

(1) No picture is to be produced which will lower the moral standards of those who see it. The sympathy of the audience must never be thrown to the side of crime, wrongdoing, evil or sin.

(2) Correct standards of life, subject only to the requirements of drama and entertainment, must be presented.

(3) Law, natural or human, must not be ridiculed, nor sympathy created for its violation.

Specific Rules and Regulations:

I. *Crimes* must never be presented in such a way as to create sympathy for the wrongdoer, or to inspire imitation.

Murder, and particularly brutal killings, must never be presented in detail. Revenge in modern times (*sic*) must not be justified.

The details of theft, arson, smuggling, robbery, safecracking, the dynamiting of trains, mines, buildings and so on must not be too explicitly presented. The use of firearms must be restricted.

Illegal drug traffic must never be portrayed.

The use of liquor in American life must not be shown unless absolutely necessary.

II. *Sex:* The sanctity of the institution of marriage and the home must be upheld. It must not be inferred that "low forms of sex relationship" are the accepted or common thing.

Adultery must not be explicitly treated or justified or attractively presented.

Scenes of passion must be kept to a minimum. Excessive kissing, embracing and suggestive postures must not be shown. In general, passion must be so treated as not to "stimulate the lower or baser element."

Sex perversion, white slavery, miscegenation, seduction, rape, sex hygiene must not be depicted.

III. *Vulgarity:* The treatment of "low, disgusting, unpleasant, though not necessarily evil" topics must be "subject always to the dictates of good taste and a regard for the sensibilities of the audience."

IV. *Obscenity:* Obscenity in word, gesture, reference, song, joke or by suggestion (even when likely to be understood by only part of the audience) is forbidden.

V. *Profanity:* Pointed profanity (this includes the words, God, Lord, Jesus, Christ—unless used reverently—hell, S.O.B., damn, Gawd), and every other profane or vulgar expression is forbidden.

VI. *Costume:* Complete nudity is never permitted, whether fully revealed or in silhouette. Undue exposure is forbidden, and undressing scenes must be avoided.

VII. *Religion:* Ministers of religion must not be used as comic characters or as villains. Religious faiths must not be ridiculed.

VIII. *Locations:* The use of bedrooms "must be governed by good taste and delicacy."

IX. *National feelings:* The use of the flag must be consistently respectful. The history, institutions, prominent people and citizenry of other nations must be presented "fairly."

X. *Titles:* No salacious, indecent or obscene titles are permitted.

XI. *Repellent subjects:* Hangings or electrocutions, third-degree methods, brutal or gruesome scenes, the branding of people or animals, cruelty, sale of women and surgical operations "must be treated within the careful limits of good taste."

The incubus of the code harries a screen play from the instant of its conception through its parturition and growth till its maturity. Long before any work is done on the script the idea must meet with approval. Later the script must be submitted to Mr Breen, the head man of the Code Administration, who may reject it entirely or blue-pencil it. Finally the finished picture must be screened and scrutinized (and not infrequently slashed) before it receives the code seal.

WHAT THE CODE DOES

There may be some people who, reading the code, will say: "Well, what's wrong with it? It sounds sensible enough."

The trouble with the code is the trouble with obscenity statutes. Its mandates are shot through with generalities; its social policy is one of hypocrisy and hush-hush; its criteria are predicated on the suscepti-bilities of morons; its effect is one of forcible suppres-sion; it lends itself readily to abuse; and above all, it creates a viciously false picture of life.

No more conclusive evidence can be adduced of the confusion bred by the equivocations of the code than the fact that during the last four years the Code Administration has handed down 26,808 opinions, "interpreting" the provisions of the code.

Who is to say what the "correct standards of life" are that may be portrayed? If human law is unjust why shouldn't it be ridiculed? Prostitution, the drug traffic, miscegenation, are serious problems; why should there be a conspiracy of silence about them? How do we expect to rid ourselves of venereal diseases if we are deprived of the most powerful means of spreading information concerning them? Why should sex hygiene be taboo? All of us know that people drink, swear and utter vulgar expressions; why must the screen ignore these things? What is the effect, precisely, of such mealymouthed qualifications as "subject only to the requirements of drama and entertainment" and "only when essential for the plot" and "within the careful limits of good taste?"

"Self-Regulation"

Apologists for the code argue that the work of the administration is not censorship at all, but "self-regulation."

The system [contends Mr Quigley] has its essence in the freely accepted responsibility of the producer properly to govern his activities. It is unrelated to censorship in the sense that regulatory methods are not imposed by an external force but rather are voluntarily set up by, for and within the industry. The plan provides for the administration of the regulatory methods by professional and experienced personnel.

But does the code really call for voluntary acceptance of industry standards? It is significant that back in 1930 the submission of scripts to the Studio Relations Committee (now the Code Administration) was *optional;* the code had been hardly in effect a year when it was made *compulsory.* Today the administration is a dictatorial force that rules pictures virtually unchallenged. Its edicts are implemented with penalties. If a code member dares show a picture without the code seal it is liable to a fine of twenty-five thousand dollars for each showing. Some idea of the range of its activities and the thoroughness with which it does its work may be gained from the fact that it is said to have a representative at the New York première of every play, and a confidential memorandum is sent to every member of the

Hays organization the day after the opening, indicating whether or not the Code Administration deems the play fit material for the screen.

Nor is it to be thought that the tentacles of the code reach only the big studios that are members of the Hays organization. Every non-member producer is affected. An independently produced picture must be distributed, and no major company is permitted to handle an independently produced picture which does not bear the code seal. Even if the independent producer were disposed to turn from the majors and seek distribution through other agencies, he is still confronted with the fact that the majors control most of the desirable theaters in the country, and he knows that his picture cannot be booked into any of them. So unshakable is the grip of the code, that when the government was drafting the indictment in the anti-trust case which is now pending against the major companies, it considered adding a special count based upon the code as evidencing a monopolistic combination.

Specific data as to the edicts of the administration are difficult to obtain; indeed, the office is reluctant to give out even a copy of the code. A few known examples will have to suffice.

The administration has been responsible for shelving a number of projected films, among them Shaw's *Saint Joan,* James M. Cain's *The Postman Always Rings Twice* and Sinclair Lewis' *It Can't Happen Here.* During 1937 it reviewed no less than 6,663 full-length domestic feature scripts and pictures, and ordered innumerable cuts and changes. It tabooed scenes showing kisses on the neck and shoulder, ladies removing or adjusting stockings in the presence of men (on the screen), men touching ladies' legs, men and girls lying together on a bed.

Some time ago the administration received for consideration the script of a courtroom drama which was intended to end all courtroom dramas. The judge was depicted as a lover of fishing; when he was on the bench, his nose ostensibly deep in a legal tome, he was really reading a sporting-goods catalogue. At one point he declared a recess because the court attendant had whispered to him that a package had come; he went to his chambers to practice casting with the new outfit he had ordered. There were also some unorthodox goings on in the jury room. By the time the Code Administration got through with the script the spoof was killed, and what was left was just another chestnut with a hackneyed plot, a parade of witnesses, attorneys forever popping up with objections, a silly climax and a judge who combined in himself all the qualities of dignity, benevolence and wisdom in the world.

The administration frowned on *Good Girls Go to Paris Too* as a title, insisting that it carried the lewd inference that it was mostly bad girls who earned trips to France's capital. A slight amputation did the trick. The picture emerged as *Good Girls Go to Paris*.

Nor would Mr Breen allow M.G.M. to use *Infidelity* as a title. M.G.M. summoned its brightest boys and ordered them to devise a substitute. The brain-trusters went into a huddle. They pondered and pondered. Then they triumphantly announced the new title. It was *Fidelity*.

Perhaps the most inspired achievement of the administration arose in connection with the script of *Zaza*. There a female character cried "Pig! Pig! Pig!" to a gentleman admirer. "Delete two pigs," was the order.

Pro and Con

Vaccillating, jittery, bank-ridden, lacking vision and leadership, never much concerned with the freedom of expression or the spread of ideas, Hollywood has been content to string along with the administration. Only here and there has a voice been raised in opposition.

When the New York film critics presented their annual awards for 1938, *The Citadel* and *Grand Illusion* carrying off the honors, Mr Dudley Nichols, president of the Screen Writers Guild, commented on the superiority of foreign films. He said:

Hollywood, in fear of her enemies and desirous of appeasing the prejudices of the world, has created an inner censorship which makes it impossible for motion pictures to deal with reality; and the moment the cinema or any other art form stops dealing with reality, that art form signs its own death warrant. It is significant that the pictures selected for this distinction dealt with something—with real problems and actual life.

Addressing a group of film critics a few weeks later, Mr Walter Wanger, producer of *Blockade* and other excellent pictures, said that if the industry expected to survive it would have to screen controversial subjects; that millions of people were staying away from the movies because they were fed up with escapist films; that the code, built on "the American dream: success, money, the girl, happiness without end," discouraged the honest handling of modern social, economic and political problems; and that there was a growing realization of this among directors and writers in Hollywood, but that they were bitterly opposed by reactionaries and others "afraid of ideas."

"Democracy," said Mr Wanger, "depends upon the easy and prompt dissemination of ideas and opinions. The motion picture is potentially one of the greatest weapons for the safeguarding of democracy. But if it is hobbled and haltered—if it cannot speak truthfully and freely where great issues are involved—then it can be a weapon turned against democracy. Democracies, unwisely fearing the power of the medium, have not allowed it to speak for democratic principles, whereas totalitarian states, more shrewdly realizing the power of the films, have used them to the nth degree to spread their doctrines. What we who believe in our democracy would like to do is to make films that would counteract these totalitarian ideologies, and make ours more effective by using the truth that is on our side. I do not call this propaganda. I call this a necessary patriotic service."

CHAPTER VI

The Censor and the Movies (*Cont'd*)

The American film has served as propaganda for the emotional monotony, the naïve morality, the sham luxury, the haphazard etiquette and the grotesque exaggeration of the comic, the sentimental and the acrobatic that are so common in the United States.
JOHN GOULD FLETCHER, *Crisis of the Film*

WHEN A BILL calling for movie pre-licensing was first introduced in the legislature of one of the seven states where such censorship now exists—just which state it was, we shall not say—the governor let it be known that he was opposed to it, and that if it managed to pass he'd veto it. It happened, however, that this governor was not a politician; he was an incorruptible citizen who had ridden into office on the crest of a reform wave. He had hardly made his position clear when rumors reached his ears. The movie interests, it was whispered, had descended on the legislature with bags of gold, and had reinforced their arguments against the bill with largess. The gossip may have been true; it may also have been an inspired move on the part of the proponents of the statute. In any event the governor was outraged. He sent word that unless the measure passed he'd start a bribery inquiry. The threat worked. The bill became law.

WHEN THE AX FALLS

It is not to be supposed that the activities of the Motion Picture Code Administration have lessened the work of the state review boards. For one thing, the code officials do not always gauge the censorial temper accurately (witness *Yes, My Darling Daughter* which received the code seal and yet ran into unexpected trouble in New York); for another, foreign films do not come within the scope of the administration.

The record of the state review bodies during the last dozen years or more may well give us pause. The censors have banned innumerable worth-while films, at the same time allowing cheap and tawdry pictures to go untouched. *High Treason,* a fine anti-war picture, and *Narcotics,* an exposé of the drug traffic, were denied licenses and have never been exhibited to the public. *Witchcraft,* a vivid study of superstition through the ages, was suppressed for years because it depicted the devil as a rather genial old rake with amorous leanings, and because it was feared that certain historical scenes, portraying the excesses of religious fanatics, might offend the Church. It was ultimately released in a mangled version. *Scarface,* perhaps the best of the gangster films, was held up for months; then it was so badly mutilated that retakes costing a hundred thousand dollars were required to preserve continuity. *Hertha's Awakening,* a thoroughly innocuous German film, was banned initially because the heroine, after tasting the fruits of illicit love, was shown as happy and wedded at the end. The censors insisted that for decency's sake she should have been portrayed as crushed and contrite. *Remous,* a beautiful French film dealing with impotency, was refused a license by the New York State Board of Censors, although it was scrutinized by the customs when it was imported and was officially approved.

Faithful to the enviable record they established when they turned down *The Life of Émile Zola* and *Voltaire,* the Quebec censors recently banned Emily Brontë's classic *Wuthering Heights.*

Foreign films are, of course, most vulnerable. While an important West Coast studio can kick up a row, the distributor of a French or Russian film is less apt to be armed with influence or the sinews of war. The following pictures, among others, have fallen under the ax of state boards in this country, for the reasons indicated:

Ecstasy: Czech; too frank treatment of sex urge.
The Testament of Dr Mabuse: German; anarchy.
Angele: French; Marseilles underworld.
No Man's Land: French; pacifism.
The Black Sunday: Russian; revolution.
Notturno: Czech; prostitution.
Diary of a Lost One: French; girls' reformatory.
Bolero: French; immorality.
Jeunesse: French; pregnancy.
Strike: Russian; political propaganda.
Borderline: English; miscegenation.
Amok: French; immorality.

Juno and the Paycock was barred some years ago in Boston. *Spain in Flames* was stopped in New Bedford but not elsewhere. *The Heart of Spain* could not be shown in Fall River, Worcester and Brockton.

The New York censors banned *Damaged Lives,* a film dealing with venereal disease, although it treated a difficult theme with dignity and had the sponsorship of the American Social Hygiene Society. The Board of Regents surprisingly reversed the censors. But such a result is rare. In the great majority of cases the decisions of the censors are upheld. The board has refused to lift the ban on Hedy Lamarr's *Ecstasy* and on *Polygamy*, a serious study of polygamous cults in Utah and Arizona.

The process of keeping the screen undefiled in New York is vividly illustrated by two recent cases.

THE PURITAN

This French picture was based on Liam O'Flaherty's novel of the same name.

It tells the story of a young fanatic engaged in a crusade against sin. Failing to convert a young prostitute to righteousness, he kills her and calmly covers up his tracks. The composure he derives from the conviction that he has killed to save a soul soon gives way to doubt and bitter self-questioning. Pursued by his conscience no less than by the police, his mental torment reaches a frenzied climax when he realizes that he has murdered the woman not because he wished to end her life of shame, but because he wanted her for himself and was jealous of the men she received. In the end he gets caught.

Mr O'Flaherty said of the picture: "It intends to show the stupidity of groups that attempt to impose their concept of morality on others. It is significant that the picture has been banned in all totalitarian countries—Germany, Italy, Russia and Poland—and that it may be shown in the democracies, England and France."

But it could not be shown in New York State. Despite the fact that it was a work of genuine seriousness, integrity and distinction, the censors banned the film as immoral. The Board of Regents agreed with them.

THE BIRTH OF A BABY

The death rate of mothers in childbirth and of newborn infants in this country is shockingly high. It is estimated that the yearly toll is one hundred and fifty thousand lives. Physicians are unanimous in their opinion that a large percentage of these deaths could be prevented if expectant mothers realized the importance of good medical care and sought it. Mindful of this, the American Committee on Maternal Welfare has carried on a program of education over a period of years. As part of the program the committee produced an educational picture called *The Birth of a Baby*.

The picture depicted a typical pregnancy through childbirth to a period about six weeks after. It was filmed under the direction of a group of distinguished physicians, among whom were Dr Fred L. Adair, professor of obstetrics and gynecology, University of Chicago; Dr James R. McCord, professor of obstetrics and gynecology, Emory University; Dr Everett D. Plass, professor of obstetrics and gynecology, University of Iowa; and Philip F. Williams, M.D., assistant professor of obstetrics, University of Pennsylvania.

The medical societies of New York, Pennsylvania, Ohio, Indiana, Illinois, New Jersey, Virginia, South Carolina, Iowa, Colorado and Minnesota, and the American College of Surgeons endorsed the picture. Among the many nationally prominent physicians who wrote to the American Committee urging public showing were Dr Charles H. Goodrich, president of the Medical Society of the state of New York, Dr Alfred C. Beck, professor of obstetrics at Long Island University, and Dr James Knight Quigley, member of the Board of Medical Examiners of the state of New York. In Connecticut and Minnesota the picture was shown to mixed test audiences of thousands of persons from varied walks of life, and in each instance the overwhelming majority voted in favor of unrestricted public screening. The Ohio motion-picture reviewers licensed it without hesitation.

The New York censors refused to issue a license. Their action was appealed to the Board of Regents. Although the board found that the picture had been prepared "under careful scientific supervision" and undoubtedly had "a high educational value," it refused to direct the issuance of a general license. An appeal is now pending in the courts.

HARVEST

When the New York board banned *Harvest,* a notable French film based on Giono's pastoral novel, the New York *World-Telegram* expressed amazement at the "censorial brainstorm." Having attended a private showing, the editorial writer reported that the theme and the action of the picture were on an extraordinarily elevated plane, and that there had not been a blush in the theater. He went on:

In the audience by chance was someone's aunt—not the old lady from Dubuque but from Missouri—a white-haired, churchgoing, small-town housewife. She was enchanted. "But," she was told, "this picture is immoral and has been censored. You are supposed to have been corrupted." "But why?" she said, with the out-of-towner's amazement at New York morals. "Because there was no wedding scene in the continuity in spite of the many references to 'my wife.' The censor, like a hotel clerk, wants to see the marriage certificate." The question had never occurred to her, said the aunt. Which suggests that perhaps our movies might be improved if we should trade off our present censor for an old lady from Missouri.

The Board of Regents, by a rare gesture, reversed the censors and licensed the picture without a cut.

Using the Scissors

Except where foreign products are concerned, the censors hesitate to ban pictures in their entirety. The usual procedure is to order cuts in scenes or dialogue, or to refuse a license in the first instance and then dicker with the producers on eliminations. The latter course was followed in the case of *Scarface* and *Yes, My Darling Daughter* and *Carnival in Flanders*.

When, after some vicissitudes, the French film, *Club de Femmes,* was finally passed by the New York censors, Mr Frank S. Nugent, the movie critic, commented caustically on the "few decisive scissor strokes and dialogue eraser" which had been applied. He ventured the guess that the board still had a file of *Godey's Lady's Books* somewhere. *Club de Femmes* was something of an eye opener for the critics. Ordinarily they saw only the released version of a film. In the case of *Club de Femmes* they had an opportunity to view the uncut one as well. The comparison was illuminating.

"The critics discovered," wrote Mr Ezra Goodman in the New York *Times,* "that in the process of abbreviation some scenes had taken on a suggestiveness not apparent heretofore; that the spectator tended to read, so to speak, between the cuts and bridge the obvious gaps with his own imagination."

Mr Goodman recalled that *Maedchen in Uniform* had suffered the same fate a few years before. "Many scenes dealing with the guileless sex impulses of adolescents were carved from the film. These eliminations, it seems, were due to a failure on the part of the censors to recognize that the scenes were introduced not for sensationalism but as an integral and inevitable part of the picture's thesis."

He concluded: "It is beneficial, at times, to dust off

the venerable axiom to the effect that the bad as well as the good is a necessary part of artistic experience. When a motion picture is presenting a truthful and untarnished re-creation of a certain experience it will inevitably have to include certain elements that are not entirely pure and prismatic, for the simple reason that a motion picture can be no purer and sweeter than the actual life it portrays if it does not wish to pull its punches."

It is profitless to discuss the censors' scissor work without a reference to the cuts themselves. Here's where the rub comes in. Review boards have consistently taken the position that theirs are not public records, and hence no accurate general analysis can be made of their activities. True, four or five years ago the New York board opened its files to a representative of the National Council for Freedom from Censorship. A transcript was made of typical cuts ordered over a fifteen months' period, and the material was published in pamphlet form by the council. The evidence was so damning and resulted in so much derision at the expense of the censors that the lid came down with a bang, and since that time all requests for information have been refused.

Suppressions Suppressed

And so the public is prevented from knowing the dire evils from which it is being protected, except to the extent that particulars as to cuts occasionally leak out despite official precautions.

We know, for example, that *I'm a Fugitive from a Chain Gang* was literally hacked to pieces by the censors, while Mae West's bawdy *I'm No Angel* got by with two inconsequential cuts. We know, too, that such extraordinary films as *Variety, Street of Sin, The Man*

Who Laughs (all three starring Emil Jannings), *A Woman of Affairs* (adopted from Michael Arlen's *The Green Hat*), Murnau's *Sunrise*—some of them so important that they are screened today in courses dealing with the history of movies—were badly mangled. The picture of Lenin's tomb bearing the inscription "Religion is the opiate of the people" was excised from *Potemkin.* In *Sadie Thompson,* based on Maugham's *Rain,* Rev. Davidson had to be made a "reformer" instead of a minister. The word "pregnancy" could not be used in *Boy Meets Girl,* nor "monkey glands" in *The Missing Guest,* nor "nudist" (just the word itself!) in *Unusual Occupations.*

The Old Testament idea of punishment is deeply rooted in the tenets of the guardians of the silver sheet. Flagrantly suggestive scenes often get by because the erring hero or the heroine suffers and repents in the end. Witness the sequences of debauchery in *The Prodigal* and *The Ten Commandments.*

The cuts that were ordered in *La Maternelle, The Story of Temple Drake* (based on William Faulkner's *Sanctuary*), *Generals Without Buttons* and *The Amazing Dr Clitterhouse* were such as to destroy in part the meaning of the pictures.

Not less than forty-two cuts and changes were made in *One Third of a Nation.* At one point in the film a lady of dubious morals greeted two men with: "Hello, boys. Ain't you the early birds?" One of the men replied: "And ain't you the luscious worm?" The whole exchange was eliminated.

From *Joan of Arc* the Maryland board eliminated Joan's exclamation as she stood at the stake: "Oh, God, why hast thou forsaken me?" and from *Idiot's Delight,* the sentence: "We, the workers of the world, will take care of that."

Dusky breasts may flash across the screen in *Moana,*

the *Virgins of Bali, Goona-Goona, Dark Rapture,* and other films of far-off lands, but white torsos must remain chastely draped. Nor is it to be thought that the nudity ban is limited only to the anatomy of tempting ladies. Shots of nude infants in *Carnival in Flanders* and *The Crisis* were cut.

Often as not there isn't even the element of skin color to justify a distinction in censorial treatment. Ordinarily the mere presence of two unmarried people in a house at night is enough to throw the censors into a righteous dither. Accordingly, the overnight scene was cut from *The Slipper Episode* and *Yes, My Darling Daughter.* But it was left intact in *It Happened One Night.*

The New York board banned *Blackwell's Island* at first on the ground that it did not truthfully depict the prison conditions there. Later the board reversed its position. It discovered that one of the authors of the film was David Marcus, deputy commissioner of correction of New York City.

TRIAL MARRIAGE

When *Yes, My Darling Daughter* was suppressed in New York, Mr Erwin Esmond, director of the New York board, argued in all seriousness that it was an encouragement to trial marriages. "The example which it affords," he said, "is a very dangerous one to follow. The picture teaches young people the freedom from recognized convention that would be morally disastrous if generally practiced." Which prompted Mr Nugent of the New York *Times* to observe that "it was probably a mere oversight that Mr Esmond neglected to produce supporting statistics based on the play's effect on New York City, which at the time was overrun with trial marriages." And Mr Mosher in the *New*

Yorker addressed an earnest plea to the censors for an expurgated edition of Bartlett's *Familiar Quotations* without such pornographic verses in it as:

> "Mother, may I go out to swim?"
> "Yes, my darling daughter:
> Hang your clothes on a hickory limb
> And don't go near the water."

A modified version of the film was finally released. The original had made it perfectly clear that the boy and girl who went off for a week end did not sleep together. By eliminating most of the scenes at the weekend camp, particularly one which showed the boy and the girl in separate beds, the censors accomplished the very opposite of their purpose; they created in the mind of every person who saw the picture an inference that the couple did sleep together. Indeed, the province of Ontario forbade the showing of the "toned-down" version and licensed the unexpurgated one.

COUNTING THE GAINS

What is the result of all this slashing and bluepenciling; of all this frantic solicitude for the morals of society? More wholesome pictures? An unsullied public?

What evidence we have fails to justify the censors' thesis. There is no proof that without pre-licensing the screen would become a sink of iniquity. Even if the makers of pictures were utterly unprincipled, we would still have powerful curbs against them in the form of state and federal obscenity laws and public opinion. There is no proof that the moral fiber of the nation has been improved during the last decade and a half as a result of movie censorship. There is no proof that in the absence of pre-licensing the American people would have been debauched.

The evidence points elsewhere. For the producers, the censors' cuts have meant added expense for retakes; their pictures have often been robbed of point; they have been induced to play safe, to shun controversial subjects, to gloss over the unpleasant truth, to grind out an endless stream of vapid, spineless, moronic stuff. For the public the cuts have meant, not infrequently, making suggestive by suppression something that wasn't suggestive before, and, always, a falsification of life.

Shielding the Immature

On occasion the advocates of censorship presume to don the robes of reasonableness and say: "Well, maybe we don't have to worry about the susceptibility of grownups. But how about the young?"

This is a familiar approach. It is also a misleading one. Many people who can appraise with a clear eye the "menace" of the screen for adults and dismiss the whole notion with a shrug and a smile will develop a maudlin concern for the little tots. They grow alarmed when someone charges—as did Colonel Ernest K. Coulter of the New York Society for the Prevention of Cruelty to Children a few years ago—that gangster films often influence children to commit "serious offenses."

Colonel Coulter's charge was given considerable publicity. It was challenged by Dr Frank Astor, field director of the National Child Welfare Association, and director of the junior review group of the National Board of Motion Picture Review. He declared that crime pictures acted as an outlet for the antisocial emotions of children rather than as an incentive for them to emulate what they had seen. He said that the mere statement by a juvenile delinquent that he had committed a crime because he had seen it on the screen was not sufficient evidence that the picture was to blame.

"Children have an almost remarkable capacity," he said, "for saying what they believe adults want them to say. They have heard adults put a taboo on certain films and immediately think that there is something wrong with them. On being brought before a judge for committing some crime, they begin searching for an excuse—an impressive excuse. The motion picture provides just that, and the child blandly declares that 'I saw it in the movies.'"

Dr Astor further stated that surveys made by the board over a decade and a half had developed the following:

The cases of a number of delinquents who said they had received their ideas from pictures had been investigated by the board. In many instances it developed that the children had not seen the films claimed to be responsible for their dereliction.

The leading probation officers of the country agreed almost unanimously in answer to a questionnaire that films did not influence juvenile delinquency.

Surveys among high-school and grammar-school children showed that a few of them felt that pictures might have an undesirable effect on *other* children, but none would admit that he was influenced.

Many persons directing the activities of children and having long experience in the field of education expressed the belief that films tended to quiet, not overstimulate, maladjusted and highly excitable youngsters.

"There have always been reformers and censors," Dr Astor concluded, "and there always will be so long as there are persons who begrudge emotional pleasures to others. In twenty-five years the gangster film, like the old Westerns with their two-gun men, will be looked upon as historical documents and subject to no protest. But by that time another type of film will be the goat of the publicity hunters."

Dr Astor's views are shared by other experts in the field. "Numerous studies made by scientists," says Dr Blanchard of the Philadelphia Child Guidance Clinic, "have failed to establish any appreciable contribution to delinquency from motion pictures, but we do find the motion pictures to be helpful in many ways." Both the National Board of Review and Youthbuilders, an educational organization that has made a study of juvenile activities, are of the opinion that the effect of pictures on children has been grossly overrated. Besides, in most states there are laws requiring that minors under the age of sixteen be accompanied by adults. It is the duty of the parents to decide what their children should see. That some parents may be lax or some children disobedient is no reason why the mental pabulum of society should be reduced to mush.

Let's concede that in the absence of pre-licensing some movies might not be fit fare for children. The argument that the screen must therefore be censored amounts to saying that you must not have any adult book on your shelves at home because your nine-year-old might read it.

The New Objective

Fear of sex is on the wane. The new specter is "subversive" ideas. The censors are no longer concerned with sex alone; political censorship is the new goal.

It cannot be stressed too strongly that state regulation of the screen was set up at the outset specifically to combat indecency. The law is now being perverted to uses that were never contemplated.

Professor Mamlock was produced in Russia and portrayed the persecution of the Jews by Nazis. It encountered no difficulty in New York, but its showing in Ohio was banned for almost two months. There was no question of sex. The picture was condemned as "harmful" and calculated to "stir up hatred and ill will and gain nothing." It was released only after substantial deletions were made. The police refused to permit its showing in Providence, Rhode Island, on the ground that it was Communistic propaganda. The case was appealed, and the Supreme Court of the state upheld the police. The Court wrote a long opinion bristling with precedents and shot through with fine-spun legalisms. It was precisely the kind of opinion which serves to bring the law into contempt in the eyes of laymen. It ranted on to the tune of almost six thousand words about the "indecency" of a picture, and then wound up by admitting that *the Court had not viewed it* and had not considered it necessary to view it to arrive at a decision!

But it was the Soviet-Nazi non-aggression pact that furnished the cream of the jest on *Professor Mamlock*. Before the pact was concluded the film was suppressed in democratic England as "too political," and it was a feature attraction at the Soviet Pavilion at the New York World's Fair. *After* the pact, screening was swiftly authorized in London, and just as abruptly stopped at the Soviet Pavilion.

Millions of Us, a strong union propaganda film, encountered trouble in a number of states. *Spanish Earth,* a pro-Loyalist documentary picture, was banned by the board in Pennsylvania, but was cleared by Governor Earle.

But it was *Spain in Flames* and *Baltic Deputy* that furnished the most striking examples of the new trend.

SPAIN IN FLAMES

Spain in Flames, a series of actual shots of the Spanish Civil War, with a running pro-Loyalist commentary by Ernest Hemingway and Archibald MacLeish, had a checkered career. It was refused a license in Pennsylvania and Ohio, as well as in many other states. Governor Earle of Pennsylvania, in upholding the state board, remarked: "We Pennsylvanians are not interested in the propaganda of a government largely made up of Communists, Syndicalists and Anarchists, who butcher priests." In New Jersey, ironically enough, the statute which was passed to curb Nazi activities, known as the Anti-Nazi Law, was invoked against the picture.

There could no longer be any pretense. The censors were using their office to curb opinions. Appeals were taken in Ohio and Pennsylvania. The Ohio Supreme Court upheld the ban, but in Pennsylvania Judge Levinthal of the Common Pleas Court repudiated it in a ringing opinion.

Censorship, under our theory of government [he said], is presumptively bad and is tolerated only as a necessary evil. It is needless for us to dilate upon the reasons influencing us to think censorship undesirable, for we have been brilliantly anticipated by a great galaxy of liberal thinkers. Milton, Mill, Jefferson and Holmes have spoken for us. We, like them, are confident that the popular good sense will ultimately discover and prefer truth and that the general welfare can best be served only by a free expression of opinion. . . . Moreover, it must not be forgotten that a censorship which today may be used to curb our enemies' opinions may be utilized tomorrow to suppress our own most treasured convictions. However much we prize liberty we must value democracy no less.

BALTIC DEPUTY

But the Pennsylvania board was obdurate. Its answer was to refuse a license to *Baltic Deputy*, a documentary film made in the Soviet Union. The picture was fictional; it portrayed incidents in the life of a Russian scientist at the time of the Bolshevist revolution. Its theme was the scientist's conversion to Bolshevism and his advocacy of it.

The Pennsylvania law forbade the showing of obscene, indecent, scurrilous, improper or immoral pictures. However, it required the board, in disapproving a film, to state its reasons. Since none of the statutory adjectives was applicable to *Baltic Deputy,* the board flatly refused to give a reason. Its action was challenged in the courts, and the case came up in the Common Pleas Court before Judge Bok.

Referring to the board's failure to specify the basis of its objection, Judge Bok said:

To supply this inexcusable neglect, the three members of the board were put on the stand by counsel for the picture. Their testimony showed a lack of any intelligent basis of judgment or any conception of the true nature of censorship. It ranged from assertions that they do not like Communism and are admittedly prejudiced against it, to statements that while the subject of the picture would rouse the rabble, in the words of Mrs Palmer, and incite the people of Pennsylvania to riot, it had nothing to do with our government. According to the censors, a revolution by Communists is objectionable, whereas a revolution against Communists would not be; a bitter attack against government in Russia is immoral, but one in France is not immoral because France and Russia are different countries. *It is difficult to decide a law case on stuff and nonsense like this.*

Judge Bok reversed the board. He pointed out that censorship is not an American concept. It is contrary to the principle of free speech and starts out with a heavy presumption against it. It has no place in the field of controversial questions. One of the strongest tenets of the American way of life is that ideas shall prove themselves in the market place.

Anyone who has a vital belief in democracy [said the Judge] has also the faith that the American people will, by a consensus of instinct, recognize and prefer the truth. This vigorous young nation can dare to defend the right of someone to say what another one may hate, and to abide the event without fear. Democracy is not in danger until it becomes afraid to let its people generate and express a new idea, and we have reason to hope that our civilization will be improved so long as men are free to express through ideas the thought that it may be. If it be said that we have more to fear from confusion than from Communism, we might reply that we have more to fear from fear than from either of them.

TOWARD A SOLUTION

That despite its splendid potentialities the screen today is a negligible cultural force, often a vitiating influence on public taste, and almost always a *Shangri La* utterly divorced from reality, few will deny. It would be idle to assert that censorship has been wholly responsible. A number of facts have probably contributed to the results: the mushroom growth of the industry, its comparative newness, lack of vision and courage among its leaders, banker domination, the skyrocketing of production costs. Certainly censorship has been a powerful contributing cause. And so we need not dwell on the old controversy as to whether the public demands cheap, sensational and titillating pictures, leaving the producers no choice but to comply, or whether the producers are to blame for trying to vulgarize the public taste. Many distinguished films—the biographical *Abraham Lincoln*, *Alexander Hamilton* and *Voltaire;* character studies like *Arrowsmith*, *Topaze* and *The Informer;* the poetic *Cradle Song*, *Berkeley Square*, *Emperor Jones*, *S.O.S. Iceberg*, *Adventures of Chico*— have lost money or barely managed to break even. So, too, did Von Stroheim's *Greed*, Lubitsch's *Broken Lullaby*, the mystical *Outward Bound*, King Vidor's *Hallelujah*, Jesse Lasky's *Power and Glory* and *Byrd at the South Pole. The Cabinet of Dr Caligari,* an extraordinary film, suffered from neglect; even schools refused to play *Evangeline.* On the other hand, such films as Mae West's *I'm No Angel* and *She Done Him Wrong, The Half-Naked Truth, Ex-Lady,* and Wheeler and Woolsey's *So This Is Africa* have all been enormously profitable; and such gangster films as *The Public Enemy, Doorway to Hell* and *Little Caesar* have played to jammed theaters. And yet there have been many worth-while productions that have been financial successes.

If the public is to blame for tawdry pictures, all the censorship in the world won't help. Morals can't be strait-jacketed by edicts. If the producers are at fault we can rely on sanctions of public taste. Theater-goers can get what they want by the simple expedient of shunning what they don't want.

Faith in the destiny of man means giving him the privilege of choice between right and wrong, and trusting him to choose the right. If he's headed for perdition, putting blinders on him or plugs in his ears will not stop him. Democracy is predicated on the assumption that man is capable of governing himself and working out his salvation. If this is true, and we think it is, then we must also recognize that moral coddling is incompatible with the notion of free will. Man may be led upward, but he can't be pushed.

Let adults decide for themselves what they are to see and hear on the screen. Let the responsibility for safeguarding the sensibilities of children be lodged where it should be, with the parents. Let those who would help parents discharge this duty publish lists of recommended pictures for those under age. The Schools Motion Picture Committee, a voluntary organization of parents and school-teachers in New York, has been doing just this with marked success for some time. And if there are religious groups that feel adults stand in need of similar guidance, let them come forward with similar lists.

But let it stop there. Let there be no threats, no boy-cott, no reprisal. For that way lies dictatorship.

CHAPTER VII

Freedom of the Air

The vice of censorship is that reason is not left free to combat error.

EDGAR LEE MASTERS, *Censorship* (1928)

WHEN PHIL STONG PREPARED a radio version of his juvenile *Honk, the Moose,* one of the station officials objected to the periodic moose calls. "They're mating calls," he said. "They've got to come out—too sexy."

Before delivering a talk on evolution and the depression, Dr William K. Gregory of the American Museum of Natural History was required to submit his script to WABC. In it he expressed the opinion that the depression was traceable to the "reckless overproduction of goods and reckless overproduction of people" which characterized our culture. The station objected, but Dr Gregory stood his ground and won out. When he got on the air, however, he spoke of "the aggressive selfishness of the solitary animal" which had led to "unlimited cutthroat competition." This was too much. Dr Gregory was cut off the air; he poured his revolutionary views into a dead microphone. Only when he had turned once more to the non-debatable aspects of science was he restored to the ether. Norman Thomas, Socialist leader, and many others have had the same experience.

The script of a round-table discussion on divorce, to be broadcast over WMCA, contained the expression *sexual infidelity* and a statement that harsh divorce laws were tantamount to saying to ill-matched spouses: "No matter how unhappy you are, you've made your bed and you've got to lie in it." The word *sexual* was struck out, and the sentence was changed to: "You've made your bargain and you must stick to it."

Maxine Sullivan was ruled off several stations for swinging old songs. NBC won't let General Hugh Johnson sully its microphone with the word *syphilis*. Neither NBC nor CBS will sell time to Father Coughlin. General Smedley Butler must pledge himself to use no more than a specified quota of *damns* and *hells* before he is permitted to face a deodorizer: his own epithet for a microphone. Any mention of strikes in news reports is taboo on WLW. Earl Browder, head of the Communist party, can't buy time from WIRE.

Although most of the censorship of the air can be laid at the door of the broadcasters, the Federal Communications Commission has also been responsible.

When Charlie McCarthy and Mae West did a travesty on Adam and Eve in a radio skit not so long ago, in the course of which the lady of the opulent curves invited Charlie into the Garden of Eden, the commission administered a harsh rebuke to NBC and intimated that it would bear the episode in mind the next time NBC's license came up for renewal.

In 1933 the commission fired Rev. Robert P. Shuler, a Methodist clergyman, off the air for "intemperate" utterances. It started an investigation of charges of profanity and foreign propaganda against the radio version of Clifford Odets' *Waiting for Lefty,* and called a halt only when it found that the program had been put on by the Federal Theater. It refused to renew KTNT's license because the station had broadcast Norman Baker's political diatribes. It was prompted to summon WCTN of Minneapolis to a hearing on a single complaint of blasphemy, based on the use of

God and *damn*. It stripped Dr J. R. Brinkley of Kansas of his station license for giving medical advice on the air.

MYRIAD LISTENERS

There are thirty-eight million receiving sets in the United States. Twenty-seven million families have at least one set. The extra sets in homes number about six million. The remaining five million are automobile radios.

It is estimated that twenty-one million sets are in daily use, averaging four and one half hours of use. This means an average of ninety million family listening hours a day.

In less than a generation, radio has become a one-hundred-and-fifty-million-dollar industry. Only 22 per cent of the families in this country had sets in 1927; in 1938 the percentage soared to 81 per cent.

Radio advertisers expend one hundred and sixty-five million a year. Of this amount one hundred and twenty-five million goes to stations for time, and forty million for talent.

During 1937 the total revenue of the important networks was forty million dollars and their net income six and one half million. All the other individual stations took in seventy-nine million, of which fifteen and one half million was net income.

It goes without saying that radio, as a means of mass communication, far exceeds the press in scope and influence. It has virtually usurped the place of the public platform for the discussion of social, economic and political issues. With a restricted radio, free speech and free press are empty terms.

THE GOVERNMENT STEPS IN

It was recognized in the early days of radio that broadcasting necessitated some kind of regulation. Anyone could pick a suitable street corner and shout himself hoarse at a crowd. Anyone with money enough to buy a printing press could set it up and start a paper. But everyone couldn't go on the air. There were only so many usable frequencies: non-regulation meant chaos. Besides, broadcasters couldn't appropriate the air; the government owned it, could license its use, and could presumably dictate the terms of the use.

It soon became apparent, therefore, that the industry partook of a dual nature. To the extent that stations were privately owned and managed, they were private enterprises. But because they had to go to the government to get frequencies, they were subject to public control.

So the federal government took a hand.

Since broadcasts overleaped state boundaries they constituted interstate commerce. Under the Constitution their regulation was a national, not a state, affair. The Radio Act was enacted in 1927, and the Radio Commission was set up by its terms. In 1934 the act was revised, and the present Federal Communications Commission was created.

The Commission

The F.C.C. is composed of seven members. It is one of the most important and influential government agencies.

During the last few years the commission has been much in the limelight. It has faced problems complex enough to daunt a dozen King Solomons. What with the Scylla of big business on one hand, and the Charybdis of the commission's view of the general good on the other, not to mention the rip tide of politics, it has been stormy sailing. Although the present commission, headed by Chairman McNinch, has tackled its monumental job with concern, diligence and vision, it has had to withstand a great deal of adverse criticism.

It has been charged at various times with favoring the big chains and abetting monopolies, with favoring government ownership, with keeping stations in a state of jitters through short-term licenses, with subservience to the administration, with attempting to build up federal censorship. And as if its task were not herculean enough to engage the united resource of all its members, it has been troubled with internal friction.

THE LAW

Under the act, the commission is authorized to regulate radio generally, to allot frequencies for a maximum period of three years, to grant or deny renewals of licenses and to revoke licenses. It is directed to exercise its powers so as to serve "public interest, convenience or necessity."

Section 326 of the act says: "Nothing in this chapter shall be understood or construed to give the commission the power of censorship over the radio communications or signals transmitted by any radio station, and no regulation or condition shall be promulgated or fixed by the commission which shall interfere with the right of free speech by means of radio communications."

This would seem to be as explicit and unequivocal an injunction as words can express. Certainly the legislative history of the act evidences an indubitable intention to safeguard liberty of utterance. But—

(1) Section 326, immediately following the provision quoted above, adds: "No person within the jurisdiction of the United States shall utter any obscene, indecent or profane language by means of radio communication."

(2) Since there is only a limited number of frequencies, and the commission must allot them, the commission must use some yardstick of selection.

(3) The sole criterion voiced in the act is that of "public interest, convenience or necessity."

(4) The President of the United States may reserve waves for such governmental agencies as may require radio communication.

(5) The President is given practically unlimited powers over radio in case of "war or a threat of war or a state of public peril or disaster or other national emergency, or in order to preserve the neutrality of the United States."

What constitutes "obscene, indecent or profane" language? Is a travesty on Adam and Eve obscene? Is it indecent for a blue singer to swing "Loch Lomond"? Is *Beyond the Horizon* profane? Are "hell" and "damn" blasphemous? Who is to decide? When is the decision to be made, before or after utterance? If it is to be made before, who is to wield the blue pencil and to what extent? What factors may the commission consider in applying the test of "public interest, convenience or necessity"? The financial responsibility of the applicant? Its technical equipment? Its program service? If the last, its service in the past or as projected in the future? If the commission chooses to emphasize the factor of program content, is it exercising censorship? How many waves may the President reserve for governmental use? Can he, if he chooses, reserve *all* the available frequencies? What is a state of public peril or disaster? What is a national emergency? Flood, drought, earthquake, famine, tidal wave? Economic crisis? War in Europe? In the Far East? In Central or South America? How great need the peril be, and how grave the emergency, to warrant the taking over of the radio by the government?

Defining the Undefined

But the most vexing questions concern the phrase "public interest, convenience or necessity." According to the commission the phrase means that:

(1) The stations must "serve the public," and not exploit "the private or selfish interests of individuals or groups of individuals."

(2) The requirement is met by "a well-arranged program."

(3) Such a program is one which combines "entertainment, consisting of music of both classical and lower grades, religion, education, instruction, important public events, discussion of public questions, weather, market reports and news and matters of interest to all members of the family."

The commission's position, then, is that in dealing with licenses it may predicate its decision on the program service of the applicant. This view has thus far been upheld by the courts as not constituting censorship, and not contravening either Section 326 of the act or the first amendment to the Constitution.

When the commission refused to renew Rev. Shuler's license on the ground that his broadcasts "were sensational rather than instructive"—the clergyman had indulged in strictures on the Catholic Church—Dr Shuler took an appeal. The commission's decision, he urged, was unconstitutional in that it violated free speech, and in that it deprived him of his property without due process of law. It was also arbitrary and capricious since it was not supported by substantial evidence.

The Circuit Court of Appeals of the District of Columbia heard the appeal. It said: "We need not stop to review the cases construing the depth and breadth of the first amendment . . . It is enough now to say that the universal trend of decisions has recognized the guaranty of the amendment to prevent previous restraints upon publications, as well as immunity of censorship, leaving to correction by subsequent punishment those utterances or publications contrary to the public welfare. In this aspect it is generally regarded that freedom of speech and press cannot be infringed by legislative, executive or judicial action, and that the constitutional guaranty should be given liberal and comprehensive construction . . . But this does not mean that the government, through agencies established by Congress, may not refuse a renewal of license to one who has abused it to broadcast defamatory and untrue matter. In that case there is not a denial of the freedom of speech but merely the application of the regulatory power of Congress in a field within the scope of its legislative authority."

The Court of Appeals upheld the commission; and the Supreme Court of the United States, by refusing to hear the case, impliedly placed its seal of approval on the result.

PROGRAM CONTENT

There are approximately ninety channels on the air. The Federal Communications Commission has tried to accommodate six hundred stations on these channels. There aren't enough frequencies to go around. Accordingly, if one station applies for a renewal of its license and another station applies for the same wave length, the commission holds a hearing on the merits of the respective applicants. If other considerations (financial soundness, adequacy of equipment, geographical distribution, and so on) are equally balanced, the final determination is based on the relative merits of the proposed programs submitted to the commission, and also on the program record of the station that has had the frequency. For this purpose programs are classified as (a) meritorious and (b) non-meritorious.

The following types of programs have been called meritorious by the commission:

(1) Foreign-language programs destined to educate and instruct foreigners here in the principles of our government and of American institutions.

(2) Religious features, such as services and family Bible periods.

(3) Civic and charitable broadcasts.

(4) Musical programs.

(5) Educational programs for adults and children on literature, grammar, art, music, religion, and so on, including spelling bees.

(6) Weather information to aid farmers and others.

(7) Broadcasts by such organizations as chambers of commerce, the American Legion, the Federation of Women's Clubs, the D.A.R. and the like.

(8) News and sports broadcasts, including interviews with famous people.

Non-meritorious programs have been held to include:

(1) Advertisements of medical remedies which are either ineffectual or dangerous (for example, Marmola, condemned by the Federal Trade Commission and the Supreme Court), which should not be taken except on advice of a physician.

(2) Advertisements of quack therapeutic appliances such as vitalizing belts, diagnosis machines, and so on.

(3) Advertisements of medical services, including misleading or nonscientific medical advice, or false promises of free consultation and examination or of cure without pain or surgery.

(4) Advertisements of fraudulent business schemes, including deceptive financial advice.

(5) Advertisements of "schools" accompanied by extravagant promises of overnight instruction or unfailing placement.

(6) Programs tending to promote horse racing and gambling.

(7) Advertisements of liquor.

(8) Programs dealing with astrology; and

(9) Programs purportedly religious in character but offensive because of commercial purpose, such as a rabbi advertising his availability for marriages and circumcisions.

The time ratio between commercial and sustaining programs favored by the commission seems to be 35–65.

THE BROADCASTERS

The stations have for years exercised censorship over the material broadcast by them. Because of the nonavailability of data, the extent of this surveillance and its effect on programs is impossible to appraise. There is every reason to believe, however, that the examples given at the beginning of this chapter are typical of many thousands of others. As a rule stations frown on extemporaneous talks; they want scripts in advance. If a speaker manages to get on the air without a script and "transgresses," or if, having furnished one, he departs from it in a way deemed objectionable to the station, he may find himself cut off the air.

The stations seek to justify their blue-penciling on several grounds. They say, with perhaps overmuch of piety, that theirs is a public trust, and that they owe a duty not to sully the ears of their listeners. They say that since the law makes them criminally liable for obscenity and civilly liable for defamation, they are entitled to take reasonable precautions to protect themselves. And they say they're afraid of the commission's big stick, insisting that the six months' licenses the commission has been doling out keep them in a state of perpetual jitters.

One is inclined to wonder whether the stations are really as much intimidated by the commission as they claim to be, or whether it isn't just a convenient blind for the exercise of their prejudices. The commission has never ruled or intimated that the mention of strikes in news reports is taboo; the suppression is WLW's own.

One thing is certain. Whatever the stations may do on their own account to purify the air, they don't want federal censorship. Early this year, when legislation was introduced in Congress for the reorganization of the commission, the National Association of Broadcasters, representing more than four hundred of the country's seven hundred stations (about 90 per cent of the industry in point of size of stations), stated: "There must be no censorship of programs. Congressional policy as expressed in the acts of 1927 and 1934 has expressly forbidden censorship of radio programs and has undertaken to guarantee to the American people their right to be the final arbiters of what they shall hear, and by the same token, what programs shall be broadcast. The American people have been effectively their own censors; their own tastes have elevated the standards of radio and will continue to elevate them. The radio industry readily acknowledges that it is still in a developing stage, but we contend that it is not possible by any legislative fiat to establish taste or standards and we feel strongly that Congress does not desire to, and should not, depart from its established policy. Moreover, we feel that any proposal in legislation looking toward that result should be defeated."

DISCIPLINE FROM WITHIN

The big chains have for years had elaborate deca-
logues of their own for the guidance of those using
their microphones. But until recently no attempt was
made to arrive at uniform rules. The official rebukes
which followed the Mae West and Charlie McCarthy
episode and the Orson Welles Martian broadcast, as
well as the short-term licenses, have had their logical
effect. The National Association of Broadcasters has
recently adopted a Code of Standards applicable to the
industry. The code contains general statements of policy
on standards of ethics and good taste to be observed by
member stations. Its provisions are reprinted in full in
Appendix B. Here is a summary of them:

(1) Children's programs are to be closely supervised. They are
to be based upon "sound social concepts."

(2) Stations are to provide time for the presentation of public
questions, including those of a controversial nature, with
fairness to all elements in a given controversy. But time is
not to be sold for debatable issues except for political
broadcasts.

(3) The potentialities of radio as a means of education are to
be studied and developed.

(4) News is to be presented with fairness and accuracy, and
without editorial bias.

(5) Radio is not to be used "to convey attacks on race or religion."

(6) Only such commercial programs are to be broadcast as
pertain to legitimate products or services, and comply with
legal requirements, fair trade practices and standards of
good taste.

Here, as in the case of the Motion Picture Production Code, an ingenuous reader may be prompted to

say: "Well, all this seems desirable enough." If the radio code were merely a declaration of principles for the guidance of stations, few would quarrel with it. But the likelihood is that it will repeat the career of the Hays code. A board will be set up to enforce it; penalties will be devised; the accumulated decisions of the board will establish a complex of don'ts; there will be a regimentation of opinion; free speech will be crippled.

We hope we're wrong. It's not impossible that radio has learned something from the screen's example, and will not repeat its blunders. That remains to be seen.

The Nub

A theoretical discussion of free speech, divorced from any consideration of medium, is futile. Each means of expression has its characteristics and adaptabilities, its influence for good or evil, its limitations. Free speech on the air is not free speech on the street corner.

What, then, is free speech on the radio? Is it the historic right to express one's views without previous restraint, subject only to subsequent punishment for unlawful utterances? Or is it only the privilege to say what does not displease the stations, commercial sponsors or the commission?

It is not essential at this point to decide whether, with respect to its obligation to deal impartially with all those who may seek its facilities, radio is a private enterprise or something akin to a public utility. A private enterprise has the right, ordinarily, to refuse to deal with anyone not acceptable to it. If a newspaper declines a paid advertisement, if a periodical rejects a manuscript, if a picture gallery refuses to hang a painting or if a theater decides not to exhibit a film, that is not censorship. But where a private enterprise—though not required by law to deal with all those who may offer—is of such nature and magnitude as to render the availability of its facilities a social necessity, denies equal treatment to all applicants, can it be reasonably urged no censorship exists?

If the commission revokes the license of a station whose program policy it doesn't favor, have we not a situation similar to that of a newspaper which is sought to be suppressed by injunction for its supposed libelous content—an attempt which was so vigorously denounced by the Supreme Court of the United States in *Near* v. *Minnesota*? Is it an answer that the commission cannot with impunity infringe free speech because the aggrieved person can always go to court? What good does it do a man to have a right which may be curtailed at any time by official caprice, so that he has to go to law for vindication? Is not the very purpose of constitutional guaranties to place certain fundamental rights conclusively beyond the pale of bureaucratic interference?

Is Radio Unique?

Nothing has ever divided believers in the Bill of Rights as sharply as the question of radio.

There are some people who profess a fervent belief in unfettered expression in every medium—speech, writings, stage, screen—and yet shake their heads in doubt when it comes to radio.

They say that historic notions of liberty cannot be applied to the air. Their thesis runs something like this:

A hundred years ago free speech meant that a man who wanted to say something could pause at a chosen place, gather a crowd and shout his piece to his heart's content. Those who fought for and won the Bill of

Rights in England, and those here in America who put that document into the First Amendment, saw no reason to concern themselves overmuch with the perils of intemperate utterance. They were wise enough to realize that a man's voice could carry just so far; that there was a limit to the number of possible listeners; that if a fool or rogue got up to rant, whatever mischief he did could be counteracted by other speakers free to rise in denial, and by the common sense of the community. His auditors could question him, heckle him, contradict his assertions, probe into his motives, explode his logic; people in the vicinage could shun the sound of his voice if they wished. And were he to vociferate twenty-four hours a day his circle of influence would still be limited. So in the long run two things were apt to be assured: unhampered discussion and the preservation of some kind of social balance.

Applied to radio (the argument runs on) this concept of free speech loses meaning. When a speaker steps before a microphone, though it be on a single occasion, he addresses not hundreds or thousands or hundreds of thousands, but many millions. The ether provides him with an impenetrable bastion. While he speaks he cannot be assaulted with questions or ridiculed or driven to cover. He holds in his grasp an instrument more terrible than the thunderbolts of Jove; he can wreak untold harm and havoc within the space of an hour. He can whip uncounted multitudes to hysteria, terror, loathing, violence.

When Milton urged in the *Areopagitica* that truth and error be allowed to grapple, because truth would win eventually, he envisaged an even-handed encounter. But truth and tolerance cannot fight falsehood, demagoguery and vigilantism on equal terms on the air. We are not justified in supposing that listeners whose minds are infected by a Coughlin or a Moseley listen to the

other side as well. We cannot make radio an effective
market place of ideas good and bad because we are
not at all sure that reason will always correct folly. The
microphone (it is concluded) is so dangerous an in-
strumentality that in dealing with it we must discard the
principle of unfettered discussion and formulate restrictions of some kind.

Because it sounds so plausible this argument is
doubly treacherous. Carried to its logical conclusion, it
could be used to justify almost any suppression. Its structure rests on the quicksands of the size of audience. It
makes liberty a matter of arithmetic. It is the offspring
of cowardice, compromise and fear. It would barter
principle for expediency. In the early days of printing,
controversial pamphlets reached only hundreds. Today
an author addresses hundreds of thousands. Shall we
say that, ours being an age of mass communication, free
speech should be scrapped?

If we reject the argument, what is the alternative
that faces us? We cannot escape the fact that the
physical limitations of radio are such as to require a
central supervisory authority if chaos is to be averted.
Maybe ten or twenty years from now there will be an
unlimited number of available wave lengths. Then the
question of censorship will be simplified.

But before that day comes, what criteria should guide
the authority in granting, suspending, revoking and
renewing licenses? Can the criteria be limited solely to
financial and technical considerations? If program content is to be ignored are we certain the social good will
thus best be served?

Many liberals insist that program content should be a
yardstick, and that stations espousing the democratic
ideal should be favored. Here, too, we get involved in
a confusion of terms. The "democratic ideal" is one
thing to Girdler and Ford, and another to a miner in

bloody Harlan or a share cropper. But let us assume that democracy means political, civil and religious liberties, economic as well as political majority rule, equality of economic opportunity, freedom for social change through the procedures of majority rule, recognition of the dignity and responsibility of the individual.

When we say that we should favor programs in the democratic tradition, does that mean that we should frown on anti-democratic utterances? Shall we deny the microphone to the Coughlins, the Kuhns, the Leninists? What happens then to the principle, expressed by Voltaire and many others, of fighting for the other fellow's right to speak even though we disagree with him utterly?

If it is true, and we think it is, that it is socially wise to pour all kinds of ideas into the crucible of conflict, adding the ingredients of skepticism, scrutiny, testing by experience, evaluation, so that the dross of the spurious may be cast off and the gold of enduring values disengaged, then *a free radio dedicated to the cause of democracy means diversity of opinion on the air*. So long as the ether is a genuine market place for many points of view we need not fear the prophets of reaction, the demagogues, the hate mongers any more than the psychopaths who burst into print now and then, only to be promptly consigned to oblivion by the common sense of society.

CHAPTER VIII

Art and Censorship

A sign 108½ feet long and 50 feet high, containing a perfect picture or likeness of a Durham bull, painted on the side of a store, is not so immodest or indecent as to prevent the most fastidious or refined ladies from visiting such store.
Shiverick v. Gunning Co., 58 Neb. 29, 78 N.W. Rep. 460

THE NEW YORKER recently told the story of an old lady who entered a bookstore and went to the counter that bore a sign reading "Art and Photography." She picked up some books, opened them, leafed through them and put them down. Finally, flushed and eager, she approached the sales clerk. "I can't find anything but art," she said. "Where is the pornography?"

MICHELANGELO MAKES THE NEWS

When Pope Paul IV, shocked by the heroic nudes of Michelangelo's famous fresco, The Last Judgment, in the Sistine Chapel in the Vatican, ordered Daniele da Volterra to paint loincloths on the figures, he little suspected that his action would, centuries later, strike a sympathetic chord in the heart of the United States customs.

A reproduction of the copy by Venusti of the famous mural, made before Da Volterra applied his redeeming brush, was detained at the New York customs in 1933 as obscene. Had the reproduction borne no explanatory legend, its seizure might have been explainable on the theory that the customs people did not know what they were condemning, that they were allergic to nudes generally, and regarded the fresco merely as a representation of numerous unclad bodies. However, there was an explicit reference to the original mural on the face of the reproduction; the notice of seizure described it in writing as "obscene photo books, Ceiling Sistine Chapel, Filles-Michael Angelo, the importation of which is held to be prohibited under the provisions of the Tariff Act."

The incident precipitated a great deal of jeering press comment. It was a much chastened Customs Bureau that finally permitted the picture to enter.

Another episode provoked almost as much public chortling at the expense of the customs. *Stag at Eve,* a collection of somewhat bawdy cartoons, was published in this country and was freely sold everywhere. Reprinted abroad, a copy of the English edition was sent to this country and was denied entry. Amid the chorus of jibes from the newspapers, the customs authorities were chagrined to discover that they were endeavoring to keep out something that was already in.

One might have forgiven these two incidents if they had served to make the customs officials wiser. They did not. From time to time since, the work of such outstanding men as Anders Zorn, the etcher, D. H. Lawrence, the novelist, Eric Gill, the engraver, and Leon Underwood, the woodcut artist, have been held up.

COMSTOCK AND ART

It was mainly pornographic picture post cards with which Comstock descended on our lawmakers in Washington in 1873 as evidence of the flood of corrupting matter that he claimed threatened to engulf the country. Just what emotions stirred the legislators when they gazed upon Comstock's display of smut we shall never know, but there can be no doubt that the decisive role in the enactment of the obscenity role was played by pictures, not by books.

Throughout his career art troubled Comstock. With one problem in particular he wrestled for many years. His perplexity arose out of a desire to find a *rationale* for the thesis that although an original painting might be unobjectionable, copies of it might be obscene. He may not have relished the first part of the proposition. It was forced upon him, so to speak; a contrary view would have compelled him to denounce for nudity many centuries of art accepted as great by the world. So he constructed his theory of duality of effect as between original and copy, and he labored to demonstrate its soundness. A goodly portion of his *Traps for the Young* was devoted to it. With apparently no realization that his argument failed to make sense, he wrote:

. . . the artist has expended much time to bring his picture to perfection. The lines of beauty, the mingling colors, tintings and shadings all seem to clothe the figures by diverting attention from that which, if taken alone, is objectionable, with a surrounding which protects its offensive character. In other words, that which, if taken alone, is offensive to good morals is unmasked in the copy.

"Unmasked in the copy"—that was the gist of his theory. An unclad woman didn't look unclad in a painting; she was positively stripped in a photograph of the painting.

A work of art [Comstock said] is made up of many elements that are wanting in a photograph of the same, precisely as there is a difference between a woman in her proper womanly apparel and modest appearance, and when shorn of all these and posed in a lewd posture. Because we are above savages we clothe our nakedness. So with a work of art as compared to a copy . . .

Perhaps Comstock himself did not believe in this nonsense. Whether he did or not, he was inconsistent in the application of his views. He raided the reputable Knoedler Galleries in 1887 and carried off hundreds of photographs of the paintings of such well-known French artists as Bouguereau, Henner and Perrault. But he also fulminated against Bryson Burroughs' *original* picture, The Explorers, which was displayed by the Macbeth Gallery.

THE CRUSADE GOES ON

Mr Parsons, then president of the New York Society for the Suppression of Vice, said in his 1930 report: "Mr Comstock's spirit still pervades the work of the society." This no one will deny.

In 1930 Timothy Murphy collected a series of reproductions of nudes, mostly by Rembrandt and Goya, rented a store near Longacre Square, New York City, and opened a picture gallery. Mr Sumner had Mr Murphy booked on a charge of exhibiting indecent pictures. The complaint was dismissed in the Magistrate's Court, and Mr Murphy filed suit against Mr Sumner for malicious prosecution, asking one hundred thousand dollars in damages. Nothing came of it.

About the same time Spain issued the Goya Memorial stamp in commemoration of Goya Week at the Ibero-American Exposition at Seville. The stamp bore a miniature reproduction of Goya's Maia, a portrait in the nude of the Duchess of Alba, the most celebrated of the painter's works. When the stamp came to the attention of Mr Sumner he expressed his regret that nothing could be done to curtail its circulation in this country.

THE HUMAN BODY OBSCENE?

The censor's crusade against French post cards, then, has been paralleled by his work against bona fide art. He has not been able to distinguish between the two. He has harried the one with as much energy as the other. The gist of his complaint against paintings has been that a portrayal of the human body without clothing is obscene. He draws no line between art and pornography.

In fairness it must be admitted that the judiciary has contributed no little to the confused thinking on the subject. When the courts of New York condemned *The Nudist,* the official organ of the International Nudist Conference (this case is discussed in Chapter XI), it was clearly implied that what had shocked them was not the text but the pictures of the nudist activities. The pictures were harmless enough. They merely depicted nudists exercising, swimming, eating and resting; the genitals were not shown. At the same time art studies of nudes were widely sold and were not unmolested. The inference was that the human body was indecent and unlawful if depicted for health purposes and legitimate if stripped for art.

This inference was all too soon repudiated. In 1937 the manager of a long-established firm dealing in artists' supplies was convicted of selling a copy of Volume II of *The Body Beautiful.* The book had been published by Robert M. McBride Company, and contained the contributions of many famous New York photographers. Henry Campbell wrote in the introduction: "An evil imagination will sense only the sordid and the ugly. A healthy and wholesome mind will sense only the ennobling power of the beautiful." The conviction brought the courts of New York in line with the customs policy, for the customs had for years barred art studies. It appeared to pave the way for the suppression of other collections of photographs, regardless of artistic merit, and caused considerable apprehension among booksellers.

A year later, just by way of adding another piece to the crazy mosaic, the police proceeded against "nudies," a certain kind of highball glass that was being displayed and sold throughout New York City. The glasses bore upon the outside highly colored representations of ladies in costume, but if they were turned around the ladies were revealed to be nude. No pretense was made that the glasses were objects of art. The defendant was acquitted.

THE POST OFFICE

The *Studio* is a top-notch art magazine that has been in existence for almost half a century. The February 1939 issue of it carried reproductions of Matisse's Hindu Pose, Eric Gill's Apocalypse woodcuts, Aristide Maillol's Ovid, Demetrius Galanis' Three Graces and two prints by H. M. Williamson. The post office ruled the issue was obscene, and the *Studio's* second-class permit was revoked. The publishers were told that future issues would have to be submitted in advance for scrutiny before they would be carried in the mails, and before any application for the reissuance of the second-class permit would be considered. Art, the post office said, in complete disregard of decades of judicial precedent, was not entitled to any special treatment; there was no reason why reproductions of nudes in an art magazine should be regarded any differently than in other publications. Tintoretto might be all right on the walls of a museum room where millions might see his work indiscriminately without an admission fee; he was obscene on the pages of a seventy-five-cent periodical circulated among a limited number of art lovers and connoisseurs.

Luckily the *Studio* put up a fight. After considerable trouble the February issue was reluctantly restored to the mails.

Within a month of this incident an event took place in the art world which showed how completely out of step the post office was with the march of times. Knoedler's in New York opened a loan exhibition called "Classics of the Nude," in which all the masters from Pollaiuolo to Picasso were represented. The critics hailed the exhibition as one of extraordinary merit and importance, and reproductions of many of the paintings appeared in the press.

Sound and Fury

Although the other arts have suffered much less from intermeddling, they have not escaped unscathed.

Gilbert and Sullivan's *The Mikado* was suppressed by the Lord Chamberlain in 1905 for fear of offending the Japanese. The Lord Chamberlain overlooked the fact that the operetta had been produced in 1885 and had been a continuous success for twenty years. As a matter of fact Japanese bands played the music on Japanese ships during the ban.

The German court that found nothing wicked in the stage presentation of Schnitzler's *Reigen,* objected to the music as too sensuous and suggestive.

Dmitri Shostakovich's opera, *Lady Macbeth of Mzensk,* was a great artistic success in 1935 in New York and Cleveland. When it moved to Philadelphia the local moralists, led by Mrs George Holt Strawbridge, director of the Clean Amusement Association of America, were outraged by the fervor of the love scenes and the "too graphic" quality of some of the musical measures. Pressed for the basis of her objections, Mrs Strawbridge admitted she had not seen the opera herself, but depended on hearsay. In any event the love scenes were toned down, and the musical measures which were deemed vulgar were deleted.

SOME EXCEPTIONS

It is a phenomenon of our morality that not only organized groups like the New York Vice Society, the Boston Watch and Ward and Philadelphia's Clean Amusement Association, but also indignant individuals ordinarily have no difficulty in enlisting the sympathy of the authorities in their attack on supposed indecency. Only in rare cases does the protector of morals suffer a setback. Two of these cases deserve mention.

In 1936 Mrs William Burd, wife of a Paterson clergyman, objected to the painting of a bathing nude hanging in the bar of a saloon, and called upon Commissioner Burnett to order its removal. In refusing to act, the commissioner wrote to Mrs Burd:

I am not concerned with artistry or lack of it. Nor with questions of taste, appropriateness or motive. There is no reason why places for the consumption of liquor should not be made comfortable and decorative. The live problems that confront us are the actions of human beings, not inert paintings. So long as these places are decent, self-respecting and obey the law there will be no interference with individual initiative in furnishings or appointments. Pictures as well as flowers may brighten a corner. "Obscene" should not be an execration lightly to be hurled at a painting, merely because it does not conform to one's own viewpoint. It is not to be determined by considering its effect on somebody else. Obscenity is something at which we all instinctively revolt and which common decency forbids. It is instantly determinable by inspection. The more argument necessary to prove it, the less it is. This picture is not obscene.

Some years ago a complaint was filed with the attorney general of Florida against a certain advertising poster which depicted—to use the attorney general's own vivid words—"four chorus girls performing a high-kicking dance, clad in meager bodices and short bloomers, midway of which is an attendant fringe of some fluffy silken material, probably intended to serve as a skirt but which signally fails of its purpose, thereby leaving exposed to public view the lower half of each female anatomy involved, with the exception of that small portion thereof which is afforded virtually inadequate concealment by the daring brevity of the bloomers worn."

Adverting to the Florida law which forbade the public exhibition of any obscene figure manifestly tending to corrupt the morals of youth, the attorney general observed that such morals had to be appraised in the light of prevailing standards. The problem, he said, was to ascertain what conduct would be regarded by authoritative opinion as contrary to current morals.

For evidence of "current morals" he turned to the social scene about him. "A casual view," he said, "of the passers-by on our streets, of the pictures on our best magazine covers, of the sight of actresses and actors on the stage and in the movies, and of even our church and social leaders among women will unquestionably impress one that this is the day of excessively abbreviated skirts, affording what may be regarded by some as being a too generous and unobstructed view of the major portion of the lower anatomy of the twentieth-century female. Few of the masculine sex are now so inexperienced or unsophisticated as to be admittedly perturbed by the panorama of varying styles in feminine wearing apparel (or lack of it) which would have undoubtedly furnished a rude spiritual jolt to the perspective of our forefathers."

He admitted that many "venerable and conscientious" people regarded the changing mores with apprehension. To discount their fears he turned to Isaiah's denunciation, in the Bible, of women who "are haughty and walk with stretched-forth necks and wanton eyes, walking and mincing as they go, and making a tinkling with their feet," and concluded that although women had gone their way heedless of the prophet's castigation, mankind had managed to survive. The line of demarcation, he admitted, between propriety and immorality was hard to draw. Prohibition gave him a clue: "Years ago there was a like difficulty of determining where ran the line of separation between beverages which are intoxicating, and therefore immoral, and those which were not intoxicating, and therefore licit. To settle this vexed question the leaders of the prohibition movement were forced to adopt an arbitrary standard, by which they fixed one half of one per cent of alcohol as being the immovable boundary between that which was approved as lawful and that which was condemned as outlawed."

He applied this test in true judicial fashion: "Judging by the modern trend of female dress on the stage and in the movies, it would appear that the ladies of the theatrical profession have adopted the same percentage for their dress as they are forced to observe for their beverages, and that under this modern percentage rule so adopted, and which is generally approved by the press and public, it must now be held that so long as the modern-day chorus girl has one half of one per cent of the lower half of her anatomy duly covered with clothing of some denomination, she is to be regarded as being sufficiently well and properly dressed to escape the denunciation of our laws, directed at such a state of undress as would tend to corrupt the morals of youth."

CHAPTER IX

Birth-Control Literature

The desire for conception control is found in virtually every society and in every age of history. This desire is so universal that attempts to uproot it will doubtless prove futile.

DR NORMAN E. HIMES, Article, Encyclopedia
Sexualis (1936)

Every wise interpretation of law, every liberal ruling breaks another link in the legal chain which binds birth control.

Editorial, *Birth Control Review* (1931)

THE YEARLY DEATH TOLL among women in the United States from causes due to childbearing is approximately twenty thousand. It is impossible to estimate the number of deaths due to abortions each year; the figure must be appalling. One reliable medical authority has estimated it to be fifteen thousand. Nor can it be assumed that the practice is resorted to principally by those who have had illicit relations. Dr F. J. Taussig, who has made a careful survey, states that the increase in the number of abortions is noticed primarily among married women who have three or more children.

Notwithstanding these facts, laws stringently penalizing the giving of contraceptive advice and the dispensing of contraceptive materials remain unchanged on the statute books. Whatever advances have been made toward the free dissemination of such information and supplies to those who need them have been achieved by the courts.

The Birth-Control Laws

Federal law is exclusively applicable to the transportation of contraceptive materials and information through the mails and the channels of interstate and foreign commerce. It has remained substantially unchanged since 1873, when Anthony Comstock, climaxing his crusade against vice, succeeded in getting Congress to pass a law declaring such materials and information contraband. The significant thing is that during the first ninety years of our national existence we had no restrictions whatever on birth control; reputable journals like the *Tribune* carried advertisements of contraceptives in the 1840s. At the present time:

Section 334 of the United States Criminal Code prohibits their mailing.

Section 396 of the Criminal Code prohibits their transportation in interstate commerce; and

Section 305 of the Tariff Act bars the importation of *articles,* but makes no mention of contraceptive *information.*

The federal government has no power to regulate commerce *within* the borders of the several states. That is reserved to the states themselves. Of the forty-eight, nineteen have left the subject of birth control alone; they have enacted no legislation outlawing or furthering it. Eight states (Arizona, Arkansas, California, Louisiana, Maine, Michigan, North Carolina and Wisconsin) have sought to regulate certain incidents of the marketing of contraceptives but have not affected their sale in general. Eleven states (Colorado, Delaware, Idaho, Indiana, Iowa, Minnesota, Montana, Nevada, New York, Ohio and Wyoming) have in addition prohibited some or all sales of contraceptives to laymen, but make an express exception for medical practice. Thus, in thirty-eight states no effort has been made to prevent the use of contraceptives by physicians in their efforts to preserve the life and protect the health of their patients. Four states (Kansas, Missouri, Nebraska and New Jersey) have statutes so worded that it seems fair to assume that their prohibitions do not apply to physicians. This leaves only six states (Connecticut, Massachusetts, Mississippi, Missouri, Pennsylvania and Washington) with statutes which, if literally construed, might prevent even the prescription of contraceptives by physicians. The Connecticut statute goes so far as to penalize the *use* of a contraceptive. Until very recently, however, Massachusetts was the only state in which physicians were sought to be punished for violating the contraceptive bans. At this writing Connecticut is seeking to swing in line.

These laws, federal and state, constitute the background against which the recent court decisions involving contraception must be viewed.

United States against Contraception

The Customs Bureau did not like the defeat it suffered in the *Married Love* case. Dr Marie C. Stopes had been on the customs index so long that another official foray was to be expected.

When her extensive treatise, *Contraception,* was sent to this country in 1930 it was seized as illegal. Proceedings for confiscation were commenced by the government.

As it later appeared, someone in the customs had pulled a boner. The postal law forbade the mailing of any *information,* drug, medicine or article for the prevention of conception. Whoever it was that directed the seizure seems to have assumed that the Tariff Act (which governed importations) contained an identical provision. It did not. The word "information" was missing; the customs ban applied only to contraceptive drugs, medicines and articles.

When the case came up in the federal court before Judge Woolsey, the Customs Bureau was in a quandary. There was nothing for it to do but to try to bring Dr Stopes' volume within the purview of the contraband categories. And so it argued in all seriousness that the book was an "article" within the meaning of the Tariff Act, and should be excluded.

Judge Woolsey rejected this nonsense. He characterized the work as "a scientific book, written with obvious seriousness and with great decency, and it gives information to the medical profession regarding the operation of birth-control clinics and the instruction necessary to be given at such clinics to women who resort thereto. It tells of the devices, used now and in the past, to prevent conception . . ."

Such a book [he went on] although it may run counter to the views of many persons who disagree entirely with the theory underlying birth control, certainly does not fall within the test of obscenity or immorality laid down by me in the case of *United States* v. *One Obscene Book entitled Married Love,* 48F. (2d) 821 at 824, for the reading of it would not stir the sex impulses of any person with a normal mind.

He found that the emotions aroused by the book were sympathy and pity, evoked by the many case histories recited in it of the sufferings of married women due to ignorance of its teachings. He concluded:

It follows that as *Contraception* is not an obscene or immoral book, and, obviously, is not a drug, medicine or an article for the prevention of conception . . . it may be imported into the United States . . .

It was believed that from then on there would be no customs interference with the flow of birth-control literature from abroad. The belief was soon exploded. The very next copy of the book which was sent into this country was seized at the port of entry. The customs officials admitted freely that despite Judge Woolsey's decision they would continue to pounce on every book and pamphlet dealing with contraception. They said they would find some other section of the Tariff Act to justify their course.

An important legal victory was thus temporarily nullified by administrative obduracy.

Methods Natural and Unnatural

It was at about this time that *The Rhythm* made its appearance in Chicago. It was a manual by Dr Leo J. Latz of the Loyola University Medical School. It purported to set forth the so-called "natural" method of birth control. Since it bore the Catholic imprimatur, "Published with ecclesiastical approbation," it committed the Catholic Church to the doctrine of family limitation.

The Ogino-Knaus method was sponsored. It was presented as scientific, reliable and consonant with good religion. During the menstrual cycle of a woman, *The Rhythm* explained, there was a period of sterility and a period of fertility. These periods were to be fixed by computation. By restricting sexual intercourse to periods of sterility family limitation could be achieved. In urging this "natural" means of birth control, the book launched a violent attack on the method recognized by the medical world. This method was branded "artificial and irrational," injurious to health and destructive of morals.

Dr Latz's treatise failed to state that the overwhelming majority of the medical profession had repudiated the Ogino-Knaus idea as unsound, unscientific and unreliable. It failed to state that the rhythm method depended on accurate record keeping and computation; that it was virtually useless for women with irregular periods; that the very persons most desperately in need of relief—the underprivileged, the unfit, the uneducated—could never be reasonably expected to apply the mathematical formula. It failed to state that the method had not worked in many cases and had caused great misery.

In any event, the manual went through several editions. It moved freely through the mails. The post office, which had previously evinced extraordinary alacrity in barring contraceptive matter, declined to interfere with its distribution. As a result, several other Catholic publications of the same nature were issued. All were circulated without official hindrance.

In October 1934, Mrs Hazel Moore, legislative secretary of the National Committee on Federal Legislation for Birth Control, arrived at the port of New York. She was returning from England where she had visited various birth-control clinics maintained under the supervision of the Ministry of Health. She had in her possession certain medical supplies and also several books and pamphlets. One of the books was *The Rhythm*. Among the pamphlets were copies of Dr Stone's *Therapeutic Contraception,* and also copies of Mrs Margaret Sanger's *The Medical and Biological Aspects of Birth Control. The Rhythm* had been published in this country; Mrs Moore had taken a copy abroad and was bringing it back with her.

The customs officials seized the medical supplies, claiming they were contraceptives. Mrs Moore objected. She said she did not know whether they were or not; she had collected them in England for the purpose of testing them out here. To this the customs people replied that as long as *she* was bringing the supplies in, they were going to take it for granted they were contraband.

When it came to the books and pamphlets, all were taken, excepting *The Rhythm*. Once more Mrs Moore objected. She pointed out that under Judge Woolsey's ruling in the *Contraception* case, birth-control literature could legally enter this country. The answer of the customs officials was that they were making the seizure not only under the Tariff Act, but also under some other statute. In that case, countered Mrs Moore, they could not confine themselves to Dr Stone's pamphlets and Mrs Sanger's book; they would also have to take *The Rhythm;* it too contained birth-control information. *The Rhythm* was thereupon reluctantly taken.

The government was in a spot. To be consistent it had to release *all* the printed matter, or detain all of it. If it made an exception in favor of *The Rhythm* its action would be tantamount to an official endorsement of one method of birth control as against another.

The Rhythm won. An administrative ruling was handed down which was a monument to bureaucracy. It held that *The Rhythm* was admissible under the Tariff Act because it advocated "natural" birth control, but that all the other pamphlets were illegal for entry because they recommended "artificial" means.

THE MARRIAGE HYGIENE CASE

The Customs Bureau could flout the *Contraception* decision, of course, but there it was on the lawbooks, and every time a seizure occurred in defiance of it the advocates of birth control raised a row. The bureau thought it would be a good idea to get the matter settled once for all.

So the bureau worked out a brand-new legal theory which it believed to be foolproof. It was not going to rely on section 305 of the Tariff Act which had ruined its case before Judge Woolsey. Instead, it would move forward under a *blanket* provision of the act: section 593 (b), which directed the forfeiture of any "merchandise imported contrary to law." It would argue that since the importation, mailing and interstate transportation of books on contraception were forbidden in general terms by the Federal Criminal Code such books were "contrary to law," and hence subject to confiscation under section 593 (b).

Accordingly, in 1936 the authorities seized several copies of the magazine, *Marriage Hygiene,* which were consigned to Professor Norman E. Himes of Colgate University, the American editor of the magazine, and a copy of the book, *Parenthood,* by Michael Fielding, consigned to Mr John P. Nicholas. Separate proceedings were started to forfeit the seized material.

The two cases were tried as one on June 2, 1937, before Judge Galston in the federal court. The attorneys for Dr Himes and Mr Nicholas called the judge's attention to the Woolsey decision, and declared that the prosecution's new theory was no more than legalistic gibberish, concocted for the purpose of justifying a preconceived customs policy. They pointed to the fact that section 593(b) was located in that part of the Tariff Act dealing with the frauds on revenue, and urged that in the light of its titles, context, origins, intendment and previous application, it could be construed to cover only *manner* of importation and no reference to the nature of the commodity sought to be imported. They also pointed out that section 305 was intended to be exclusively applicable to the subject matter of contraception, and that even if generally speaking section 593 (b) might apply to a situation such as that which was the basis of the proceeding, section 305 rendered it inapplicable.

A jury was impaneled at the insistence of the prosecution, but at the close of the case Judge Galston found that there was no question of fact to pass on. The jury was dismissed, and decision was reserved on the questions of law.

On June 28, 1937, Judge Galston handed down his decision. He ruled against the government. He did not decide the basic issue as to whether or not section 593 (b) applied to the facts of the cases. He merely held that even if the section were applicable, the government had failed to prove its case because the section required intent on the part of the consignees, and the government had not shown that either consignee had had knowledge that the law would be violated by the importation of the material in question.

The government appealed the cases to the Circuit Court of Appeals. They were argued there on April 18–19, 1938, before Judges Learned Hand, Swan and Chase.

The Court showed great interest in the case. Judge Learned Hand wanted to know what the magazine, *Marriage Hygiene,* was about, and where it had come from. The attorney for the claimants said that the publication dealt with matters touching on family health, particularly birth control; that it had been published in Bombay, India; and that a number of copies had been sent to Dr Himes, its American editor, for distribution here.

"Well," observed Judge Hand with a smile, "it seems to me that information of this kind is more sorely needed in India than here."

Assistant U. S. Attorney Schoonmaker argued that even if the Customs Bureau were held to be in the wrong the seized material should not be released to

Dr Himes and Mr Nicholas, but should be sent to the Dead Letter Office.

His adversary was understandably nettled. "If it please the Court," he said, "whenever in the past the government won a customs case the impounded matter was confiscated, and whenever it lost, the matter was released to the claimants. But now the Customs Bureau is saying to the claimants, heads we win, tails you lose."

Judge Hand leaned forward, a twinkle in his eye. "Does the government ever play the game any other way? After all, it's one hundred and thirty-seven million people against a solitary book and a handful of magazines. You could hardly expect the struggle to be an even one!"

The Circuit Court rejected all the government's contentions but one, and upheld Judge Galston. It ruled:

(a) That *Marriage Hygiene* was to be released to Dr Himes because he, as American editor of the magazine, was "qualified" to receive it, contraceptive books and pamphlets being "lawful in the hands of those who would not abuse the information they contained. This excuses the magazines, addressed as they were to their legal editor; being lawful in the hands of physicians, scientists and the like, the claimant at bar was their most appropriate distributor. True, he might misuse his privilege, but that chance does not cancel it; if he does he will then be subject to punishment, but he is not so subject yet nor can he now be deprived of his property."

(b) That although *Parenthood* was not to be forfeited, it could not be released to Mr Nicholas, the consignee, but was to go to the Dead Letter Office. This was because there was nothing in the record as to Mr Nicholas' qualifications to receive birth-control literature.

Although the government had indicated at the outset that it would carry the cases to the United States Supreme Court, it did not do so.

Thus another victory was chalked up by the birth-control forces. The salutary holding in the *Contraception* case was vindicated and reinforced. There can no longer be any doubt that contraceptive literature is subject to the same rules as a contraceptive article: it may be lawfully imported, transported or mailed, provided the consignee or addressee is a person qualified to receive it. Those who are interested in the birth-control field may well be content with the present status of the federal law. As things now stand, a qualified person (meaning a physician or some other person who has a special standing) can by the presentation of an affidavit at the customs obtain a release of contraceptive supplies or literature which he wishes to import for legitimate use in his work.

CHAPTER X

Birth-Control Advice and Materials

Not only has birth control nothing in common with abortion, but it is a weapon of the greatest value in fighting this evil. With its help we may hope to limit and, I trust, eradicate this criminal practice. It is not generally known outside the medical profession and social workers how widespread this practice is. It amounts in fact to a national disgrace. I say national because the United States leads all other countries in the number of abortions performed yearly. The laws enacted to suppress it have had but little deterrent effect. The practice is most common among married women, particularly of the poorer prolific classes, who already have children and cannot afford to add to their number. These mothers, on finding themselves pregnant again after repeated pregnancies, resort in desperation to this immoral and dangerous means of relief. Some women seek this means not only once but a dozen or twenty times. Some women do not live to seek it for the second time.

DR RACHELLE S. YARROS,
Birth Control Review (1931)

LAW OR NO LAW, people will resort to some means to limit their families. The crucial question which has been facing society for generations is not whether we should have birth control, but whether the people of the land should be afforded dependable medical advice instead of devious, hit-or-miss information.

THE GROUNDWORK

In 1915 a New York court found Margaret Sanger's *Family Limitation* "contrary not only to the law of the state but to the law of God." Mrs Sanger went to jail for violating a law which imposed an absolute ban on the dissemination of birth-control materials and information by laymen. The Appellate Court denied her appeal, but said that what Mrs Sanger and her co-workers could not legally do, a licensed physician was permitted to do *for the prevention of disease in a patient.* In a later case Judge Cropsey enlarged the exception to include the *preservation of health.*

Accordingly, birth control in New York State, upon the advice of a physician, is lawful in cases where transmissible diseases are present and where the spacing of children or the prevention of childbearing is necessitated by the health of the mother. There is also some indication that physicians may legally dispense contraceptive information and supplies where economic conditions are such that another child would imperil the health of the family. This economic factor has been recognized by the Catholic Church. In recommending the "natural" method of birth control based on the so-called sterile period, Dr Latz says in *The Rhythm:*

Burdens that test human endurance to the utmost limit, and to which all too many succumb, will be lightened. I speak of economic burdens, the burdens of poverty, of inadequate income or unemployment, which make it impossible for parents to give their children and themselves the food, the clothing, the housing, the education and the recreation they are entitled to as children of God.

A Clinic Is Raided

Despite the liberality of judicial policy, reactionary groups have made sporadic attempts to halt the forward march. In 1929 a chapter of the Daughters of the American Revolution filed a complaint with the police commissioner of New York City against Mrs Sanger's Birth Control Clinic. Just eleven days after the defeat in the New York legislature of the Remer bill (which was to release birth control from its legal shackles in New York) the clinic was raided by the police. Three nurses and two licensed physicians were hustled off in a patrol wagon and thousands of confidential case histories, which legal and medical tradition had always held inviolate, were ransacked and carried away. The clinic had been operating in a dignified manner for six years. It had received the approval of the late Dr Louis I. Harris who, as health commissioner of New York, had scrutinized its work.

When the case was called for trial in the Magistrate's Court, the courtroom was jammed. Looking around, the defense attorney recognized many of the rich Park Avenue ladies who had for years sponsored the birth-control movement. He was puzzled, however, by the presence of a large number of young working girls.

"What's up?" he asked one of the attendants, indicating the girls.

The attendant chuckled. "The cops raid this clinic because they don't want people to know about birth control. Those girls get arrested for picketing a cafeteria. Their case comes after this, so they'll hear what the doctors have to spill. Methods and all. What a break they're getting!"

Five eminent physicians testified for the defense. They unanimously endorsed the activities of the clinic.

It was doing no more, they said, than doctors throughout the city, no more than they themselves had done for years in their private practice. If the five defendants were guilty, the whole medical profession would have to be put in jail.

This was a tough one for the magistrate. If he was going to be consistent he could not hold the defendants for trial without directing that warrants be sworn for the arrest of the witnesses. They had admitted in open court that their practices were no different. He tried to find a way out.

He questioned Dr Harris closely. Did the clinic give contraceptive advice to married women only? Yes. How did Dr Harris know? By the records that were kept. What were these records based on? The statements made by the patients to the clinic. But were any steps taken to check up and find out whether the women were telling the truth?

This was too much. The attorney for the defense broke in. "Is it customary in medicine," he asked Dr Harris, "for a physician to send out detectives to investigate his patients?"

A ripple of laughter stirred the crowded courtroom.

"Or to ask a patient who says she is married to produce her marriage certificate?"

This time the audience roared. The magistrate was annoyed. If there were any more outbursts, he said, he'd have the courtroom cleared.

He then engaged in an earnest colloquy with Dr Foster Kennedy, one of the defense witnesses. Dr Kennedy had testified that the proper spacing of children was of the utmost importance in preserving the health of the family. He had said that too frequent pregnancies impaired the mother's constitution, jeopardized the welfare of such children as she had and imperiled the unborn.

"So you think," the judge said, "that if a patient says she has had a child within a year, she should receive contraceptive advice so as to make proper spacing possible?"

"Yes."

"But what if the patient is lying? Wouldn't it be better practice to check the official birth records to find out whether the patient is telling the truth?"

"Judge," replied Dr Kennedy, "we doctors examine a patient before we prescribe. You can forge a birth certificate but you can't forge a womb."

The listeners roared again. The magistrate angrily crdered the courtroom cleared. The attendants herded out the spectators into the corridor. They made no attempt to eject a gentleman who sat well up in front. He had a beard; he looked like a doctor. As a matter of fact he was Carlo Tresca, the well-known radical.

The complaint was eventually dismissed. But by that time the medical profession was aroused. The special committee appointed by the Academy of Medicine reported that unless adequate steps were taken to prevent the recurrence of similar depredations in the future, the rights of the profession would be threatened and the public good jeopardized. The committee found that there had been an unwarranted interference with the freedom of physicians engaged in the lawful practice of medicine, and a flagrant violation of the privileged character of their records.

THE YOUNGS RUBBER CASE

The Youngs Rubber Corporation was a large-scale manufacturer of rubber condoms sold in interstate commerce. Its trade-marked product was sold in many millions each year. When the trade-mark was improperly appropriated by a competitor, the company applied to the federal court for an injunction. The infringer's defense was that since a condom was an "article or thing designed, adapted, or intended for preventing conception," its distribution was a criminal act under the provisions of sections 334 and 396 of the Federal Criminal Code, and the trade-mark law could not be invoked to protect an illegal article. Agreeing with this contention, the District Court refused to grant the injunction.

The Youngs people appealed to the United States Circuit Court of Appeals. The Court weighed the language of section 334 of the code, which forbade the mailing of contraceptive articles, and section 396, which prohibited their transmission in interstate commerce.

Taken literally [said the Court], this language would seem to forbid the transportation by mail or common carriage of anything "adapted," in the sense of being suitable or fitted, for preventing conception or for any indecent or immoral purpose, even though the article might also be capable of legitimate uses and the sender in good faith supposed that it would be used only legitimately. Such a construction would prevent mailing to or by a physician of any drug or mechanical device "adapted" for contraceptive or abortifacient uses, although the physician desired to use or to prescribe it for proper medical purposes. The intention to prevent a proper medical use of drugs or other articles merely because they are capable of illegal uses is not lightly to be ascribed to Congress. Section 334 forbids also the mailing of obscene books and writings; yet it has never been thought to bar from the mails medical writings sent to or by physicians for proper purposes, though of a character which would render them highly indecent if sent broadcast to all classes of persons.

It was more reasonable, the Circuit Court said, to give the word "adapted" a more limited meaning than that above suggested, and to construe the whole phrase, "designed, adapted or intended," as requiring an intent on the part of the sender that the article mailed or transported be used for *illegal* contraception. The basic consideration, therefore, was how the business of the Youngs Rubber Corporation was carried on.

Its sales [the Court went on] are to wholesale and retail druggists and to jobbers who will agree to sell only to drugstores. Section 1142 of the New York Penal Law makes it a misdemeanor to sell or offer for sale any article, drug or medicine for the prevention of conception, or for causing unlawful abortion, but section 1145 provides that the "supplying of such articles to such [lawfully practicing] physicians or by their direction or prescription, is not an offense under this article." As already stated, the highest court of the state has said that the protection thus afforded physicians extends also to "the druggist, or vendor, acting upon the physician's prescription or order."

The words "druggist or vendor," the Circuit Court said, doubtless referred to the retailer from whom the physician or his patient would purchase. Nothing was mentioned with reference to the right of a manufacturer to sell to druggists without a physician's order.

But in view of the way modern business is conducted [the Court concluded], such a right we believe to be implicit in the statute; otherwise no local supply of abortifacient or contraceptive drugs or instruments would be available for use by physicians. It can hardly be supposed that the physician was to seek out a manufacturer each time that he had professional need for a drug or instrument of the generally prohibited character, or that, in anticipation of a possible future need, he should in advance direct the manufacturer to place a supply with the local druggist whom he favored. We conclude, therefore, that a manufacturer of drugs or instruments for medical use may in good faith sell them to druggists or other reputable dealers in medical supplies, or to jobbers for distribution to such trade.

The decision of the lower court was reversed, and the injunction was granted. Although it was not fully realized at the time a vital breach had been made in the

Comstock Law. The Circuit Court had read the word "exclusively" into it. It had ruled, in effect, that while a drug, medicine or article adapted *exclusively* for preventing conception was under the ban of the federal laws, any drug, medicine or article which was susceptible of a *legitimate* as well as *illegitimate* use, was under proper circumstances entitled to the privilege of the mails.

The case developed another angle. The Youngs people had attacked on two fronts: they had sought the injunction in the federal court, and they had instituted criminal proceedings in New York for trademark piracy. When the latter case came up for trial the Youngs people had already obtained the injunction; they indicated their willingness to drop the prosecution in New York. The state court was of different mind. There were, it said, interests other than the complainant's to be safeguarded. It insisted on imposing a penalty on the offender. "A firm that steals a trademark," it said, "is likely to turn out an inferior condom. The public, no less than a manufacturer, has a right to be protected."

Legitimate versus Illegitimate

Three years later the Circuit Court of Appeals in another circuit adopted the same reasoning in the *Davis* case. Two defendants had been convicted of sending contraceptives through the mails. The Circuit Court reversed the convictions because no intention of illegitimate use had been proved.

The *Youngs* and *Davis* cases made clear that, under the mailing and interstate commerce statutes, doctors and drug concerns were free to traffic in articles which might be used as contraceptives, provided that they were intended to be legitimately used. What was not made clear was the meaning of "legitimate" use. The authorities argued that a legitimate use invariably meant a noncontraceptive use, and that under no circumstances ·could· a contraceptive (as distinguished from a condom) be so used. This question was answered in 1936.

THE JAPANESE PESSARIES

In 1933 a package of pessaries was sent from Japan to Dr Hannah M. Stone of the New York Birth Control Clinic. They were seized at the customs as illegal.

Dr Stone conceded at the outset that the pessaries were articles of contraception, but she insisted that under the holding in the *Youngs Rubber* case they were entitled to enter the country because they are susceptible of a legal use; i.e., to save life and preserve health. The government argued on the other hand that the interdict of the customs law was absolute; that it made no distinction between the legal and illegal use of a birth-control article; and that it contained no exemption in favor of physicians.

The case was tried in the federal court before Judge Moscowitz. The sole medical witness for the government was Dr Frederic W. Bancroft, who identified one of the pessaries as a contraceptive article. He admitted that he had had occasion in his practice to prescribe similar articles. His testimony on cross-examination was illuminating.

Q. Doctor, you stated that you have prescribed pessaries or similar articles. Now, I would like you to set forth as fully as you please the medical indications upon which you have found it necessary to make such prescriptions. A. I think there are many medical needs.

Q. For example? A. Tuberculosis, threatened tuberculosis, heart disease of the mother—many similar medical conditions.

Q. It could be cases of kidney diseases? A. Yes.

Q. It could be cases of pelvic deformities which make child-birth arduous? A. Not necessarily, with a Caesarean incision.

Q. Not necessarily, but it could happen? A. It might.

Q. Diabetic cases? A. Yes.

Q. Toxic goiter where pregnancy places a great strain upon the thyroid and may seriously endanger the woman's life? A. It could be, but the condition could be removed. She should be operated on for the thyroid and then the pregnancy is a simple condition.

Q. Cases where they are suffering from insanity and epilepsy? A. Yes.

Q. How about the very basic use for the proper spacing of childbirth in relation to the mortality of the offspring? And, with regard to the mother, might there not be medical indications for a prescription of some such article in order to prevent the birth of a child if there had been a child born to the same woman within a few months? A. That is right.

Q. For the sake of the offspring possibly you would find cases where you would prescribe the use of this article to prevent syphilis and gonorrhea through infection at the time of birth or even transmission? A. Yes.

Dr Stone's attorney then read the paragraph from *The Rhythm* quoted in this chapter, and asked Dr Bancroft whether he saw eye to eye with Dr Latz with respect to the economic justification of family limitations. Dr Bancroft said that he did, but that he disagreed with the method suggested by Dr Latz.

The first witness for Dr Stone was Dr Frederick C. Holden. Dr Holden testified that in his opinion it was proper to prescribe a contraceptive:

(a) If the mother was afflicted with tuberculosis, heart disease, kidney disease, Bright's disease, diabetes or goiter.

(b) If either parent was mentally deficient or suffered from epilepsy.

(c) If it was found that the father's sperm was not up to standard.

(d) If the children were improperly spaced.

(e) If the family lacked sufficient food, clothing and shelter to assure its health and general welfare.

Dr Foster Kennedy, the second witness, agreed with everything Dr Holden had said. He added that many women were subject to recurrent nervous disorders which made it impossible for them to bear the strain of pregnancy. Dr Kennedy mentioned severe melancholia, St Vitus' dance, manic-depressive psychoses, rhythmic mental delusions and depressions. He added:

There are a large number of diseases which should not be propagated, such as the atrophies, the muscular atrophies, the bleeders which are inherited diseases, in no way venereal, but due to an abnormality in the genitive structures of one or the other mate. Such things should not be allowed to continue. When our knowledge is sufficient to know about them I have prescribed contraceptive advice in the cases of patients suffering from myasthenia gravis, which is an intense fatigability of muscles due to a chemical abnormality in an individual who is unable to generate the proper chemical acetylcholine, as it is called, in the neuromuscular junction—the place where the nerve goes into the muscle—with the result that after some effort the ability of the individual to make a muscle contract at will goes, and until quite lately these patients all died. We now have discovered a method of aiding this contraction. By allowing such patients to become pregnant is to allow a disgraceful act on the part of the doctor, I think.

The following colloquy then took place between Dr Stone's lawyer and Dr Kennedy:

Q. All your confreres in the medical profession are agreed, are they not, that prevention of birth is necessary to prevent disease, even though there are wide differences of opinion as to the particular method or device to be used? A. Yes. The general principle of the need of preventing birth has been accepted by practically all—I believe all—the medical bodies that I know. Q. In other words, the disagreement that exists, if any, does not go to preventing this disgrace of ill-health, but as to whether this type of device or some other device or some calendar computation basis or abstinence or some other method be the means used to keep up the health of the family?   A. I think the principle has been accepted. They still quarrel over practical details.

Doctors Hannah M. Stone, Ira S. Wile, Louis I. Harris, Alfred M. Hellman and Robert L. Dickinson also appeared for the claimant.

When the trial was concluded it was found that the particular rubber pessary which had been put in evidence had disappeared. It had repeatedly passed back and forth among counsel, the Court, attendants and the expert witnesses. No one knew what had become of it. Dr Stone's attorney showed some concern.

"Never mind," the assistant United States attorney said to him cheerily, "there are plenty of pessaries in the shipment that was seized. We'll take out another and use that as evidence."

"That's not what's bothering me," said the lawyer. "The government has held this case up so long that the shipment is useless: the rubber is all dried out. What I'm afraid of is that someone will use that pessary and it may not work!"

Relying on the authority of the *Youngs* and *Davis* cases, Judge Moscowitz ruled against the government.

The claimant [he said] having imported the libeled articles for experimental purposes to determine their reliability and usefulness as contraceptives to cure or prevent disease, a lawful purpose, it must be held that the libeled articles do not come within the condemnation of the statute . . .

The government appealed the case. The Circuit Court of Appeals observed:

While it is true that the policy of Congress has been to forbid the use of contraceptives altogether if the only purpose of using them be to prevent conception in cases where it would not be injurious to the welfare of the patient or her offspring, it is going far beyond such a policy to hold that abortions which destroy incipient life may be allowed in proper cases, and yet that no measures may be taken to prevent conception even though a likely result should be to require the termination of pregnancy by means of an operation. It seems unreasonable to suppose that the national scheme of legislation could involve such inconsistencies and should require the complete suppression of articles, the use of which in many cases is advocated by such a weight of authority in the medical field.

Prompted by these considerations, the Circuit Court upheld Judge Moscowitz.

Although the case turned on the interpretation of the Tariff Act, and the mail and interstate commerce statutes were not involved, it followed by implication that a similar interpretation would be accorded those statutes as well. It was significant that nowhere in its opinion did the Court specifically state under what circumstances a doctor was to be free to prescribe a contraceptive. The inference was clear that the medical profession was to be sole judge of the propriety of a prescription in a given case, and that as long as a physician exercised his discretion in good faith the legality of his action was not to be questioned.

But the case means more than this. It has—in the light of the testimony at the trial—broadened the definition of "medical necessity." The medical experts who appeared for Dr Stone testified not only as to pathological, physiological and psychological conditions, which they said would justify the interruption of pregnancy, but also as to the need for the proper spacing of births as a *sine qua non* of family welfare. Even the economic factor—insufficient income—was mentioned as grounds for birth control.

Departing, for once, from its policy of truculence, the Customs Bureau took its defeat without any gestures of defiance. It didn't go to the Supreme Court as it might have. Instead, the Treasury Department issued a circular letter, No. 1682, dated February 10, 1937. This letter instructed all collectors of customs to release consignments of contraceptives on receipt of an affidavit from the physician who was their ultimate consignee, stating that the contraceptives were to be used only to protect the health of his patients.

WITCHES BURN IN SALEM

Though these cases deprived the militant opponents of birth control of much of their ammunition, they were by no means ready to lay down their arms. They launched a fresh offensive instead, choosing Massachusetts as their battleground.

On June 3, 1937, the police raided the North Shore Mothers' Health Office in Salem, Massachusetts. This clinic had been conducted for years by the Birth Control League of Massachusetts under strict medical supervision. The police officers presented a warrant ordering the confiscation of all materials found on the premises and the arrest of the staff. They ransacked the offices, seized all case histories, card files, records, printed literature, clerical supplies and even the contents of the cashbox. Dr Lucille Lord-Heinstein, the physician in charge, Mrs Carolyn Gardner, a social worker, and Mrs Flora Rand, a nurse, were taken to the Salem police headquarters.

The charge was that the defendants "did sell and give away, exhibit or offer to sell, lend or give away, instruments and other articles and drugs and medicine for the prevention of conception."

The case was tried on July 13 before Judge George B. Sears of the Salem District Court. The first witness for the prosecution was Miss Clark, a police matron. She testified that on May 27 she went to the health office, posed as a Mrs Flanagan, gave her case history and was told that she would get contraceptive advice. On cross-examination she admitted that she had never gone back for the advice, and that "she had told a lot of lies and come out without getting anything."

The next witness was a Mrs Rose Barlotta, an Italian woman who had gone to the health office at the instigation of the police matron. Her case history showed repeated self-induced abortions and toxemia of pregnancy. The need for the prevention of future pregnancy had been imperative, and Mrs Barlotta had been fitted with a pessary.

Several distinguished Boston physicians testified on behalf of the defense. Dr Robert de Normandie, Dr Peer Johnson and Dr Malcolm Restal declared that it was the duty of the medical profession to give contraceptive advice to married women to preserve health. Mrs Standish Bradford explained that the function of the clinic was to afford contraceptive information to women who couldn't afford to go to private physicians.

Judge Sears found the defendants guilty and fined them one hundred dollars each. He recognized, he said, that the defendants had been prompted by worthy motives, but the law was the law. He turned a deaf ear to the plea of the attorneys for the health office for the return of the case histories which had been illegally taken.

WITCH BURNING APPROVED

Those who hoped that the higher courts of the commonwealth would reject narrow legalisms and bring the judicial policy of Massachusetts in line with that enunciated by state and federal courts were doomed to disappointment. In May 1938 the full bench of the court of last resort affirmed the convictions.

The defendants contended that the statute, which dated back to 1879, did not apply to drugs, medicines, instruments or articles for the prevention of conception when they were intended for such use upon prescription by a duly qualified physician for the preservation of life or health, according to sound and generally accepted medical practices. They also urged that the statute was unconstitutional under both the state and federal constitutions.

Chief Justice Rugg, who wrote the decision, curtly rejected these arguments. He stood upon the letter of the law. Its terms, he said, were "plain, unequivocal and peremptory. They contain no exceptions. They are sweeping, absolute and devoid of ambiguity. They are directed with undeviating explicitness against the prevention of conception . . ." Massachusetts turned its back squarely on the *Youngs* case, the *Davis* case, the *Japanese Pessaries* case. It chose to tread alone the path of illiberalism, heedless of the social harm that might flow from such a course.

The decision was the first to issue from any state tribunal, declaring it unlawful for a duly licensed physician to give birth-control advice under any conditions. The medical profession was shocked. Dr Eric M. Matsner, medical director of the American Birth Control Clinic, said:

A protest against the infringement of medical rights involved in the closing of contraceptive centers in Massachusetts has been signed by 1790 members of the Massachusetts Medical Society, more than one third of the society's total membership. These centers, which gave medical advice on child spacing to underprivileged mothers, are kept shut by today's ruling of the Massachusetts Supreme Court. Yet unscrupulous interests continue to profit from sales in the state of unreliable and dangerous contraceptives masquerading as products for "feminine hygiene."

The Birth Control League of Massachusetts declared:

In failing to except the practice of medicine from indecency laws, the Court has lost a chance to bring Massachusetts abreast of a more enlightened world. Common sense is outraged by a decision so out of touch with the realities of the world today . . . It means that a safeguard to the health of women is considered illegal. It means the continued prevalence of abortion and of harmful bootleg contraceptives.

The New England Conference of the Methodist Episcopal Church adopted a resolution stating that the closing of birth-control centers in Massachusetts was "a distinct threat against the public code."

Dr Hannah M. Stone, medical director of the Birth Control Clinical Research Bureau, said:

All that the Massachusetts police can accomplish by closing birth-control clinics is to prevent for a time the poor and indigent women from obtaining information that wealthier women can obtain from their private physicians . . . It is no more possible to stem the flow of contraceptive knowledge than to stem the tides of the ocean that wash the shores of Massachusetts.

The case was carried to the United States Supreme Court.

"A NOTORIOUS PLACE"

Heartened by their victory in the Salem case, the foes of birth control launched an intensive drive along a wider front. They struck successively at Brookline and Boston.

On August 2, 1937, the police repeated the Salem performance at the Brookline Mothers' Health Office of the Birth Control League of Massachusetts and seized all supplies and literature. Dr Ilia Galleani, the medical director, was charged with exhibiting contraceptives and offering them for sale.

The case was tried on September 15. This time the prosecution did not rely on the testimony of *agents provocateurs;* plain ordinary snooping was the source of the evidence. The police testified that during the month of July they had eavesdropped at the window of the clinic and had overheard conversations between the patients and the doctors.

The attorney for Dr Galleani tried to introduce medical testimony regarding the use of the contraceptives, but his efforts were blocked by the Court. He explained that the health office was conducted under the supervision of a committee of physicians, and that cases were taken for medical reasons only. He pointed out that contraception was a generally recognized medical practice, and that the clinic administered mainly to women who could not afford to consult their own physicians.

Judge Parker said he saw a great difference between "advice given privately by a physician in a particular case to preserve life, and an office that is openly conducted like this, with free demonstration and advice to anybody who might apply." And although Dr Galleani testified that the office was run along strict medical lines, that patients were referred by hospitals, physicians and social agencies, and that a large percentage of them were free cases, the judge characterized the clinic as "a notorious place."

As in the Salem case, the judge was requested to direct the return of the seized materials. In the course of argument ordinary wooden tongue depressors were mentioned as having been included among the supplies taken. The prosecutor objected to their return *on the ground that they could be used to lift up the vaginal walls!*

The defendant was found guilty and fined four hundred dollars.

Boston Follows Suit

The police then descended on the headquarters of the Birth Control League in Boston and carried off a quantity of leaflets. Mrs Leslie D. Hawkridge, president of the league, and Mrs Caroline C. Davis, its educational director, were charged with circulating contraceptive literature in violation of the law.

The case was tried on September 22 before Judge Joseph Riley of the Municipal Court of Brookline.

Mrs Hawkridge's testimony with respect to the functions and work of the league were supported by Dr Howard B. Sprague of the Harvard University Medical School and of the staff of the Massachusetts General Hospital. To no avail. On October 6 the defendants were found guilty and fined two hundred dollars each.

Epilogue

The United States Supreme Court refused to hear the appeal from the Salem case. Just why the Court did this no one can say. It is hard to believe that the Court was sympathetic to the legal reasoning or the social results implicit in Justice Rugg's decision. It may be that the Court felt that birth control was a subject on which each state should be permitted to evolve and enforce its own policy free of federal dictation. It is also possible—and we hope that this conjecture strikes nearer the truth—that the Court was willing to make a favorable pronouncement on the legal status of contraception but wanted a more vivid, specific and clear-cut case for the purpose. Justice Rugg's decision therefore stands as the law, and Massachusetts has taken its place as the most backward state of the Union in its treatment of a vastly important medical and sociological problem. This distinction has now been challenged. Connecticut too has embarked on a police campaign against birth control. It remains to be seen whether the courts of the state will sanction so senseless and disastrous a move.

Shaken by repeated defeats but not daunted, the Birth Control League surveyed the situation and decided to withdraw the appeals pending in the other cases.

"We believe," said the league in a statement, "that the continuation of our case in the courts would have added little to the legal clarification of the situation. The courts in this state were some time ago presented with cases which, because of their facts, raised in general terms the question of protecting the health and welfare of the people through the distribution by licensed doctors of birth-control advice. However, the courts have not had an opportunity to pass judgment on birth-control statutes as applied to any particular case, such as (1) where the absence of the advice would lead to the death of a mother suffering from tuberculosis or cancer, or (2) the death of a newborn child due to the improper spacing of births or innumerable other causes. We are convinced that the physicians of our community will never consent to allow women to leave their offices doomed to death or disease because of the failure of the physicians to give advice.

"Nor do we think that the medical profession will degrade itself by becoming a body of stealthy bootleggers, dispensing contraceptive articles and information in surreptitious fashion. We feel confident that if the fundamental issue is sharply and directly placed before the courts in a proper case the existing decisions will be distinguished and clarified, and the law will not be construed, as it is by some people today, to prohibit a particular doctor from giving particular contraceptive advice to a particular patient suffering from a particular disease in a case where pregnancy might mean death to the mother, or death or disease to the child.

"From advice and information we have received we are convinced that the courts will welcome an opportunity for such clarification, and thus be in line with all the other states in the nation. It is our intention to bring one or more such test cases in the near future.

"The Birth Control League of Massachusetts has functioned for more than two decades on the basis of a sincere conviction that family limitation under medical supervision is essential for the prevention of disease. We regret the confusion that now exists in the public mind in regard to the frontiers of the recent court decisions. We have never urged the dissemination of contraceptive advice other than through doctors. It is the function of all those who believe that the medical profession can thus reduce human suffering and misery to join in this battle for clarification. We believe that the courts of this state will dissipate an impression now current that lawyers, sitting as judges, desire to override the overwhelming opinion of the medical profession in a field affecting public health."

THE WATERBURY CASE

Following the Massachusetts pattern, the police of Waterbury, Connecticut, raided the Birth Control Clinic there, arrested its chairman and staff physicians, and seized a quantity of contraceptive supplies. Judge

Kenneth Wynne dismissed the criminal charges against the defendants, saying:

". . . the unaided language of the statute would offer no defense to a doctor facing prosecution for a violation of it. Thus, the question which must be determined is this: 'Is a doctor to be prosecuted as a criminal for doing something which is sound and right in the best tenets and traditions of a high calling dedicated and devoted to health? Should he be forced to practice furtively and in stealth rather than give up what his conscience and his honest professional judgment dictate?'

"The Court has no right to read exceptions into the statute but is convinced that without these proper exceptions the statute is defective on the broad constitutional grounds set up in the demurrers . . ."

The seizure of contraceptive materials was contested in a separate proceeding. Judge Frank P. McEvoy decided that the materials should be destroyed, but ordered that the destruction be delayed pending a decision by the Connecticut Supreme Court of Errors.

The contrary conclusions reached by the two judges threw the status of birth control in Connecticut into utter confusion. At the present moment, a physician there may lawfully give birth-control advice, but the minions of the law can swoop down on his office at any moment and cart away the supplies without which his advice may be utterly useless! Until the highest court of the state has spoken, it will not be possible to know whether or not Connecticut proposes to follow the egregious example set by Massachusetts.

PUERTO RICO

There are few places on the face of the earth more desperately in need of family limitation than Puerto Rico.

In 1937 the Insular legislature passed an act authorizing the setting up of birth-control clinics under the supervision of the Insular Health Department. The United States could have, if it so wished, let the matter rest there. Instead it ordered District Attorney A. Cecil Snyder of Puerto Rico to bring a test case.

Six directors of the Puerto Rican Maternal and Child Health Association were indicted under the Comstock Law of 1873, which applies to Puerto Rico as well.

On January 20, 1939, Federal Judge Robert A. Cooper acquitted all the defendants. In his opinion he followed the reasoning adopted by the federal courts in birth-control cases during the last decade. He held that while anyone prescribing or furnishing a contraceptive merely to prevent birth would be acting illegally, "contraceptive articles may have a lawful use, and the statutes prohibiting them must be read as prohibiting them only when they have an unlawful use."

CHAPTER XI

Nudism and the Law

And the eyes of them both were opened and they knew
they were naked. And they sewed fig leaves together and
made themselves aprons.

Bible, Genesis 3:7

The censors cried: "Shame! You're a crime and a blight,
A sin against everything sacred."
And shielding their eyes from the horrible sight,
They imprisoned the Truth. It was naked.

E. B. L., *Rhymes for This Age* (1939)

CHARLES J. FINGER, the author, tells the following story: "A little school-teacher in my part of the country [the Ozarks] was doing a good job, until one day I noticed that she had disappeared. I asked one of the school trustees and learned that she had been removed for having some bad books in her possession. 'What were they?' I asked. He became very earnest and asked me to follow him to his house, which I did. He went to his bed and lifted up the mattress. 'Here they are,' he said, and I beheld some copies of the *National Geographic Magazine,* containing articles, with pictures, about the South Sea Islanders."

THE CULT OF NUDISM

Nudism is not new. It has been practiced for thousands of years. It has been and still is an accepted mode of living among primitive tribes in many quarters of the globe. In Japan and elsewhere naked persons of both sexes bathe together. As a modern movement among civilized peoples, nudism is of postwar origin. According to its advocates, its aim is to afford psychological escape by ridding people of a sense of bodily shame, and to confer physical benefit through heliotherapy.

Organized groups have been operating in Europe for the last twenty-five years. In America the movement dates back to 1930. In 1932 the International Nudist Conference was organized, and *The Nudist,* its official publication, made its appearance. At the present time there are in this country more than a hundred organized groups, with many thousands of members. It is claimed that supporters of nudism throughout the world exceed three million in number.

NUDITY AND THE CENSOR

Protectors of morals have always regarded the unclad human body as a public menace. A "soldier of righteousness," Comstock warred against Paul Chabas' September Morn, against the statue of an antique faun reproduced on the cover of a magazine, against Macfadden's Mammoth Physical Exhibition and even against unclothed wax figures in store windows.

With characteristic myopia the censor has been unable to distinguish between art and illicit bodily exposure, between nudity practiced for health and the strip tease. He has consistently fought the nudist movement, and has tried to stamp it out by means of the so-called indecent-exposure statute. Most states have such statutes. They were enacted to punish lewd and lascivious bodily exposure of the kind clearly conducive to immorality, such as the willful, perverted display of genitalia; they were never aimed against mere nudity.

Had any other construction ever been placed on these laws it would have been criminal to conduct ordinary art classes.

Officials in California, New Jersey, Maryland and Virginia have ruled that the practice of nudism under proper circumstances does not constitute indecent exposure. The Rhode Island legislature passed an anti-nudist bill, but it was vetoed by Governor Green. Florida has, by implication at least, approved nudism, and Kentucky has specifically made it legal.

Needless to say, the hostility of the censor to the unclothed human form has affected the screen. Some years ago a Shirley Temple script was submitted to the Motion Picture Code Administration in which there was a sequence showing Shirley taking a bath. The sequence was blue-penciled. Both Hedy Lamarr's *Ecstasy* and Sally Rand's *The Sunset Murder Case* have been banned in New York as "exploiting nudity."

In 1938 the owner of a motion-picture theater of Los Angeles was haled into court for exhibiting certain photographs in the lobby of his theater. The photographs advertised a motion picture called *Unashamed,* which recorded the activities of certain nudists at Lake Elsinore. Since there was no law against such a film the police based their charge on a city ordinance prohibiting the showing of nude pictures in a theater lobby. The defendant pointed to the fact that certain parts of the movie stills on exhibit had been covered up with black paper patches. The judge dismissed the case, remarking that the photographs were no more damaging to public morals than everyday scenes on a bathing beach.

In 1939 the attorney general of Colorado, after consulting the Bible (!) and the laws of his state, concluded that there was no legal objection to a couple being married in the "same natural uniform they were born in." His ruling was made in response to a question raised by a clergyman who wanted to know whether it was lawful for him to "marry an unclothed couple on a secluded mountaintop."

Nudity has its economic side too. One may wonder what the official attitude toward unclad ladies might have been at the current Golden Gate International Exposition in San Francisco if the attendance had been up to expectations. But people were staying away, and so Sally Rand's Nude Ranch was installed to draw the crowds.

NUDIST ACTIVITIES IN NEW YORK

The police have twice raided indoor nudist gymnasiums in New York City. In both cases the officers who made the arrest testified that there had been no lewd conduct. In the first case Magistrate Goldstein dismissed the twenty-two defendants and scolded the detectives for arresting them. In the second case convictions were obtained in the Court of Special Sessions on four counts: indecent exposure, openly outraging public decency, maintaining a public nuisance and permitting a building to be used for a nuisance. The convictions were promptly reversed by the Appellate Division. The Court pointed out that nudism was not an offense under the indecent-exposure statute unless lascivious behavior was proved.

Judge Merrell wrote a dissenting opinion. It may fairly be said that this opinion crystallized the philosophy which led to the subsequent enactment of a law outlawing the practice of nudism in New York State. The judge quoted the following edifying excerpt from an Indiana case:

Immediately after the fall of Adam there seems to have sprung up in his mind an idea there was such a thing as decency and such a thing as indecency; that there was a distinction between them; and since that time the ideas of decency and indecency have been instinctive in, and indeed, parts of humanity. And it historically appears that the first most palpable piece of indecency was the exposure by Adam or Eve of his or her as now commonly called privates, and the first exercise of mechanical ingenuity was in the manufacture of fig-leaf aprons . . .

The Court of Appeals disregarded this argument and upheld the majority in the Appellate Division. For the time being nudist activities were not taboo.

THE NUDIST MAGAZINE

In a case involving another aspect of nudism, however, the censor was more successful. *The Nudist,* a periodical devoted to nudism, was prosecuted in the Court of Special Sessions and was held to be obscene. This was not surprising since the same court had convicted the defendants in the second gymnasium case. Strangely enough, however, the Appellate Division— the identical Bench which had reversed the convictions in the gymnasium case—affirmed the judgment.

The Court was apparently concerned over the fact that the magazine was being sold at newsstands and was available to the young and impressionable. The Court ignored the *Ulysses* case and the adult-with-normal-sex-instincts test which Judge Woolsey had laid down. It made no reference to the gymnasium case which it was deciding at the same time. And more surprising still, its decision was affirmed without opinion by the Court of Appeals.

The suppression of *The Nudist* is incomprehensible when one considers that it was a dignified, non-sensational publication and the official organ of the International Nudist Conference; that all its illustrations were reproductions of legitimate nudist photographs, not art poses; and that it carried none of the pseudo-scientific or quack advertising which fills the pages of hundreds of other magazines that circulate with immunity. The only explanation that occurs to one is that the Court of Appeals was, consciously or unconsciously, hostile to the basic philosophy of the movement itself. Certainly it could not have deemed the illustrations sexually exciting.

ANOTHER BLUENOSE LAW

The victory of the censors in *The Nudist* case did not console them for the defeat in the gymnasium case. Having found that the indecent-exposure law did not serve their purpose, they introduced a specific anti-nudist bill in the New York legislature. Former Governor Al Smith was the sponsor. At the hearing on the bill, however, its advocates failed to come forward in its support. The opposition was so determined and articulate that every sign pointed to the abandonment of the bill. But there were dark doings afoot. Considerable pressure was being exerted behind the scenes. The senate and the assembly passed the bill in quick succession, and Governor Lehman signed it. It is now a criminal offense in New York State for a person to appear nude in the presence of two or more persons of the opposite sex who are also nude. It makes no difference what the place, time or the occasion. If a group of friends decide to dispense with their bathing suits on a deserted beach they lay themselves open to a fine or a jail sentence or both.

There has thus been inscribed on our statute books what many thinking people believe to be one of the worst pieces of useless and meddlesome legislation ever concocted.

THE CUSTOMS VERSUS THE MAILS

In 1926 Dr Alice Bloch of Stuttgart wrote a book called *Harmonious Development of Women's Bodies*. It was a manual of physical education based on modern rhythmic gymnastics and was illustrated with photographs of exercises. Trained in the Royal Chirurgical Clinic and the Orthopedic University Clinic in Berlin, the author had studied with Dr Bess Mensendieck, and had had many years' experience in her own Orthopedic Gymnastic Institute in Stuttgart. The book was praised and went through several editions. A sixth edition was translated into English by Mathias H. Macherey, assistant supervisor of physical education, Newark, New Jersey.

Since the propriety of the use of the undraped figure in the German editions had been questioned in some quarters, the English version was submitted to the United States Customs Bureau for scrutiny. The bureau was asked to consider the book in the light of section 305 of the Tariff Act which forbids the importation, among other things, of obscene literature. In March 1936 the bureau declared the book to be lawful for admission into this country. This ruling was in accord with the ostensible policy of the bureau, under which a number of books containing nude photographs, including Laura Brunet's *Desnudismo Integral* and *Desnudo Integral* had been approved for entry.

The American edition was well received. *Hygeia*, the organ of the American Medical Association, wrote: "This excellent work on gymnastics, though addressed to the layman, will be equally helpful to teachers . . . The book is illustrated with one hundred and fifty photographs of the author's pupils, taken in the nude. The pictures thus show clearly the action of the various

muscle groups involved in the exercise photographed."
This was echoed by the *Quarterly Review of Biology:*
"A rational attitude toward gymnastics is herein expressed. The purpose of exercise, the author states, is
to develop a beautiful and graceful body . . . There
is a section of beautiful illustrations of nude figures to
serve as a guide toward performing the exercises cor-
rectly." The lay attitude was summed up by the *Parents'
Magazine:* "This carefully compiled guide to movement will probably have its largest audience among
teachers who are concerned with the physical training
of girls. But mothers and daughters who would like to
take systematic physical exercises at home will enjoy
working out Miss Bloch's explicitly given directions."

The book was advertised, and copies were sold to
leading universities and other institutions, including
Dartmouth College, University of Texas and the Army
Medical Library of the War Department.

Things went along smoothly for over a year. Then,
inexplicably, the sensibilities of the federal authorities
underwent a change. On July 1, 1937, without any
warning, the post office declared the book to be unmailable. No attempt was made to explain this action, and
no reference was made to the *contrary* ruling of the
Customs Bureau. In all likelihood the post office did not
even know of the ruling. Had there been any divergence
between the provisions of the Postal Law and those of
the Tariff Act, there might have been a colorable justification for the situation. But the provisions were
virtually the same. The bewildered publishers said:

We find ourselves faced with two diametrically opposed federal
administrative rulings on identical subject matter. Once the
conflict becomes generally known, we feel certain the government will come in for a considerable amount of derisive comment at the hands of literary critics and newspaper people. We
could understand how on occasion a state court may disagree

with a federal court on the same book or picture. Judges sometimes evince a kind of cussedness born of vanity or bad temper.
It seems to us, however, that here we have a different situation.
Certainly one arm of the government should know and respect
what the other arm has done.

Here we have the reverse of the *Stag at Eve* situation. *Stag at Eve* was permitted to circulate freely in
the mails, but when an attempt was made to import it
it was barred because of the supposedly bawdy character of some of the drawings. Dr Bloch's book was sufficiently unsullied to come to our shores, but was deemed
too salacious to be vouchsafed the mails. And no
amount of persuasion could budge the postal officials.

DISHARMONY WITHIN THE CUSTOMS

Perhaps it was too much to expect the Customs
Bureau and the post office to agree on the "decency" of
given material. But was it unreasonable to hope that the
Customs Bureau would be consistent in dealing with
books in its *own* bailiwick?

A book called *The New Gymnosophy* by Dr Maurice
Parmelee, was published in England some time in 1927.
It was a scholarly study of nudism and was illustrated
with photographs of bona fide nudist activities. A copy
was sent to Dr Parmelee in the United States. It was
stopped at the customs, and the detention was protested. On December 24, 1937, the collector of customs
ruled that the book was legal for entry into the United
States. Four years later an American edition was
issued by the reputable publishing house of Knopf's
under the name of *Nudism in Modern Life*. No trouble
was encountered with the authorities.

Shortly afterward Dr Parmelee wished to prepare a
new edition with additional photographs showing nudist
activities in Germany. When photographs dealing with

these activities were sent to him in 1932 they were stopped for examination at the customs, but were ultimately released. The new edition appeared in 1933 in England. It was substantially the same as *The New Gymnosophy* originally issued, except that the German pictures were included. A copy of the new edition was sent from England to Dr Parmelee in the United States and was seized by the authorities.

It was pointed out to the customs people that the publication was virtually identical with the book which had been previously approved; that the only difference lay in the inclusion of the German pictures, and that these pictures, too, had been officially approved. It was pointed out, too, that the bureau had freely admitted other studies dealing with nudism. The arguments fell on deaf ears. In 1934 the government instituted libel proceedings against the new edition. It then delayed the trial of the case for four years in spite of repeated demands for adjudication. The case was finally tried on December 1, 1938, in the District of Columbia. The court ruled that the book was obscene and should be confiscated. An appeal will shortly be argued.

The absurd implications of this case require little comment. When it comes to the importation of printed matter the government can play fast and loose as it pleases. It can go on record one year as officially approving a publication; next year it can change its mind and reverse its position. It need give no warning, no reason. And it can subject the consignee to unconscionable delay.

If we view this case in the light of the Customs Bureau's actions in the *Contraception* case described in Chapter IX, we are impelled to the conclusion that there is nothing that an importer of books, acting in the utmost good faith, can do to assure the unimpeded flow of printed matter from abroad. If he proceeds like a sensible citizen to get an official customs ruling, he does not know how long it will stand. If he does not rely on an official ruling but carries the case into the courts (as did the consignee in the *Contraception* case) and wins a favorable decision, he cannot be sure that the customs officials will respect the court's order and let the books through. In sum, he can be thoroughly bedeviled. His only recourse is to fight in the courts: a protracted, wearisome and expensive process, and one calculated to cool the ire of many an aggrieved consignee. It is disheartening to think how many seizures go unchallenged because of this.

CHAPTER XII

Casting up Accounts

What a court declares to be the law always was the law,
notwithstanding early decisions to the contrary.
          Ross v. Board of Chosen Freeholders,
                          90 N. J. L. 522 (1917)

THERE'S AN OLD QUIP about a law never meaning what
it says but what the courts say it means.

The obscenity law has been on our statute books for
generations. Hundreds of cases have arisen under it;
judges have written learned and extensive opinions
probing into its origins, trying to wrest specific mean-
ings from its array of adjectives, applying it to particular facts.

Where do we stand today?

TOWARD A DEFINITION

It seems to be fairly well settled that the gist of the
offense under the obscenity law is not sex, nor scatology
nor breach of taste, but *sexual impurity*. In absolving
Frankie and Johnnie the highest court in New York
said: "The question is not whether it would tend to
coarsen or vulgarize the youth who might witness it
but whether it would tend to lower their standards of
right and wrong, specifically as to the sexual relation."

This formula runs through all the cases, state and
federal. We find it said that material, to be unlawful,

must "excite lustful or lecherous desire," or "suggest impure or libidinous thoughts," or "invite to lewd and lascivious places and conduct," or "be offensive to chastity," or "incite dissolute acts," or "create a desire for gratification of animal passions," or "encourage unlawful indulgences of lust," or seek "to satisfy the morbid appetite of the salacious," or "pander to the prurient taste" or "exploit dirt for dirt's sake." It's amazing how many different ways the courts have of saying the same thing.

No attempt has been made to define pornography or to distinguish between it and obscenity.

L'Homme Moyen Sensuel

There used to be a trick question that went something like this: There's a lake, and an old decayed tree falls into it. There's not a living creature within miles to hear the sound it makes. Is there a splash or isn't there?

Indecency does not exist *in vacuo;* it must be considered in the light of its probable effect on those it reaches.

The ancient test laid down in the case of *Regina* v. *Hicklin* sought to measure the lawfulness of any material by the susceptibility of those "into whose hands it may fall," thus judging the reading matter of normal adults by standards applicable to children or idiots. This test has now been generally rejected, and in its place we have Judge Woolsey's *l'homme moyen sensuel.* If a book arouses lustful desires in a reader it is not necessarily obscene. The reader may be a cretin or a psychopath. Only a man of normal sex instincts may be used as a criterion.

But even Judge Woolsey's opinion in the *Ulysses* case—in which he first put forth this principle—left

something to be desired. He said that *Ulysses* acted as
an emetic rather than as an aphrodisiac, implying that
if he had found it to be an aphrodisiac he might have
condemned it. What an unfortunate implication! Is not
the most precious quality of all great art its power to
arouse and stimulate, to quicken an intense emotional
experience? Shakespeare's *Venus and Adonis*, Elizabeth Barrett Browning's *Sonnets from the Portuguese*,
the best of Keats and Shelley are not emetics; Titian's
nudes, Maillol's rich sculptures, Wagner's *Tristan*
music are, in the truest sense of the word, aphrodisiacs.

Probable Effect

Judge Woolsey's *l'homme moyen sensuel* hasn't
solved the problem altogether. It has given us what he
has termed a "hypothetical reagent," but the rest is
still guesswork.

If we had a foolproof corruption detector with a
dial marked "harmless" at one end and "corrupting"
on the other, *and* if we could find a man of normal sex
instincts, we could strap electric contacts on our subject,
thrust a supposedly immoral book in his hand and watch
the dial. That would be an approximation of the scientific method.

What we have instead is a measure of guidance for
the honest judge. He no longer has to worry about the
young, the psychopathic, the mentally deficient. But
the legal result still depends upon the operations of *his*
mind. He must ask himself: "What do *I* conceive to be
a sexually average man? Do *I* think this book would
arouse sexually impure thoughts in him? What distinction do *I* see fit to draw between sex thoughts that
are impure and ones that are not?"

If there's a jury Judge Woolsey's hypothetical reagent is of no practical use at all. True, the court will

instruct the jurors to weigh things from the point of view of the normal adult. But the essence of the jury system is that the jurors *are* average citizens and represent a cross section of the community. What a juror should do, theoretically, is to use himself as a guinea pig. He should ask himself: "This book the district attorney is waving in the air till he's purple in the face —will it impair *my* morals?" The fact is that our juror will do nothing of the kind. Once he steps into the jury box he is a vastly changed person. He ceases to be common clay. *Ipso facto* and *instanter* he becomes a little inflated and more than a little righteous. He falls prey to responsibility. Power is his for a brief instant, and he is going to use it. He may relish a dirty story; he may even collect erotica. But in judging others he will be strict as hell. Not that the book the district attorney is shouting about could hurt *him*. He's got to protect that utterly mythical creature: the other fellow.

Since we have no corruption detector it would seem that the courts might welcome the next best thing. The mind of man may be a jungle, but it is not altogether uncharted. A qualified psychiatrist could well go on the stand in an obscenity trial and say: "I've made a special study of mental ills for twenty years. I've read this book. My opinion, based on my experience with and observation of thousands of cases, is that it would not hurt the average man."

For years the law has refused such evidence, insisting that the question of obscenity was one for the jury (a group of laymen), not for experts. But this rule is no longer as firmly entrenched as it once was. Judges are beginning to recognize its unwisdom more and more, and in several recent cases—notably *The Birth of a Baby* case in New York—expert testimony was received.

"Good Taste"

The obscenity law is not concerned with any question of taste. Material may be vulgar or coarse or ill advised without being unlawful.

When *Life's* picture story on childbirth was attacked as being in bad taste, Harry Hansen, noted book critic, wrote in his column in the New York *World-Telegram*: "I felt that it was done in a dignified way, and that damning the truth for not being in good taste must bring laughter to the gods. For good taste, after all, is simply the echo of the code of behavior decided on by the dominant groups in society; it differs with the times and with different strata of people, and is actually indirect pressure brought to bear on those who don't conform. It is probably not half as important as washing behind the ears."

The Whole, Not Excerpts

Material claimed to be obscene must be judged in its entirety, not by isolated fragments singled out by the prosecution. The judicial test must be applied to the whole matter. In the *Mademoiselle de Maupin* case the Court said: "No work may be judged from a selection of such paragraphs alone. Printed by themselves they might, as a matter of law, come within the prohibition of the statute. So might a similar selection from Aristophanes or Chaucer or Boccaccio or even from the Bible. The book, however, must be considered broadly as a whole."

Taking Stock

As things now stand, a book written by a known author, published by a reputable firm, advertised in newspapers and magazines, generally reviewed and openly sold over the counter in bookshops, is not likely to be deemed obscene. The classics are definitely immune. In a prosecution the opinions of critics will probably be regarded as "persuasive pieces of evidence."

As to magazines, the situation is not as wholesome. There is a strong movement afoot for pre-censorship. A short time ago an ordinance was framed in Akron which would have required the advance submission and approval of all periodicals offered for sale on newsstands; it was abandoned because the city's counsel gave the opinion that such a measure would be unconstitutional. Bills calling for the advance censorship of magazines have been introduced in the Pennsylvania and Indiana legislatures; and movements for similar laws have been started in a number of other states. Disregarding any statutory warrant for their action, the police in several sections of New England have assumed arbitrary control over periodicals, and have demanded that copies be submitted for approval prior to sale. Massachusetts has established an official black list of far-reaching effect: a magazine condemned by the chief of police of one city is teletyped to the chiefs of other cities.

It may safely be said that an accurate exposition of facts relating to sex, couched in decent language and proper spirit, will not be regarded as obscene even though to some extent and among some persons it may tend to promote lustful thoughts. Nor do works on physiology, medicine or science come within the ban of the law.

In the theater considerable progress has been made since the days of Olga Nethersole, when *Sappho* was held to be immoral because its heroine was carried upstairs by a man. The chances are that a play with an overt sex theme will get by. A *Tobacco Road* will run into trouble here and there, but it's a production like Odets' *Waiting for Lefty* that will meet with real opposition.

Movie censorship seems to be firmly established, with the Production Code Administration and the state boards very much in the saddle. There's a great deal of dissatisfaction among directors, actors and writers in Hollywood. Occasionally, despite all restraints and obstacles, an honest and significant picture manages to break through. But for the most part the screen is solidly in the grip of the uplifters. Virtue is ever rewarded, vice is punished, the boy gets the girl, social criticism is taboo, values are falsified, escapism rules.

Pictorial representation has fared somewhat better at the hands of the censor than literature. To be sure, French post cards are still remorselessly hunted, and of late, nude photographic studies have come in for attack. But no recognized art dealer or reputable publisher of reproductions of paintings need fear being haled into court, as was Knoedler many years ago.

BIRTH-CONTROL LITERATURE

Books dealing with contraception may be lawfully distributed to "qualified persons." This category has never been judicially defined, but it doubtless includes physicians, surgeons, workers in medical schools and hospitals, public health officials, psychiatrists, social welfare workers, medical students, nurses, dealers in medical books and supplies, druggists and the like. A layman with a doctor's prescription would also be a qualified person.

Provided the addressee comes within this category, a birth-control book may legally move through any of the channels of interstate commerce, including the mails, and may enter at the customs if sent here from abroad.

The rule as to contraceptive articles and supplies—jellies, pessaries and so on—is the same.

BIRTH-CONTROL ADVICE

The giving of birth-control advice by a physician involves different legal considerations, depending on whether such advice is given on (a) physiological, (b) psychiatric or (c) economic grounds.

It is clear that a physician may lawfully give contraceptive advice where in his opinion the need for such advice exists for physiological reasons. So long as he acts in good faith his judgment with respect to diagnosis and advice is conclusive.

Where psychological (as distinguished from physiological) factors are involved the legal propriety of giving contraceptive advice is not quite so clear. This is because there has been no case directly in point, not because there can be any doubt about the basic principle. In a proper case the courts will undoubtedly recognize that mental diseases are no less real than physical ones, and that it is no more important to prevent syphilitics from procreating than it is to avert the aggravation of a psychosis or a neurosis in the mother or the production of mentally defective offspring.

So far as economic factors are concerned the situation is likewise obscure. Here again, whatever doubt there is arises merely from the fact that there has been no direct precedent. However, the rationale of the law as expressed in the decided cases points to the recognition of the economic factor as legal justification under certain conditions for the giving of birth-control advice. Where the economic status has direct physiological implications the prescription of a contraceptive would probably be lawful. If a mother already has several children for whom she is unable to care properly it is obviously to the best interests of the family from the standpoint of health to afford contraceptive advice. As we have already indicated, this was recognized by the Church in Dr Latz's *The Rhythm*.

In laying down the foregoing, it has been assumed that a physician is dealing with a patient who is a married woman. The question as to whether the law is otherwise if the patient is unmarried raises a number of questions. Two principles, however, appear to be fairly clear:

(1) If the patient seeking advice states that she is married the physician has the right to assume that she is telling the truth. He is not under a legal duty to ask for a marriage certificate or to conduct an independent investigation. If he were it would be impossible to practice medicine.

(2) If the physician knows the patient is unmarried he may nevertheless give contraceptive advice where there are clear-cut medical indications for it, as where pregnancy or child-birth would imperil the mother's life.

By What Yardstick?

The courts may theorize and coin high-sounding phrases; the purity crusaders may clamor that what was immoral in Caesar's time is immoral today; in the final analysis it is society that establishes the standards of decency for itself. These standards cannot be reduced to a fixed and unvarying formula; they are in a state of flux because society itself is constantly changing. Each generation sets up its own conventions. In 1900 any girl who appeared on a bathing beach without sleeves and a long skirt would have been jailed. By 1911 bare knees could be legally displayed at the seashore; but legs still had to be covered, and girls wore stockings rolled down below the knees. A few years ago the one-piece bathing suit came into its own; and today the so-called sun suits leave very little of the human form concealed.

What the community, in a given place and at a given time, approves or tolerates is decent. What it frowns on is obscene.

This principle strikes at the roots of censorship. A New York court says that photographic studies of the nude (which, if unmolested, might reach a few thousand) are illegal; yet statues of naked men and women adorn the façades of our public buildings—indeed, our courthouses—for millions to see, and our museums are full of undraped images. The integrity of the judiciary, say the movie censors, must not be impugned lest we lose faith in the administration of justice; yet the daily press carries detailed accounts of flagrant examples of judicial misconduct: patronage in connection with receiverships and lunacy proceedings, bribes and corruption in high tribunals, resignations under fire. Gangster pictures, says the Production Code Administration, are bad for children because they invite imitation (an unproved theory) and stress violence; yet the tabloids, to which any child may have access for one tenth the price of a movie admission, are strident with the exploits—in words and pictures—of Al Capone, Dutch Schultz, Bitz and Spitale, Lepke and Gurrah, Luciano, Dixie Davis and Torrio, of holdups and kidnapings, of bloody industrial warfare.

THE CURRENT SCENE

If the application of the obscenity law is to make any sense at all, material claimed to be offensive must be viewed against our contemporary background. Any attempt to keep alive the conventions of a dead era is bound to be futile as well as ridiculous. We may as well try to bring back gaslight and the horse-drawn carriage and donkey engines on the elevated, as to seek to restore the mores of those days.

We've gone a long way since the days when the pinch-nosed Miss Frances Willard excoriated Richard Watson Gilder for allowing the word "rape" to appear in the *Century Magazine* where it might offend the gaze of good women.

For the press of today a spade is a spade. Such squeamish phrases as "statutory offense" have been discarded for good. The headlines and the columns speak openly of rape, blood lust and adultery. Stories of passion and lust, of crime and perversion, are told with a degree of frankness unheard of a generation ago. Every man, woman and child in the community may read all about suicides, of sash-weight murders, of torch murders, of barrel murders, of concrete-coffin murders, of marital infidelities, of boudoir intimacies, kidnapings and abnormalities. The *Hall-Mills* case, the *Snyder-Gray* case, the *Winnie Judd* case, the *Dr Sylla* case, the *Jessie Costello* case, the *Dr Wynekoop* case and more recently the *Carroll* case are but a few of innumerable examples.

There was a time when even the most daring papers shied from the word "prostitution." Venereal diseases couldn't be mentioned, much less discussed. Today the press speaks freely of syphilis, and it is something worth pondering that the letting down of the bars has been coincident with a concerted drive to eradicate the disease.

In his article, "The Facts of Life in Popular Song," Dr Sigmund Spaeth has revealed the extent of forthrightness which our lyricists have come to practice (and the community to accept) in telling of the technique and joys of love-making.

On the stage we have had plays like *Design for Living, Frankie and Johnnie, The Green Bay Tree, Oscar Wilde, Reunion in Vienna, The Children's Hour* and *The Women.* At the time of this writing, *Tobacco Road, The Primrose Path, Kiss the Boys Goodbye, The Boys from Syracuse, The Happiest Days* and *I Must Love Someone* are on the boards.

Our current attitude in letters is illustrated by the kind of books in general circulation. Works like Thomas Mann's *Death in Venice,* Victoria Lincoln's *February Hill,* Faulkner's *Sanctuary* and *Light in August,* Caldwell's *Kneel to the Rising Sun,* Cain's *Serenade,* Hemingway's *To Have and Have Not,* Margery Sharp's *The Nutmeg Tree,* John Steinbeck's *The Grapes of Wrath*—not to mention Thorne Smith's effervescent ribaldries—have all been freely distributed.

Schools and museums have definitely repudiated the philosophy of suppression and obfuscation. Sex education is gaining acceptance everywhere. The American Museum of Natural History in New York has many exhibits dealing with human anatomy and embryology; the Museum of Science and Industry at Rockefeller Center has, in addition to the Transparent Man and Transparent Woman, a complete set of actual fetuses showing progressive stages in the growth of the human embryo from one to nine months. The same is true of the Hall of Medicine at the New York World's Fair.

We are no longer afraid of sex. We no longer pretend, as did the good folk before the turn of the century, that biological functions don't exist. We have abandoned hush-hush. We have found certain social ills thrive on secrecy and suppression, and the best way to deal with these ills is to drag them out into the open and expose them to the full glare of public scrutiny.

We've developed sturdier tastes and tougher hides. And perhaps we've grown a little wiser in the process.

CHAPTER XIII

Commentary

Mankind can hardly be too often reminded that there was once a man named Socrates, between whom and the legal authorities and public opinion of his time there took place a memorable collision. Born in an age and country abounding in individual greatness, this man has been handed down to us by those who best knew both him and the age as the most virtuous man in it; this acknowledged master of all the eminent thinkers who have since lived was put to death by his countrymen after a judicial conviction for impiety and immorality. Impiety, in denying the Gods recognized by the state; immorality, in being, by his doctrines and instructions, a "corrupter of youth."

JOHN STUART MILL, *On Liberty* (1859)

ART VERSUS MORALS

CONTROVERSIAL as is the whole subject of censorship, no phase of it has been more bitterly contested than the question as to whether art should be subservient to morals. "Strychnine," says Comstock, "is a deadly poison. Its effect when administered sugar-coated is the same as when administered otherwise. When the genius of art reproduces obscene, lewd and lascivious ideas, the deadly effect upon the morals of the young is just as perceptible as when the same ideas are represented by gross expressions in prose or poetry."

199

"There is no such thing," replies Oscar Wilde, "as a moral or an immoral book. Books are well written, or badly written. That is all. The moral life of man forms part of the subject matter of the artist, but the morality of art consists in the perfect use of an imperfect medium."

The Old Man glowers and tugs at his ginger whiskers. "Art is not above morals," he warns. "Morals stand first. Law ranks next as the defender of public morals. Art only comes in conflict with law when its tendency is obscene, lewd or indecent."

Gautier makes a jeering sound. "Books follow morals," he cries, "and not morals books. The Regency made Crébillon, and not Crébillon the Regency. Boucher's little shepherdesses had their faces painted and their bosoms bare because the little marchionesses had the same. Pictures are made according to models, and not models according to pictures. Someone has said somewhere that literature and the arts influence morals. Whoever he was he was undoubtedly a great fool. It was like saying green peas make the spring grow, whereas green peas grow because it is spring, and cherries because it is summer. Trees bear fruits; it is certainly not the fruits that bear the trees, and this law is eternal and invariable in its variety; the centuries follow one another, and each bears its own fruit, which is not that of the preceding century; books are the fruits of morals."

Comstock's brow is a thundercloud. "The closer art keeps to pure morality," he insists, "the higher is its grade. Artistic beauty and immorality are divergent lines. To appeal to the animal in man does not inspire the soul of man with ecstasies of the beautiful."

Mr Brooks Atkinson, the drama critic, joins the discussion. "The function of art," he says, "is not to promote a code of standards or to establish social ideals, but to tell the truth about all the people who inhabit the world. What is, is, and if we are ever to get anywhere with enlightened civilization we must know the full truth. Whether it is flattering or distressing, inspiring or depressing, is beside the point; and the need is not for temperate speaking but for complete frankness about everyone and everything, for none of the ills of humanity can be cured until it is understood. The moral artist is one who has the courage and the capacity to tell the truth."

Mr Martin Quigley, coauthor of the Motion Picture Code, disagrees: "The function of art is certainly not that of a tattletale columnist—to tell everything about everybody. Mankind is not lacking in knowledge of human frailties; its lack is only in capacity to avoid the exceedingly well-known frailties. Mr Atkinson inveighs against temperate speaking and wants complete frankness about everyone and everything, evidently subscribing to the theory that the more the audience is rolled in the gutter the cleaner it will get up."

Anton Chekhov puts in a word. "People abuse me for objectivity," he says, "calling it indifference to good and evil. It's my task simply to show people as they are."

Comstock's answer is apocalyptic. "If through eye and ear the sensuous book, picture or story is allowed to enter, the thoughts will be corrupted, the conscience seared—so such things reproduced by fancy in the thoughts awaken forces for evil which often explode with irresistible force carrying to destruction every human safeguard to virtue and honor."

Let Professor H. W. Garrod close the argument: "If you ask me whether art or literature must be moral, I can only answer you by a method not much liked by such persons as mostly ask the question; the method, that is, of common sense. It is hateful, I know, to carry the common sense into the rarefied atmosphere of artistic discussion; and yet a man might as well ask, 'Should mankind be moral?' A book of an unpleasant theme or of an immoral tendency may, as well as a man of like constitution, both exhibit talent and afford entertainment; and a prude in literature is as tiresome as a prude in life. But the fact is that in the long run, in books and in life alike, morality can be trusted to look after it. There are periods of immoral literature, just as there are periods of social convulsion. But the average citizen never dies; and the good sense of the ordinary decent man, like charity, never fails in the long run. Literature does not please by moralizing us; it moralizes us because it pleases; and the world is pleased by what is unpleasant only for a limited time. I see no reason why literature should be moral except that; nor any ground, out of faith, why you and I should be moral, save that society insists on making us so."

No Truce

It is a truism that liberty is never permanently won, that it must be fought for each day, that a free people, overconfident of possessing it and relaxed in vigilance, soon finds itself enslaved.

Each triumph the censor scores means not only that something, and quite possibly something worth while, has been destroyed or driven to cover, but also that the censor himself has grown in strength. Victories are the food he thrives on, especially victories by default, won by intimidation. He does not relish a fight. Determined opposition will often put him to rout.

For years the Old Man and Mr Sumner warred on books indiscriminately; pleas of guilty were wrung by the hundreds from hapless defendants; depredations mounted while authors and publishers stood idly by. The moment vigorous opposition was organized, however, the power of the vice crusader over the written word was broken. Today no bona fide book need fear his ax. This emancipation has not come about by chance. It is the direct result of the *Jurgen* fight, the *Mary Ware Dennett* fight, the *Ulysses* fight. The reason the screen is so completely throttled by a triple censorship—the Code Administration, state boards, city authorities—is that no producer, distributor or exhibitor has ever had the courage or desire to put up a real fight.

"Judges and juries," wrote the New York *World* at the time when a succession of literary decency cases instigated by uplifters resulted in acquittals, "are not fools. They can see injustice as well as anybody else. And the man who would try to smash through the law which squeezes him might find that it would fall apart from the weight of its own rivets."

THE ENIGMA

There is no society for the eradication of burglary or arson or murder. The theory is that the law-enforcement agencies—the police and the district attorneys—are sufficiently alert to detect and prosecute crime. The theory is sound. If it doesn't always work, the thing to do is to overhaul the authorities, not to have their duties taken over by vigilante groups in the community.

The obscenity law has always been a thing apart. Vice crusaders have ever contended that while the police can ferret out ordinary crimes they are not "equipped" or "qualified" to track down indecency. The reasoning behind this contention is anything but clear. The implication seems to be that a special kind of nose is required for smut snuffling. In any event let it be noted that the authorities rarely get after a book or a play of their own free will. Whether this is because they take a common-sense view of things or because they have abdicated their functions is unimportant. *What is important is that the overwhelming majority of prosecutions are brought at the instigation of pressure groups.* These groups are spark plugs that fire the engine of morality. They snoop around, they entrap, they get the evidence, they fulminate, they demand action. And they get it.

One of the phenomena of censorship is the ease with which professional uplifters, and even meddlers, mossbacks and cranks manage to enlist the co-operation of the authorities. These people have perfected a technique which, considering the tenuous basis of their assumed right to speak for the community, is nothing short of amazing.

When, armed with a complaint, they descend on the police or the district attorney or the licensing power they presume to "speak for all the decent elements in society." Is any attempt made, one may well ask, to find out whom they actually represent? If they do act for a group, is there any inquiry as to who constitute the group or whether the group is typical of the community? Are they questioned as to their motives? If they are lone crusaders, are they examined to find out whether they aren't abnormal prudes or just plain nuisances? No.

Here we encounter a species of official cowardice which might well engage the attention of the psychologist and the sociologist. When a district attorney receives an ordinary complaint he usually appraises it dispassionately, and if he thinks the complainant is a fraud or a crackpot he wastes no time booting him out of the office. With an obscenity charge it's a different story. The district attorney doesn't look too closely at the supposedly offending material. He gets worried. He knows that if he ignores the complaint he will be accused of succoring evil. With a protest from a religious source his concern will be all the deeper. He may see political ruin in a refusal to act. And so he submits to a form of duress, the drastic results of which are ridiculously disproportionate to the negligible amount of public sentiment behind it.

Nor will the process stop there. Unless he is courageous and clear eyed, the judge who gets the case may follow in the district attorney's steps. It will make no difference what his private views are. He too will yield to timidity, to his notions of expediency. Indeed, the more liberal his private outlook, the more reactionary his judicial decision may be. A New York judge, now dead, who was notorious for his violent diatribes against "offensive" books, had one of the country's largest collections of erotica in his library.

If an obscenity complaint bristles sufficiently with invective and is generous in the use of such good standbys as "an outrage on public decency" and "an affront to all right-minded people," the chances are that it will precipitate an investigation and a prosecution.

It would be far wiser in every case to investigate the complainant first.

BOOMERANG

Since the obscenity law is a slough of quaggy definitions and assumptions it's natural that those treading the maze in search of quarry should sometimes get trapped.

There's the case of L. A. Tatum of Tallahassee, Florida, for example. Mr Tatum disapproved of the texts and reference books that were used in the Florida State College for Women. He claimed he had proof that they were very "improper and objectionable." He commenced a purity crusade, calling upon the college, the State Board of Education and the legislature in turn to root out the evil. He met with opposition and indifference. To justify his stand he and a Mr Prichard issued two pamphlets containing excerpts taken from the books warred against. They mailed five thousand of these pamphlets. The federal authorities promptly indicted them for sending obscene literature through the mails. The cases were finally dropped.

There's also the case of Philip Yarrow, Chicago's Sumner. As the superintendent and guiding spirit of the Illinois Vigilance Society, Mr Yarrow for years fought "indecent" books, plays, pictures and movies. His efforts were so successful against dealers in pornographic material that he cast about for new fields to conquer. He began to frequent the establishments of reputable booksellers. He would ask for some erotic item, and if he was told that the concern did not carry it he would insist on leaving an order for it. When the item was finally obtained for him he would swoop down on the unfortunate dealer with detectives and stage an arrest.

The Chicago *Evening Post* ran a series of articles exposing Mr Yarrow's methods, suggesting that a clue to his zeal might be found in the provisions of an old Illinois law which enabled him, as informer, to collect fifty per cent of the fines levied on defendants as a result of his efforts. When the *Post* published photographs of checks paid to Mr Yarrow, public indignation ran high.

Walter Shaver, one of Mr Yarrow's bookseller victims, sued him for malicious prosecution and got a jury verdict of five thousand dollars. Mr Yarrow said he'd rather rot in jail than pay this sum, and Mr Shaver's lawyer took him at his word. Mr Yarrow landed in the county jail where he had sent so many others.

A higher court later set aside the verdict.

Nullification or Repeal?

A useless or undesirable law may be repealed; the legislative force that created it can also end its existence. Or it may continue on the statute books and yet be completely ignored by public opinion. The latter process is known as nullification. Nullification is the non-legislative rejection by society of a bad law. It may be evidenced by a number of things: social usage (widespread drinking during the prohibition era), the refusal of district attorneys to prosecute, the prompt flare-up of public resentment when a prosecution is attempted, the refusal of juries to convict and, notably, the whittling away of the law by judicial decision.

Should we work for legislative repeal of the Comstock Law or let nullification take its course?

This question vexed the advocates of birth control for more than a generation. Some argued that it was socially unwise to accumulate dead laws on our statute books; that repeal was the logical and orderly process; that nullification meant breaking the law and set a bad example; that as long as a defunct contraceptive law existed—even though it was not generally enforced—it could be used on occasion as a pretext to "get" persons for some other reason. Those favoring nullification pointed out that we were a people given to enacting laws, not repealing them; that we did not, as we should, clean house from time to time to get rid of defunct statutes; that nullification was a wise process of life, having been always practiced by mankind, and being society's only effective answer to the stupidity of those that governed it; that law always lagged a half century behind social progress; and that in some things—as in birth control—we couldn't afford to wait until the law caught up.

These arguments, and many others pro and con, were advanced in the course of the symposium which was conducted by the *Birth Control Review* almost a decade ago. The intervening ten years have furnished an acid test. The birth-control laws are still with us, but—with the notable exception of Massachusetts and Connecticut—they have been virtually reinterpreted by the courts and society. Today, whatever the statutes say and however stringent their ban, it is legal for a duly licensed physician to prescribe a contraceptive in a proper case, and a "proper" case may be one based not only on strict medical grounds but economic considerations as well. It is legal to transmit birth-control literature and materials in intrastate and interstate commerce if consigned to qualified persons, and a "qualified" person need not be a physician; he may be a medical student, the editor of a scientific journal, a wholesale or retail druggist and even a layman if he holds a doctor's prescription. It is legal for birth-control literature and materials consigned to qualified persons to enter at the customs. To say that the situation today is not vastly more wholesome than ten years ago is to ignore the facts.

What has brought about the result? Repeal? Year after year those who espoused the legislative methods made their pilgrimages to Washington and to state capitols, argued with heat and eloquence, adduced incontrovertible data, submitted repeal bills, worked tirelessly. The lawmakers listened politely, made promises and did nothing. There was inertia, and religious pressure and the whole complex of political "expediency." But social progress did not wait. The people and the courts did what elected representatives failed to do.

Birth control is not the lone example. The highest court in New York placed its seal of approval, by implication at least, on the suppression of *Reigen,* yet

Schnitzler's study is freely circulated in the Modern Library edition. A bookdealer was fined two hundred and fifty dollars for selling Pierre Louÿs' *Aphrodite;* a copy may be picked up for less than a dollar in almost every drugstore.

True, nullification is not an ideal method. It is a makeshift at best, a lame substitute for the courageous, forward-looking legislative policy we so sorely need and don't seem to be able to achieve. Stupid, ancient statutes are an embarrassment to conscientious district attorneys and an obstacle to enlightened judges who must indulge in strained interpretations to avoid unconscionable decisions. They are a menace because we never know when they may be seized upon by professional uplifters or reactionary officials to thwart free trade in ideas.

CHAPTER XIV

Who Is the Censor?

In many ways this society is of avail for good in this com-
munity, as will be seen in the report which our efficient
secretary and his too small staff now make. But some-
times we are tempted to feel as Elijah felt when, in his pro-
test against a corrupt civilization, he thought himself
alone. But our list of subscribers proves to us that there
is a large body of men and women who are not misled by
the clamor of the prejudiced press and reporters and too
eager self-styled literati.

ANSON P. ATTERBURY,
New York Vice Society Report (1929)

SOMEONE ONCE SAID that there could never be a good
censor because any man wise enough to be one would
also be wise enough not to tackle the job.

The loose use of the word "censorship" has led to
much confusion. There are several kinds of censorship,
many kinds of censors and many kinds of things censored. The members of motion-picture review boards
are admittedly censors; organizations like the New
York Vice Society and the Boston Watch and Ward
deny that they perform any such function, though there
can be little doubt about their aims and the results of
their work.

On the other hand, it would be absurd to say that a
story is "censored" because a magazine refuses to print
it, or that a painting is "suppressed" because a gallery
refuses to hang it. Only recently the League of Ameri-

can Writers called a meeting on the subject of "Censorship in Book Reviewing," saying that many progressive writers felt that a certain amount of censorship existed in regard to their books. Isabel Patterson, the New York *Herald Tribune's* Bookworm, deplored the misapplication of the word "censorship."

Whatever a "progressive" writer may be [she wrote] he is evidently just like any other writer in feeling that the reviewers have done him wrong. We can only guess that by "censorship" in this respect is meant that their books don't get enough space or sufficiently favorable comment to please their aforesaid progressive authors . . . Well, nobody's books do . . . Including our own . . . But it would be just as reasonable for the reviewer to "complain" that a book has been "censored" because it is not about some subject, or because it does not contain what the reviewer thinks it should contain, as to make such a complaint of reviewing.

THE CENSOR DEFINED

Webster's New International Dictionary gives the following definitions of the word "censor":

(1) One of two magistrates of Rome who took a register of the number and property of citizens, and who also exercised the office of inspector of morals and conduct.

(2) One who acts as an overseer of morals and conduct, especially an official empowered to examine written or printed matter, as manuscripts of books, plays, foreign newspapers or magazines, etc., in order to forbid publication, circulation or representation if containing anything objectionable.

(3) One who judges.

(4) One given to faultfinding; a censurer; an adverse critic.

For our purposes here a censor may be defined as one who, by reason of his judicial, administrative or quasi-official position, exercises control over public morals by dictating what kind of matter shall be placed before society and suppressing what he deems objectionable.

CHOICE VERSUS COMPULSION

Every one of us exercises a personal censorship every day of his life. We decide to read one book, not another; we vow never to see another play by a certain dramatist; we fulminate against an editorial that clashes with our views. Our action may depend on a number of factors: our upbringing, our education, our glandular make-up, our tastes, our prejudices, our mood. We may not be content to reserve our judgment to ourselves; we may try to persuade our children and our friends.

With this type of censorship no liberal will quarrel. It is predicated on the freedom of personal choice. It is dynamic and democratic; through the processes of education the standards which govern its exercise are constantly molded and improved. But the moment some official steps in and deprives us of *the right to exercise our choice* by making a book unavailable to us even if we want it, we get another kind of censorship, the Hitler-Mussolini-Stalin kind: one that proceeds from coercion, one that comes from the outside instead of from within, one that is unsound, dangerous, hostile to progress and, from the censor's own point of view, futile.

PREVIOUS RESTRAINT

Historically, censorship meant previous restraint. Material had to be submitted to an official censor for approval prior to publication, and could be published only if licensed by him. When Caxton set up his printing press in Westminster in 1476 both the Church and the Crown quickly perceived the vast potential power of the printed word. Both strove to control it, the Church by extending the Papal Index, the Crown by forbidding all printing except by royal license. Maintained under close governmental supervision, presses were made subject to the decrees of the Star Chamber. In 1557 the Stationers' Company of London, a guild of stationers, received the exclusive privilege of printing and publishing in the British dominions. Queen Elizabeth went further; she demanded that all books be read and passed upon in advance by loyal bishops and councilors.

Notwithstanding these restrictions, printing presses multiplied in number, unlicensed books poured forth, courageous printers risked mutilation and death. The people, hungry for knowledge, impatient of restraint, overrode all efforts on the part of the Crown to fetter the press. The Star Chamber's strict edict of 1637 was of no avail; the Long Parliament's re-enactment of it called forth Milton's *Areopagitica,* but did not stem the tide of books. Prepublication control of the press was finally abolished in 1695.

The motion-picture censorship of today is a true example of the historic type: supervision through previous restraint, for the review boards are authorized by law to examine and license. When a jittery publisher, afraid of trouble, submits a manuscript to Mr Sumner before publication we get a hybrid kind of precensorship: there is no warrant in law for the publisher's submission or Mr Sumner's examination, nor does it necessarily follow that if the publisher proceeds in defiance of Mr Sumner's recommendation he will become liable criminally.

SUBSEQUENT PUNISHMENT

The non-historic type of censorship, far more extensive, imposes no previous restraint on dissemination; it merely prescribes some form of penalty if material is found to violate some law after it is placed in circulation. The manuscript of a book need not be submitted to a censor before publication, but if it is adjudged obscene afterward the author as well as the publisher and the bookseller may be fined or sent to jail.

The immediate practical effect of both these types is the same: the suppression of "objectionable" matter. The important difference is that pre-censorship stifles creative effort before birth, so that—to borrow Edgar Lee Masters' expression—freedom is not left free to combat error; whereas subsequent restraint gives the novel or the play under attack a chance to get before the public, to rally sentiment and to be tested out in the courts. For obvious reasons it is easier to fight the latter type of censorship. During the last decade or so the frontiers of literary decency have been substantially extended; in the field of motion pictures very little advance has been made.

In 1912, prior to the enactment of state censorship, an ordinance for the licensing of films was presented in New York City. Mayor Gaynor vetoed it, saying:

It has hitherto been the understanding in this country that no censorship can be established by law to decide in advance what may or may not be lawfully printed or published. Ours is a government of free speech and a free press. This is the cornerstone of free government. The phrase, "the press," includes all methods of expression by writing or pictures. In past ages there were censorships to decide what might be published or even believed . . . The few were very anxious not to give freedom of speech or of the press. They thought the many were not fit for it . . . But in the course of time . . . censorship and all interference with freedom of speech, of the press and of opinion began to give way . . . until in the end . . . they were abolished. There seem to be a few . . . who wish to retrace our steps and resort to censorship again in advance of publication . . . Do they

know that censorships of past ages did immeasurably more
harm than good? If this ordinance be legal then a similar ordinance in respect of the newspapers and the theaters generally
would be legal . . . Once revive censorship and there is no
telling how far we may carry it.

WITH AND WITHOUT BENEFIT OF OFFICE

There are official, semiofficial and unofficial censors.

Official censors are those empowered by law to exercise powers of supervision and suppression. They include judges (despite their oft-repeated declarations
that it is not the function of the courts to exercise
censorship); administrative bodies such as film review
boards; administrative officials such as the postmaster
general and the collector of customs and license com-
missioners. Administrative bodies and officials purport
to operate under specific statutes which outline their
powers and prescribe the procedure they must follow.

The judges interpret and apply the law in cases that
come up before them, as where the seller of an
"obscene" book is prosecuted criminally. They are also
supposed to act as a check on bureaucracy—an important function, but one which has been all too often
abdicated through judicial policy. The rule is that an
administrative decision, though palpably wrong, will
not be disturbed by the court unless it can be shown to
be clearly "arbitrary, capricious or oppressive," and if
the question permits of any doubt, the decision will be
binding on the court. Stupidity is not enough to warrant
a reversal, so long as it is the kind of stupidity an
"honest" man may be guilty of. Blundering is not
enough. The fact that the court disagrees with the decision is not enough. Stubborn refusal to read the signs
of the times is not enough. The situation must be shocking in the extreme to induce the court to interfere.

The semi-official censors are bodies that have no specific powers under the law but have been organized for the express purpose of moral uplift. The New York Society for the Suppression of Vice, the Boston Watch and Ward Society, the Clean Amusement Association of America, belong in this category. Some of these agencies possess limited police powers. They work in co-operation with the authorities. They ferret out alleged violations, act as complaining witnesses, practice entrapment, prod the police and the district attorneys.

They refuse of course to be styled censors. The annual reports of the New York Vice Society, for example, are strident with disclaimers. Says the 1929 report: "Frequently this society has been accused of trying to set itself up as a censor of public morals. Emphatically we deny this offensive charge. We are simply trying to sustain the laws established for public order." And again the 1935 report: "Let me make it plain that the position of our society is not in any way that of a censor, which is far from our thought or purposes, but simply that of a law-enforcement agency, acting in the public interest with public officials on individual complaints received. These complaints come from very many sources. We are constantly co-operating with the police in purely police cases, and we are always working in thorough harmony with the prosecuting authorities —especially with the police department—and last and most important of all, with the courts, whose decisions represent the final word."

The vice societies are more or less permanent organizations. There are others that are formed as part of particular morality drives. These are energetic and clamorous while the crusade lasts, and then their work tapers off.

A small reactionary group in the Catholic Church, through the Legion of Decency, wields a powerful influence for censorship. With its desire to set up an ethical or religious code for Catholics to follow, few will quarrel. But there are many who question seriously its effort forcibly to superimpose the pattern of its moral precepts on the entire community. There can be little doubt that it has tried to do so. In New York it inspired the raid on the Dr Hannah Stone's birth-control clinic, the prosecution of Mrs Dennett (because she rejected religious dogma as a basis for sexual ethics) and Joyce's *Ulysses* (because of blasphemy); in Massachusetts and Connecticut it has been responsible for the wholesale closing of birth-control clinics; in a number of states it furnished the impetus for attacking the issue of *Life* carrying the *Birth of a Baby* picture story; in several cities it has resorted to economic boycott to enforce its black list of magazines. Fortunately this illiberal group represents but a small, though energetic and vociferous minority in the Church; the majority has scant sympathy for its objectives and methods.

The Motion Picture Production Code Administration, too, comes within the group of semi-official censors. Although publicized as "self-regulatory," it exercises a degree of surveillance and controls a battery of sanctions wholly out of keeping with voluntary adherence to industry standards.

Non-official censors are scattered individuals—clergymen, crackpots, busybodies, meddlers, irate housewives, psychopathic "smut snufflers," scandalized parents who find their adolescent children reading a book on sex and expect the worst—who raise their voices in warning or indignation from time to time, and call upon the authorities to do something. They are a menace because one never knows when their scoldings will be heeded by the police or the district attorney.

Censors, State and Federal

Under our system of government certain spheres of activity are under national control, and others are left to the states. The federal government has exclusive jurisdiction over the mails and interstate and foreign commerce. The postmaster general sees to it that the mails are not contaminated, and the Customs Bureau bars from our shores whatever material may be thought to imperil the morals of the American people. On the other hand, whatever happens within the confines of a particular state is regulated by that state itself. The movie censors, for example, are state censors.

The line of demarcation between federal and state censors, while clear cut in theory, is not sharply observed in practice. A book banned at the customs is effectively kept from the people of the states; the motion-picture producers in California work with the New York State board in mind; the decisions of the federal courts on books, plays and films are usually followed by the state courts, and vice versa.

Sex versus Politics

There is sex censorship and political censorship. The latter category seeks to perpetuate the present order by suppressing criticisms of it; its weapon is prosecutions under sedition and criminal-syndicalism laws. The former aims to protect the morals of society from the taint of obscenity. Suppression of political ideas is often attempted in the guise of a prosecution for "sexual impurity." Here are three typical cases:

Fred Warren of Kansas, publisher of the *Appeal to Reason,* a Socialist weekly, was indicted for alleged violation of the obscenity law.

In 1912 Hobart Croomer, publisher of a Socialist paper in Oklahoma, received a jail sentence of six months, ostensibly for publishing a "lewd and lascivious advertisement in his paper."

In 1923 Carlo Tresca, anarchist, strike organizer, editor of the radical weekly *Il Martello,* gave offense to the Italian government because copies of his paper, vigorously attacking the Fascist regime, found their way into Italy. There is persuasive evidence that official instructions were given to "get" him. He was arrested, indicted and convicted for publishing a two-line advertisement of a book on birth control. He received a sentence of a year and a day. His appeal was denied and he actually served four months in Atlanta.

CHAPTER XV

The Case against Censorship

These absurdities in the administration of censorship serve only to strengthen the independent thinker's resentment against the essence of the practice. The saving of a man's soul, which one must presume is the object of the censorship, is after all a man's own affair and is not to be achieved by external compulsion or guardianship. It is of a man's free will that he buys a ticket for a play or borrows a book from the library. If he wants to pander to the lower side of his nature no censor will prevent him.

WILLIAM ALLAN NEILSON,
The Theory of Censorship (1930)

SO FAR as the record goes the case against censorship is formidable. A great deal of the evidence damns the process itself; the rest convicts the censor.

THE ORIGINAL SIN

Two doctrines lie at the heart of censorship. Their central idea is the same; the difference is a quantitative, rather than a qualitative, one.

The first flows directly from the biblical concept of the temptation and fall of man. According to the doctrine, man is a fallible being, a prey to sensual appetites. If he is to be saved from eternal damnation he must be stripped of his follies and vices. Satan—who can don innumerable guises (witness what happened to St Anthony), at times squeezing himself, horns, hoofs and tail, between the covers of a book—must not be permitted to tempt him.

The second doctrine lacks the picturesque theology of the first. It, too, presupposes the frailty of man but ascribes that lamentable condition to the basic imperfection of the human stock, not to predestiny traceable to the serpent and the apple. It assumes that man's nature must and can be improved, and that the exposure of the species to sexually exciting material is injurious, if not fatal, to the process of improvement.

The lack of proof as to the correctness of the underlying assumptions of these doctrines has never given any concern to their advocates. The uplifters have never paused to consider the implications of evolution as against religious dogma; if they were to be told that it was the destiny of mankind to work out its spiritual salvation as part of the march of evolution they would rise up in hot denial. And yet the plain truth is that there is no reason to suppose that man, if left alone, would sink into the mire, or that surveillance over his mental fare can either keep him from corruption or forcibly alter his nature for the better.

"My God! what a foolish thing is this pretended perfectibility of the human race which is continually being dinned into our ears!" wrote Gautier in his impassioned attack on the moralists of his day. "One would think, in truth, that man is a machine susceptible of improvements, and that some wheelwork in better gear or a counterpoise more suitably placed would make him work in a more convenient and easy fashion. When they succeed in giving man a double stomach so that he may ruminate like an ox, or eyes on the other side of his head so, like Janus, he may see those who put out their tongues at him behind and contemplate his indignity in a less inconvenient position than that of the Athenian Venus Callipygus; when they plant wings upon his shoulder blades so he may not be obliged to pay six sous for an omnibus, and create a new organ for him, well and good: the word perfectibility will then begin to have some meaning."

Gautier was no doubt carried away by the ardor of his youthful rebellion against hypocrisy and cant. Perfectibility does not appear to be an impossible dream. Man has been helped in the past to a fuller realization of his potentialities. But never by coddling.

CAUSE AND EFFECT

Science has profound respect for the law of cause and effect. It doesn't take things for granted. It doesn't assume that if a dog follows a rabbit the latter "produces" the former. It bases its conclusions on concrete things closely observed under strict controls over periods of time. Hunches, hopes, hypotheses are all right as starting points for investigations, but only as such.

Censorship is vulnerable from the point of view of science because it scorns facts. Given allegedly obscene material, it does not seek to ascertain by clinical methods the nature and extent of the influence such material may wield over human beings. It substitutes guesses for findings.

Anyone studying the subject is shocked to discover the extraordinary fact that there has never been a thoroughgoing, impartial, wide-range experiment conducted to ascertain within possible limits the psychological or psychiatric effect of matter claimed to be objectionable. Whatever surveys have been made—and they have been few—have been unsystematic or narrow or prejudiced from the start.

To be sure, the scientific problem is much more complicated here than in a field that lends itself readily to observation and analysis. Bacteria can be identified and counted under the microscope. The physical manifestations of disease can be established virtually beyond dispute. But how are we to look into the mind of a man who is said to have been infected with the "virus" of *Ulysses?* If we cannot cut a window in his skull, how shall we pursue our investigation? Shall we observe him over a space of time? How long a period? Under what controls? If he misbehaves, shall we be necessarily justified in blaming *Ulysses?* How shall we be able to isolate the book from the complex of all other impacts on his mind so as to assert with reasonable certainty that it was *Ulysses* and not something else that caused his dereliction? And even if we establish the existence of cause and effect in his case, what validity will that finding have with reference to other members of the community? How can we make sure that he is a man with normal sex instincts, so that we may claim general application for our findings?

Or are we to discard the laboratory method as unsuited to inquiries of this kind, and try questionnaires? Even assuming that questions can be worked up which, if truthfully answered, will turn a man's mind inside out, how shall we make sure that our subject won't lie, consciously or unconsciously?

The field is *terra incognita*. Without adequately surveying it, without even penetrating its labyrinth to any appreciable extent, censors have seen fit to draw the conclusion that books, plays and the like have a capacity to corrupt human behavior. The meagerness of the evidence has not disturbed them, nor the fact that there is at least as much evidence the other way.

For it cannot be denied that a substantial gap exists between things in the mind and things in real life. A small-town Rotarian can see Paul Muni in *Zola,* sympathize with the unfortunate Dreyfus on the screen and yet ally himself, all unaware of the inconsistency, with the forces of intolerance and vigilantism in his community. A mother may be moved to tears by a sob story in a magazine in which a child is cruelly treated, and yet not hesitate to cuff her own youngster when unruly.

"Once I had the opportunity," says Heywood Broun in *Anthony Comstock,* "to talk about books and plays with a young man in the Tombs prison who had just been indicted for murder. Asked to outline the plot of the best book he ever read, he animatedly retold a story of a young wastrel, who reformed upon being elected mayor and cleaned up a dissolute city by rigorously suppressing vice and crime. The young man had read and enjoyed this novel just a week before he was moved to shoot two policemen."

The Weak and the Strong

Let's assume that the noxious effect of certain types of material on people in general has been demonstrated with sufficient certainty, and that the suppression of such material is more to be desired socially than freedom of expression. The next question is, who is to do the job?

The censor, we are told. But in order to entrust him with the task we must assume that he is thoroughly competent and of superior judgment, that he himself is immune to moral poisons, and that he can produce results that, measured over long periods of time, are found to be socially desirable.

Is the censor just, able and qualified? Does he know what's good for society? Can he be relied on unerringly to separate the wheat from the chaff? We have already

discussed who the censor was. We found that he may be
a petty bureaucrat, a political hack, an obtuse police
chief, a state trooper, the recipient of a political plum, a
bigot, a psychopathic prig or a mental nonentity. Are
these the people who will sit in judgment?

What will happen to *their* moral fiber? They will receive thousandfold doses of the venom which they say
corrodes the soul of the average citizen even if administered in small, occasional amounts. Are they sustained by a sense of sacrifice, marching to self-
destruction like missionaries in a leper colony? Or are
they impervious? Does their office invest them with a
cloak of invulnerability? "If the books you oppose," a
reporter asked Mr Sumner some years ago, "really
harm those who read them, what is the effect on you
who read so many of them?" Mr Sumner replied:
"There is a difference between getting pleasure out of
these books and reading them to see whether they cover
a violation of the law." He laid bare no scars. Comstock himself, who waded through filth all his life—
worked in a sewer, to borrow his phrase—was acknowledged even by his bitterest foes to be unsullied.

If this immunity exists, the source of it must be the
badge of office, conferred, in the case of administrative
officials, by political appointment, and in the case of uplifters, by self-ordainment. A housewife may not see
High Treason on the screen lest she be tainted, but if
she belongs to the right club and is named a film censor,
her morals *ipso facto* become armor plated and she may
view thousands of questionable pictures without the re-
motest likelihood of hurt.

HOW LIKE A GOD

"But I have again to point out that censorship is the
wrong method," wrote George Bernard Shaw to the

New York *Times* in 1936. "Whatever its moral and religious pretenses may be, it always comes in practice to postulating the desirability of an official with the attributes of a god, and then offering the salary of a minor railway stationmaster plus a fee per play to some erring mortal to deputize for Omniscience. He who is fool enough or needy enough to accept such a post soon finds that except in the plainest cases judgment is impossible. He therefore makes an office list of words that must not be used and subjects that must not be mentioned (usually religion and sex); and though this brings his job within the capacity of an office boy it also reduces it to absurdity."

Omniscience in the guise of customs inspectors condemned Da Vinci's frescoes and ruled that Utrillo was not an artist. Back in the days of Daly and *Mrs Warren's Profession,* Comstock showed his knowledge of contemporary letters by saying, in a burst of temper: "George Bernard Shaw? Who is he? I never heard of him in my life. Never saw one of his books, so he can't be much."

When the motion picture *Birth* was banned by the Maryland board of censors, only to be vindicated by Judge Ullman in a ringing opinion, H. L. Mencken wrote in the Baltimore *Sun:* "It is difficult, if not downright impossible, to induce men and women of really enlightened minds to sit on any such board. The daily torture of gaping at imbecile movies would drive them frantic, and they would shrink from the grotesque task of considering the tastes and regulating the morals of morons. Thus recruits must be sought mainly in two classes—that of the professional job seekers and that of the professional uplifters.

"All boards of censors, it seems to me, are useless, and most of them are evil. No one ever heard of one that carried on its business in a sensible manner, and no wonder, for its business at bottom is simply not sensible. Such posses of smellers are quite unnecessary. There is plenty of law on the books to punish any actual obscenity, and volunteer snoopers may be trusted to complain whenever it is violated. The country swarms with them, and they are always snuffling for smut. When they complain there is an open trial in the ordinary courts, with the rights of the defendant safeguarded. Before a board of censors he has no rights at all. The board is at once the complainant, the prosecutor, the judge and the executioner. It has all the powers of a court, but none of the responsibilities."

A BETTER BREED?

Would things be otherwise if wiser men served as arbiters?

Plato suggested that Homer be expurgated. St Bernard called Abelard "an infernal dragon and the precursor of the anti-Christ." Thomas Carlyle called Charles Lamb a shameless and despicable abortion. Sir Walter Scott trembled for the morals of adolescents exposed to Richardson's *Pamela*. Robert Buchanan condemned Rossetti's sonnets as "one profuse sweat of animalism" and Gautier's *Memoirs de Charles Baudelaire* as "skillfully and secretly poisoning the mind of the unsuspicious reader." When *La Terre* was published Anatole France said of Zola: "His work is evil, and he is one of those unhappy beings of whom one can say that it would be better had he never been born." Whittier, himself a victim of persecution for abolitionist poems, threw Whitman's *Leaves of Grass* into the fire in a fit of disgust. Edmund Yates called George Moore a "bestial bard" for writing *Flowers of Passion*. Jerome K. Jerome found *Dorian Gray* corrupt. In the course of the controversy over the denial of the mails to *The*

Kreutzer Sonata, Theodore Roosevelt called Tolstoy a "sexual and moral pervert." Paul Elmer More described a novel by John Dos Passos as "an explosion in a sewer." Edgar Saltus dismissed Stephen Crane's *The Red Badge of Courage* as "vulgar inanity." William Dean Howells berated Mark Twain for writing "she combed me all to hell."

A GLANCE BACKWARD

History is the most eloquent witness against censorship. The list of works banned during the last three thousand years reads like civilization's honor roll. The men who wrote them were in most cases the pathfinders, the leaders of thought in their field, the intellectual giants, the people responsible for human progress. Here is a sketchy tabulation of material that has been proscribed in the past.

Prose Literature: Homer's *Odyssey, The Letters of Héloïse and Abelard,* Tasso's *La Gerusalemme Liberata,* Cervantes' *Don Quixote,* Pascal's *Lettres à un Provincial,* La Fontaine's *Fables,* Defoe's *Robinson Crusoe,* Swift's *Tale of a Tub* and *Gulliver's Travels,* Voltaire's *Candide,* Fielding's *Pasquin,* Richardson's *Pamela,* Casanova's *Memoirs,* Goethe's *Faust* and *Sorrows of Werther,* Gibbon's *Decline and Fall of the Roman Empire,* Sterne's *Sentimental Journey,* Andersen's *Fairy Tales,* Hugo's works, Balzac's *Droll Stories,* Stendhal's *Rouge et Noir,* Flaubert's *Madame Bovary,* Maupassant's *Une Vie* and *L'Humble Vérité,* Heine's *De L'Allemagne,* Stowe's *Uncle Tom's Cabin,* Hawthorne's *The Scarlet Letter,* Mark Twain's *Tom Sawyer* and *Huckleberry Finn,* Eliot's *Adam Bede,* George Moore's *Flowers of Passion,* Zola's *Nana,* Hardy's *Tess of the d'Urbervilles,* Upton Sinclair's *Oil,* Cabell's *Jurgen,* Lawrence's *Women in Love,* Sherwood Anderson's *Many Marriages,* Sinclair Lewis' *Elmer Gantry,* Aldous Huxley's *Antic Hay* and Remarque's *All Quiet on the Western Front.*

Drama: Shakespeare's *Richard II,* Ben Jonson's works, Molière's *Tartuffe,* Racine's *Théâtre Complet,* Oscar Wilde's *Salome,* Ibsen's *Ghosts,* George Bernard Shaw's *Man and Superman,* Gilbert and Sullivan's *Mikado,* Maeterlinck's *Mona Vanna* and Aristophanes' *Lysistrata.*

Poetry: Dante's *La Divina Commedia* and *De Monarchia,* Shelley's *Queen Mab,* Rossetti's *Poems,* Baudelaire's *Fleurs de Mal,* Whitman's *Leaves of Grass,* Elizabeth Barrett Browning's *Aurora Leigh* and Swinburne's *Poems and Ballades.*

Philosophy: The books of Confucius, Montaigne's *Essays,* Descartes' *Meditations,* Montesquieu's *L'Esprit des Lois,* Swedenborg's *Principia,* Diderot's *L'Encyclopédie,* Rousseau's writings and Kant's *Philosophy.*

Science: Roger Bacon's *Opus Majus, Opus Minus* and *Opus Tertium,* Galileo's study of the Ptolemaic and Copernican theories, Francis Bacon's works and Darwin's *Origin of Species.*

Politics and Economics: Machiavelli's *The Prince,* Jefferson's pamphlets, Paine's political writings and John Stuart Mill's works.

Religion: Savonarola's books, Erasmus' *Encomium Moviae* and Greek Testament, Luther's pamphlets, Tyndale's New Testament, the Koran, Calvin's writings.

Hundreds of the disciples of Confucius were buried alive for professing their master's beliefs. Sir Thomas Malory's *Morte d'Arthur* was attacked as no more than "bold adultery and willful murder." Prynne was fined, imprisoned and branded, and his ears were cropped for writing *Histrio-Mastix.* The Church called Molière "a demon in human flesh" for writing *Tartuffe,* a satire on religion. André Chénier went to the guillotine for *Iambes* and *Jeune Captive*.

Shelley's *Alastor* was attacked as indecent, and *Queen Mab* was prosecuted as blasphemous. Shakespeare was bowdlerized in 1818. Rev. A. C. Coxe was outraged by Hawthorne's *The Scarlet Letter*, and cried out "against any toleration to a popular and gifted writer when he perpetrates bad morals—let this brokerage of lust be put down at the very beginning." Elizabeth Barrett Browning's *Aurora Leigh* was denounced as "the hysterical indecencies of an erotic mind." Walt Whitman was discharged from the Department of the Interior because of *Leaves of Grass*. In 1885 the Public Library of Concord, New Hampshire, banned Mark Twain's *Huckleberry Finn* as "trash and suitable only for slums." Vizetelly was jailed for publishing the "pernicious literature" of Zola.

The Bible itself has not escaped unscathed. Versions of it were suppressed by Emperor Justinian, the synod of Canterbury, Cardinal Wolsey, the Inquisition and Queen Mary. In 1525 Tyndale's translation of the New Testament was denounced by the Church as "pernicious merchandise," and ten years later Tyndale was burned at the stake with his books. A special license is still required in Scotland for Bibles and prayer books.

The contemporary record of censorship is no better. It is shot through with inconsistencies and absurdities.

Sleeveless Errand was banned in England; it appeared without any trouble here. Remarque's *All Quiet on the Western Front* was uncensored in the English edition; bowdlerizing cut down the American version from 320 to 291 pages. New York critics hailed Lillian Hellman's *The Children's Hour* as a fine, gripping play; Marc Connelly's *Green Pastures* won the Pulitzer prize; England proscribed both.

Ovid's *Art of Love,* although freely circulated in this

country, was for many years barred at the customs. *Stag at Eve* went unscathed through the mails, but shocked the sensibilities of customs inspectors. *The Harmonious Development of Women's Bodies* reversed the process: it was officially approved at the customs and denied the mails.

The New York State Board of Regents upheld the ban of the censors on *The Birth of a Baby*, and lifted the ban on *Damaged Lives*.

Time and again hypersensitive Boston has cracked down on books and plays that have been acclaimed in New York. But while it has persistently harassed the legitimate drama, it has given free rein to rowdy burlesque. And Radclyffe Hall's *The Well of Loneliness*, which prompted Magistrate Bushel in New York to unburden himself of a spirited diatribe, did not cause so much as a ripple in the stronghold of decency.

THE KICKBACK

If censorship attacked only the indubitably offensive and succeeded in rooting it out, many of its critics would be silenced. The plain fact, however, is that it does not suppress. It drives material underground, encourages illicit trade, raises prices and whets prurient curiosity. And often as not it publicizes on a large scale the very thing it seeks to extirpate.

Joyce's *Ulysses* was bootlegged for many years; hardly a literate tourist returned from Paris without smuggling it in. It is estimated that some twenty to thirty thousand copies were sold this way, most of them pirated copies that paid no royalties to Joyce.

In the halcyon pre-1929 days quite an industry grew up for the exploitation of erotica. Esoteric items dealing with sexual practices and abnormalities, as well as titles long hounded by the censors, were privately printed, richly bound and sold at exorbitant prices through devious channels to "collectors." After a while the business became so good that the publishers grew bold, came out in the open and advertised their wares in reputable newspapers and magazines. The censor fought the industry energetically, never realizing that it was a creature of his own making.

Pornography thrives on suppression. Let alone, it barely subsists. The obscenity laws of France are extremely lax, yet its citizenry seems impervious to smut, and the trade in objectionable matter is confined principally to tourists.

In any event, there seems to be a real question whether, as a matter of human psychology, censorship or any other method of prophylaxis can cast out obscenity. Havelock Ellis finds that it is a "permanent element of human social life and corresponds to a deep need of the human mind," and there are other authorities that agree with him.

BEATING THE DRUM

When *The Well of Loneliness* first came up in the Magistrate's Court, the attorney for the defendants asked for a week's adjournment to enable him to prepare his case. Mr Sumner, as complainant and *alter ego* for the district attorney, objected. The judge wanted to know why.

Mr Sumner jabbed his forefinger accusingly at the defense lawyer. "He doesn't need any time," he said. "He could try the case now if he had to. He wants a week to whoop things up in the papers. He's after publicity."

The defense lawyer turned blandly to the vice-secretary. "We don't need any more publicity, Mr Sumner," he said. "You've given us plenty."

Without the benefit of Mr Sumner's condemnation the book might have sold a few thousand copies; as it was, the sales ran over a quarter million. There was even a de luxe Victory edition in two volumes, boxed, at twenty-five dollars a set.

It was Roger Bacon's fourteen dungeon years, occasioned by the censor's displeasure, that gave the initial impetus to his *Opus Majus*. Galileo was first brought to the attention of his contemporaries by the Inquisition, which spread his ideas by attacking them. The more Verlaine was flayed for indecency, the more notorious his work became. From the very outset Voltaire and Rabelais flourished on suppression. Before Baudelaire was tried for obscenity only his comparatively innocuous poems were in circulation. At the trial the most lurid ones were put in evidence; thereafter every French publisher, aware of the immunity attaching to the printing of evidence, printed the trial testimony in full, and there were made available to the public unexpurgated editions which would not otherwise have been attempted. It was an attack of bigots that turned public attention on Gautier's *Mademoiselle de Maupin*, Flaubert's *Madame Bovary*, Charlotte Brontë's *Jane Eyre*, Hawthorne's *Scarlet Letter* and Hardy's *Jude the Obscure*.

Comstock's attack on Daly's production of Shaw's *Mrs Warren's Profession* caused such a stir that orchestra seats sold for fifteen dollars and balcony seats for ten dollars on the opening night.

When *Candide* was stopped at the customs in 1929 the Detroit *Free Press* wrote: "The seizure will advertise the existence of the work to thousands of salacious-minded young people who had never heard of it. There will be a rush on the libraries for the unsatisfying expurgated copies they stock. The failure of some enterprising publisher to bring out and bootleg a new edition will be surprising. The very class of citizenry which the law is designed to protect from its own mental weakness is harmed by a stupid misapplication of the law."

Unmolested, *Yes, My Darling Daughter* would have had the uneventful career of an average movie. As a result of the censors' to-do, the Strand Theater in New York, where it was first scheduled to be shown, was mobbed; two stock companies instead of one gave the play in Brooklyn; and Alfred de Liagre, Jr, the impresario of the original production, was moved to consider a Broadway revival.

Before 1933 Sally Rand had been an obscure nightclub dancer. Her arrest when she appeared in Chicago's Century of Progress Exposition was played up in the press all over the country. "Some people would like to put pants on a horse," said Judge Joseph B. David, dismissing the charge. Miss Rand's anatomy was depicted in all its allure in hundreds of newspapers and magazines, and she became a public institution overnight.

When things got dull in the amusement area of the New York World's Fair the early part of this summer, the masterminds of the Frozen-Alive Show thought it would be a good idea to encase in an ice coffin a shapely young lady clad in a G string instead of a bathing suit. The police came (as had been fervently hoped) and made arrests. The news broke in all the papers. For weeks afterward the show was jammed while the other concessions languished.

CHAPTER XVI

The Case against Censorship (*Cont'd*)

Who can compute what the world loses in the multitude of promising intellects combined with timid characters, who dare not follow out any bold, vigorous, independent train of thought, lest it should land them in something which would admit of being considered irreligious or immoral? No one can be a great thinker who does not recognize that as a thinker it is his first duty to follow his intellect to whatever conclusions it may lead. Where there is a tacit convention that principles are not to be disputed, we cannot hope to find that generally high scale of mental activity which has made some periods of history so remarkable.

JOHN STUART MILL, *On Liberty* (1859)

THERE'S THE STORY of the tight-lipped, prudish maiden lady who lived on the outskirts of a small town, and who complained to the sheriff because, it being summer, small boys were bathing nude in a near-by stream, in plain view of her porch. Being a sensible man, the sheriff told the boys to move up the stream a bit so that the lady wouldn't be able to see them. The boys obeyed. A few days later the lady spoke to the sheriff again. "What's the trouble now?" he asked. "Haven't the kids moved?" "They have," snapped the lady, "but if I go upstairs I can still see them from the window." The sheriff said he'd do something. He spoke to the boys again. Would they go a little farther away? They said they would. In a week the lady was back in the sheriff's office. There was a strange light in her eye. "They've gone upstream," she said, "but I can still see them from the attic window with spyglasses."

The Hunt and the Quarry

Since it's the censor's task, official or arrogated, to track down "offensive" matter he unfailingly manages to overreach himself. No matter how level-headedly he starts out at first, his judgment gets warped in the end. You can't have a chimney sweep without chimneys to sweep.

"It is hardly possible," says Sydney Smith, "that a society for the suppression of vice can ever be kept within the bounds of good sense and moderation. Beginning with the best intentions in the world, such societies must, in all probability, degenerate into a receptacle for every species of tittle-tattle, impertinence and malice. Men whose trade is ratcatching love to catch rats; the bug destroyer seizes upon the bug with delight; and the suppressor is gratified by finding his vice."

The censors have much in common with the diviners of old who could detect hidden sources by means of their rods. After attending a meeting of the followers of his archfoe, Ezra Heywood (Heywood had branded the obscenity statute as the National Gag Law), Comstock wrote: "I looked over the audience of about 250 men and boys. I could see lust in every face." Mr Sumner once confessed in a burst of confidence that he found the ads in the subways of New York shamelessly suggestive, and lamented the fact he could do nothing about it.

The myopia of the censor, being an occupational malady, precludes the exercise of discernment. Evil is glimpsed everywhere. The good is persecuted with the bad: *Reigen* and *Ulysses* are placed on a par with *Only a Boy* and *Fanny Hill;* reproductions of nudes by Rembrandt, Goya and Titian draw the same fire as pornographic post cards; a play like *The Captive* shares the fate of *Pleasure Man* and *The Drag;* bona fide nudist activities are classed with stag exhibitions.

But it isn't always myopia that prompts a moralistic foray. The censors know that suppression is their *raison d'être*. They also know that they must try to justify themselves in the public eye. So if the Hays office or a movie review board raises a fuss about a film and the story gets written up in the papers, and if you happen to have seen the picture at a private screening and wonder what all the shooting's for, don't waste any time puzzling about it. It's just the censors' way of saying to the community: "See, we're alive and kicking. We're protecting you, and don't you forget it." The movie industry is aware of what's going on, and winks its eye. The episodes recur regularly; some cynics claim they can foretell when the next blast will come.

TYRANNY FOR THE MORAL GOOD

Misguided zeal and unwitting blunders are one thing; arbitrary highhandedness is another.

When Comstock set the police on Daly he admitted he had not read Shaw's play and had never seen it performed.

Mr Sumner hounded Halsey, the bookseller in the *Mademoiselle de Maupin* case, to such an extent that Halsey got a judgment of twenty-five hundred dollars against the Vice Society for malicious prosecution.

When he instigated criminal proceedings against *The Well of Loneliness*, Mr Sumner admitted that he had not read it. He raided the publishers' premises,

seized 865 copies, and returned only 815 after the case
was thrown out of court. The attorney for the publishers made an issue of the missing books. Mr Sumner's
retort was that he had never received 865 copies. The
attorney exhibited a receipt signed by Charles J. Bamberger, Mr Sumner's assistant. Mr Sumner said Mr
Bamberger had had no authority to sign a receipt.
Pressed further, he admitted he had distributed twenty-
one copies among "officials." Who were these officials?
Mr Sumner refused to say. As a matter of fact the only
officials entitled to copies were the judges of Special
Sessions and the district attorney.

On another occasion Mr Sumner descended on the
home of I. Lhevinne, a high-school instructor, and
seized printed copies of his novel, *Ariadne*. For good
measure he also carried off the manuscript of *The Girl
from the Boulevards* which Mr Lhevinne had written six years before, and which he had no intention of
publishing. *Ariadne* was cleared of the charge of obscenity, but Mr Lhevinne never got his manuscript back.
Mr Sumner refused to give it up. To be sure, Mr
Lhevinne could have started suit for it. But litigation
costs money, and Mr Lhevinne couldn't afford it. So
Mr Sumner, although defeated at law, chalked up another victory by summary expedient.

This is how he described the case in the 1929 report
of the Vice Society:

In another prosecution a defendant was both author and publisher of a book. He was held for trial by the magistrate, but the
case was transferred to the Court of General Sessions and the
grand jury failed to indict. A manuscript of another book taken
on search warrant from the same defendant might have been
made the subject of a separate proceeding. It was considered by
the district attorney to be legally obscene, and its return to the
defendant was denied on that basis. This author is teacher in one
of the city high schools, and the question may reasonably be

asked of what moral worth in the educational plan is one whose depraved state of mind is so clearly exemplified by his writings.

Here we have a novel theory of law, one that bobs up repeatedly in the annual reports of the Vice Society: it's the district attorney, not judges or juries, who decides what's obscene.

CHAMPIONING THE LAW

Although the administrative censor insists that he does no more than enforce the law, and the non-official censor (such as a decency league of some kind) says that all it does is help the police authorities in ferreting out objectionable matter so that the law may take its course, censors are in fact lawless. They praise the judicial process when it reinforces their prejudices, when it aids and abets them by imposing a fine or a jail sentence in any case in which they are complainants. But do they like reasonable people admit their mistake and let it go at that if the defendant is absolved? No. They denounce the obscenity statute as ineffectual, and accuse the judge of being derelict in his duty.

When the *Contraception* case came up, the customs bureaucrats said they had no feeling about birth-control literature one way or the other; what they wanted was an adjudication. The public therefore had the right to assume that if Dr Stopes' treatise was cleared in court it would not be harassed afterward. But what happened? The moment Judge Woolsey ruled that the book was admissible into this country under section 305 of the Tariff Act, *under which the customs had tried to exclude it,* the officials said that they would ignore the decision, and find some *other* section of the law under which to bar it.

In a letter that Mr Sumner wrote in 1929 he euphemistically referred to methods of legal procedure "in line with developments in our form of democratic government." He professed himself committed to these methods which, he said, led to "the established principle of trial by jury." After pointing out that the result was "always satisfactory to the successful litigant," he went on:

The loser in such litigation may take his defeat quietly as most of us have to take our defeats, or, on the other hand, such defeat may be made the basis of a noisy condemnation of law and procedure. That may be a manifestation of one side of human nature, but it is not in accordance with the theory of the acceptance of the results of lawful procedure which is the American standard.

Reading this, you'd be apt to think that the Vice Society has accepted each court defeat with unfailing good grace, and that the opposition has always indulged in "noisy condemnation" whenever the results have been against it.

In the 1930 report of the Vice Society, William H. Parsons, its president, referred to a case in which the society's complaint had been dismissed by a magistrate after a hearing in court. "To say the least," said Mr Parsons severely, "this magistrate's mind did not function in the interests of the public."

The 1931 report took Magistrate Overton Harris to task for exonerating Clement Wood's *Flesh* (without naming the author or the book, it should be noted). This was the comment:

In another prosecution a "privately printed" book containing several short stories came before one of the newer magistrates. He frankly admitted that he knew very little of the law regarding obscene books. However, he heard the case, gave several adjournments for argument and finally after much wavering decided that in his opinion only one of the stories was legally obscene, and that he did not think he should hold the defendant for trial because of one story out of several. The district attorney has expressed the opinion that the book is clearly legally obscene; further action in this case is contemplated. In the words of the Appellate Division of the Supreme Court: "Of course there are some people who seem to be unable to find anything obscene in anything written."

After noting some setbacks suffered by the society during the year, the 1934 report again adverted to "court decisions which seem to many people to be regrettable and surcharged with public harm." This report was particularly testy, for it contained an account of the *Ulysses* case. Irritated by the courteous treatment accorded by Judge Woolsey to the litigants, Mr Sumner wrote:

After a series of very sociable and friendly hearings and discussions, some at the Bar Association's building, the judge, as was anticipated, wrote a very picturesque opinion, holding that the book was not obscene within the purview of the Customs Law. Thereafter the victorious publisher, with considerable emphasis on the unsavory history of the book, published it and offered it for indiscriminate sale. No consideration was given to the fact that the government might take an appeal from this decision. Probably no appeal would have followed had not a new United States attorney come upon the scene in 1934. Hon. Martin Conboy, who has a high regard for the maintenance of common decency in public print, was this official. He appealed from the decision of the single judge to the United States Circuit Court of Appeals. Here three judges passed on the legal character of the book. Possibly it is not surprising, as these things go, that two of these judges sustained the opinion of their brother of the lower court. One judge dissented.

This was a partial victory for the people, and further appeal to the Supreme Court was in order. The question of appeal was in the hands of the high officials of the Department of Justice. They decided to give up the contest, ignoring the partial and important victory of their New York representative in a district where so-called broad-mindedness seems to be an attribute of several of our judges.

Magistrate Jonah Goldstein's exoneration of Flaubert's novel of adolescence, *November*, drew the following sharp reproof in the 1935 report:

In the course of a written opinion something over a year ago, a judge said of such a book submitted for his judicial opinion: "In many places it seems to me to be disgusting, but although it contains, as I have mentioned above, many words usually considered dirty, I have not found anything that I consider to be dirt for dirt's sake."

We think that the fault is with the judge . . . The unfortunate phase of this judicial expedition into the fields of literary review is this: if the judge is presiding over an important court his example is likely to be followed by magistrates of the inferior courts.

Indeed, the tone of the 1935 report rose to a pitch of desperation:

Within the past fifteen years several opinions have been written in defense of some book or other by or for magistrates, and these have been hailed by the unregenerate as mighty blows in defense of the freedom of thought and the freedom of the press. The force of some of these opinions has been later overcome by grand jury action, a second trial or some other legal means. But enough of these opinions have survived to furnish the groundwork of the defense of any publication, however vile it may be.

Are judges serving the public good only if they see eye to eye with the uplifters? Was there not, in every case the Vice Society cried out against, a full hearing in court for both sides, a weighing of the evidence, a judicial ruling—all the incidents of the orderly administration of justice Mr Sumner considered to be "the American standard"?

If the Vice Society professes, as it did in Mr Sumner's letter in 1929, to take its defeats "quietly," why has it repeatedly tried to get grand jury indictments in cases (*Flesh, November* and *Hsi Men Ching*) which were dismissed by magistrates? Is it in line with our democratic form of government to harass and plague defendants persistently, and to have complainants go shopping from judge to judge (as in the *Female* case) or from judge to grand jury (as in the *Pay Day* case) in the hope of getting an indictment or a conviction by the process of attrition?

OUSTING THE COURTS

Comstock had things pretty much his way. He was —or at least so he believed—public conscience incarnate; he could bully officials and judges. Some of those that followed in his footsteps were not quite as successful. Comstock belonged to the Victorian era; at the turn of the century conventions underwent a revolution, old restraints were swept away, the secrecy and stealth that had characterized the treatment of sex were replaced by healthy curiosity, frank discussion and a desire to build a system of sexual ethics on some firmer basis than that afforded by threat of eternal hell-fire and fear of venereal disease.

Comstock's successors discovered that the courts could no longer be bludgeoned as before into accepting their views, and that fearless judges were more and more apt to appraise open-mindedly the material the uplifters fulminated against. Too many complaints were being dismissed.

This gave the vice hunters a pause. It also gave them an idea. "Why should we go into court," they reasoned, "and risk being thrown out when there are other ways of getting what we're after?" The other ways were intimidation of potential defendants and pressure brought to bear on administrative officials.

Thomas Seltzer, publisher of the early edition of *Casanova's Homecoming,* was "persuaded" to withdraw the book from circulation rather than to run the risk of a legal test. The distribution of Floyd Dell's *Janet March,* of Nezelov's *Josephine* and of many other works was discontinued for the same reason. The exhortation of the censors to the publishers ran something like this: "We think your publication is objectionable. You believe it's all right. You must accept our judgment and stop selling the book. If you don't we'll have you prosecuted criminally. The chances are ten to one we'll convict you. You may go to jail or pay a fine. But even if you're lucky and win we'll put you to a lot of trouble, and you'll have heavy lawyers' fees to pay. Think it over."

What the censors didn't say was this: "We're bigots and meddlers practicing duress pure and simple. You're entitled to a court test of the book we're attacking; more than that, society itself has a vital concern in the freest possible dissemination of ideas. Any agreement with us is cowardly, corrupt and socially reprehensible."

Mr Sumner's threat on *The Well of Loneliness* followed the usual pattern; Covici-Friede, the publishers, defied him and won out in court. But for every concern that stiffened its back and fought there were a dozen others that capitulated.

Pressure groups prevailed on License Commissioner Moss to exile *The Nudist* from city-licensed newsstands long before there was any adjudication on the legality of the magazine. This zealous public servant has consistently lent an ear to moralistic plaints. At one time he sought to have every theatrical producer in New York send his office tickets for pre-openings so as to enable him to make "suggestions" for changes—a brazen attempt at pre-censorship of the stage. Let it be said to the credit of the producers that the effort did not succeed.

And let it be said to the credit of the commissioner

that his righteous fervor was not thereby dampened. On the contrary, he was prompted to reach out into realms alien to sex. It seems that in the play, *Russet Mantle,* which appeared on Broadway some seasons ago, a character bit into an apple and was warned by another that some apples bore a residue of poisonous spray. The applegrowers became alarmed and communicated their fears to the commissioner. He in turn spoke to the producers of the play. But the producers knew their rights. They were aware that the commissioner had not the least vestige of censorship powers under the law, and that he was sticking his nose into something that was no concern of his. Nor were they unmindful of the fact that the commissioner's intercession was freighted with the unspoken threat of revocation of the license of the theater where the play was being shown. But they stood their ground. The dialogue about the apple spray stayed in. And nothing happened.

THE ECONOMIC BOYCOTT

It has remained for a reactionary group in the Catholic Church to perfect the technique of censorship by pressure. The technique has been implemented with the device of economic boycott. The group does not concern itself with judicial tests of the lawfulness of material. It arrives at its own judgments, uses its own methods to impose them on the community and applies its own sanctions when challenged. The technique, the drastic nature of which far exceeds the reasonable scope of spiritual guidance, is best illustrated in its operation with respect to magazines.

(1) The group issues a list of "objectionable" periodicals. The list is the modern equivalent of the historical Index Expurgatorius.

(2) The list is forwarded to parishes, and local committees are organized to enforce them.

(3) The committee members visit all the newsdealers in their community and tell them to take the proscribed publications off their stands on pain of losing all Catholic patronage.

(4) The committee members also communicate with all advertisers in the periodicals who are located in their district, and urge them to withdraw their advertisements. Here, too, the penalty for non-compliance is the loss of patronage.

In a world of totalitarian governments, widespread unrest and dissension, race hatred and religious persecution, this method is fraught with implications of authoritarianism and disaster.

Choosing the Victim

But the censor can't always accomplish what he's after without going to court. If a prosecution is inevitable he has another string to his bow. He can always choose his quarry. And choose him he does, with a measure of guile that does credit to his gift for strategy if not to his sense of fair play.

He won't, as a rule, attack a large and influential publisher, or an important department store, or a well-known bookshop. Such defendants are not readily intimidated, they have resources, they can hire able lawyers, they can whip up the press. And tough opposition is precisely what the censor doesn't want.

So, like the street-corner bully, he picks on small fry. The little man, the impecunious newsdealer or bookseller, does not relish the prospect of a criminal prosecution. It's easy to persuade him to plead guilty upon promise of a suspended sentence or a small fine. He has no great interest in the book attacked, no ax to grind.

The censor thus gets what he wants without any trouble: a prompt surrender, an adjudication of obscenity and a suppression of the book.

In the *Mademoiselle de Maupin* case, the Vice Society singled out Halsey, an employee in a bookshop, as its target. In *The Sex Side of Life* case, the defendant was a lady of very limited means; in the *Hsi Men Ching* case and the *Let's Go Naked* case, the owners of small bookstores; in the Astoria *Female* case, the proprietor of a less-than-average circulating library; in the *Flesh* case, an inconsiderable publisher; in the *November* case, an obscure distributor; in most of *The Birth of a Baby* cases, newsdealers.

That this process is hostile to all our concepts of freedom and fair play cannot be denied. In an obscenity case the nominal defendant is a person—a book clerk or the like—but the real defendant is the book itself. It's on trial for its life. A conviction means a death sentence. From the point of view of the community it is of the utmost importance that a full and impartial trial be had, for suppression is doubly penal: it strikes no less against the potential readers than against the author and his work. Society is thus denied access to condemned material, except through devious and illegal channels. The censor's tactics are therefore tantamount to a deprivation of due process insofar as the material is concerned, and a despoiling of the public.

BAITING THE TRAP

We have spoken of the prospective defendant in a book prosecution as the censor's "quarry."

Evidence in a case of this kind usually consists of a copy of the book and testimony that the defendant sold it or had it in his possession for sale. It sometimes happens that the censor wants to take a book into court but has no evidence. The censor proceeds to stalk his victim the way a hunter stalks game. If the game is innocent (the bookseller singled out may not carry the volume in question) or is wary (the bookseller may not place the work on his shelves but may sell it secretly), the censor does not hesitate to resort to entrapment. That means the defendant-to-be is deliberately tricked into committing a crime.

When, after a ten-year period of sporadic badgering, the post office resolved to proceed against Mrs Dennett, the evidence was obtained by means of a decoy letter sent to her by a "Mrs Miles" from Grottoes, Virginia. "Mrs Miles" was a postal inspector.

For years Mr Sumner and his first lieutenant, Mr Bamberger, have used the name, *Eciv Rotacidare* (vice eradicator reversed), verbally and in writing, for entrapment purposes. The usual procedure is to pose as a Swede bearing that fantastic name when calling in person on a dealer to induce him to sell a pornographic work, or to send an order on a letterhead emblazoned with the name. Personal calls are usually made by Mr Bamberger, for Mr Sumner does not act the role of erotica fancier any too convincingly (he looks like a weary, humorless accountant), while Mr Bamberger has a broad, smoking-room joviality and an air of really enjoying smut. This makes Mr Bamberger a fine *agent provocateur.*

In 1912 the Vice Society wished to proceed against *The Satyricon of Petronius,* which Boni and Liveright had published in a limited edition. Since the edition had been fully subscribed there were no copies for sale to the public. Undaunted, Mr Bamberger visited the shipping room of the publishers and tried to persuade a shipping clerk to sell him a copy. The clerk refused. Mr Bamberger coaxed and cajoled. He was a real booklover, he said. He was particularly interested in the classics. If he couldn't buy a copy of *The Satyricon* could he at least take a look at it? The clerk reluctantly exhibited a copy. Pouncing on it, Mr Bamberger flung twenty dollars at the clerk and fled.

At the trial the Vice Society agent testified that the clerk had demanded thirty dollars and had agreed to take twenty.

Magistrate Oberwager threw the case out of court. He said of the book: "Its value to the student and the scholar is such that it would be too serious a matter to deny access to it, for ancient literature enlarges and enriches the mind . . . Time has determined that this work must survive, and were it simply a piece of obscenity it would have perished long since and never have reached the portals of this tribunal."

MORE CASE HISTORY

In 1920 Mr Bamberger visited Leo Fritzlo, a needy printer, said that he was a businessman and ordered some calling cards. A short time later he placed an order for letterheads. After a few transactions of this kind a pleasant relationship was established. Fritzlo thought he had a steady customer.

One day Mr Bamberger told the printer that some friends of his were arranging a stag party and needed some photographs for souvenirs. Fritzlo protested; that sort of thing was not in his line. But the agent of the Vice Society was insistent. Reluctant to lose a customer, the printer said he'd see what he could do about it.

Mr Bamberger showed up again in a few days. Fritzlo was apologetic; the pictures had slipped his mind. The agent was quite vocal in his disappointment. The printer promised faithfully not to forget the next time. He didn't forget. He handed the pictures over to

Mr Bamberger on his next visit, and was promptly placed under arrest.

At the trial these facts came to light, and Magistrate Joseph F. Schwab was incensed.

"He wasn't doing business there regularly on that kind of stuff?" he asked Mr Bamberger.

"No."

The Magistrate scowled. "Complaint dismissed," he said.

LADY CHATTERLEY'S LOVER

The most widely publicized case of entrapment occurred in Boston.

John Tait Slaymaker, agent of the New England Watch and Ward Society, called on DeLacey, a bookseller, and asked for a copy of D. H. Lawrence's much-debated novel. Mr DeLacey said he did not carry it. Mr Slaymaker urged him to procure a copy. The bookseller demurred, but the agent finally prevailed. Mr DeLacey got hold of the book, sold it to Mr Slaymaker and was convicted.

The Watch and Ward had not reckoned with public opinion. The press was aroused; there were scathing editorials. Even Judge Fosdick, who sat on the case, was outspoken in his censure. "I do think," he said, "that the way in which the defendant was induced to sell the book calls for every part of the condemnation that has been placed on it by counsel for either side. The Court entertains no cordiality for the society."

Although the district attorney had, in the course of the trial, referred to Lawrence as "a filthy degenerate with a sewer brain," he too echoed the Court's attitude: "I want the public to understand that the district attorney does not indorse the Watch and Ward Society's policy or tactics. I serve warning here and now that as long as I am district attorney and agents of this society go into a bookstore of good repute and induce and procure the commission of a crime, I will proceed against them for the commission of a crime."

Several of the directors of the society, among them Bishop William A. Lawrence, resigned as a gesture of protest.

William Jay Schieffelin, then president of the New York Vice Society, was asked by the press for his views on tricking people into committing a crime. "I disapprove most emphatically," he said, "and if the same things are done by our agents here I object to them also."

Mr Sumner not only disagreed unequivocally with Mr Schieffelin, but confessed that he himself had instigated the whole matter. "What was done," he declared, "was thoroughly justified. We had information that the Cambridge bookseller was handling this book. He had sold several copies to Harvard professors (the crime of crimes!) and one to a book collector. To convict him it was necessary to show a sale. What difference does it make that Slaymaker had to go to his store several times and finally got him to send to New York for a copy?"

The cat was out of the bag. Mr DeLacey had been convicted to protect the morals of Harvard professors.

PAYING THE PIPER

Most people have to pay for their mistakes. The censors don't.

If the postmaster excludes a book from the mails and the publisher loses substantial revenue the likelihood of the latter recovering damages from the former is nil, even though a court later decides against the postmaster. The collector of customs, motion-picture boards of review and other administrative officials appear to enjoy the same immunity. Even the semi-official censors

—the vice societies and the lone uplifters—can make their forays without fear of retaliation. The Halsey case is the whitest of white crows. Since then the New York Society for the Suppression of Vice has led a charmed existence. Even though it has been sued repeatedly for malicious prosecution as a result of the court dismissal of groundless charges of obscenity brought by it—in one case the jury returned a verdict of five hundred dollars—it has not been called on to pay a penny.

If judges and juries show such tender solicitude for the war chests of vice societies, why shouldn't the censors arrive at snap judgments? Why shouldn't they give free rein to their prejudices? Why shouldn't they indulge in arbitrary tactics? Why shouldn't they try to assume powers they don't possess? The worst thing that can happen to them is to be told by the courts that they were wrong. A verbal rap on the knuckles and usually a polite one at that. It makes no difference how much damage they have inflicted. They don't have to make good.

SHIELD INTO WEAPON

Ostensibly society's buckler against the slings and arrows of sex corruption, the obscenity law is often a sword that slays an altogether different foe.

Balzac's *Droll Stories* has long been hounded as tending to arouse lustful and lecherous desire, although it seems clear that the basic objection to it has been its irreverent treatment of the Church. Does not Balzac speak again and again of the "itching of the theological palm," the hawking about of indulgences and excommunications, the sensuality and greed of the clergy from cardinal to the lowliest friar? Does he not in almost every story speed such telling shafts as this from "The

Fair Imperia": "The poor old archbishop, having arrived at an age when he was physically incapable of sinning, now passed for a saint"?

Instances of ulterior purpose in criminal prosecutions for obscenity are numerous. Fred Warren, editor of the *Appeal to Reason,* and Hobart Croomer, the editor of another paper, were found guilty under the Comstock Law, although their real offense was Socialist activities. Carlo Tresca, the famous radical, went to jail ostensibly for publishing a birth-control advertisement in his paper *Il Martello;* the actual reason for the prosecution was the anti-Fascist policy of his publication. Mrs Dennett has told his story in full in her book, *Who's Obscene?*

Ezra Heywood's chief crime was his violent opposition to Comstock; he demanded the repeal of "The National Gag Law"; he received a two-year sentence under the statute which the red-whiskered crusader had wrung from Congress in 1873.

In the *Madeleine* case the same statute was used as a ruthless weapon in a private grudge fight. It is not improbable that the animus behind the prosecution of Mrs Dennett was not so much official opposition to the dissemination of sex information as religious disapproval of her persistent efforts over many years to amend the birth-control law. And the argument of the United States attorney in the Circuit Court of Appeals on *Ulysses* made it abundantly clear that Joyce's derisive attitude toward religion, not his forthrightness as to sex, was the real offense.

John Steinbeck's *The Grapes of Wrath* has been banned in several places, including the Imperial Valley in California, and Kansas City. The book tells the story of migratory farm workers who lost their lands in Oklahoma and Kansas, and went to California in quest of a new haven. It is an indictment of unplanned society, and an impassioned plea for the disinherited and the dispossessed. The reason given for the Kansas City suppression was the use of a few four-letter words by some of the characters in the novel.

Motion-picture review boards were originally set up to prevent the exploitation of sex on the screen. The statutes creating them have not been changed, and yet today they are warring against such films as *Spain in Flames, The Spanish Earth, Millions of Us, Concentration Camp* and many other films, the basic objection to which is their political ideology. The Legion of Decency made no bones about the real basis of its objection to *Blockade*.

The Metropolitan Motion Picture Council, an independent body affiliated with the National Board of Review and responsible for important studies of the screen, condemns movie censorship on the grounds that it is:

(1) An aspersion on public morality.
(2) An insult to American intelligence.
(3) An excuse for indirect taxation of the industry.
(4) An opportunity to dispense political patronage.
(5) An obstacle to the production of truly entertaining adult films.
(6) A violation of the Bill of Rights; and
(7) An ideal instrument for the promotion of bigotry and intolerance and a possible implementing of Fascism, Nazism and Communism.

We may well look askance on any gag law which is so broad in its terms and so vague in its criteria that it may be readily invoked by governmental officials or other persons to achieve ends that were never contemplated by the framers of the law.

CHAPTER XVII

Conclusion

Since I have been interested in this work I have found that the blackest mud is to be found behind the trees on which the sun shines brightest. In that shadow the slime lies thick.

ANTHONY COMSTOCK, *The Evening Mail* (1906)

GEORGE MOORE ONCE SAID that even if the censors succeeded in sweeping from the face of the earth every vestige of material that might conceivably tend to arouse emotions of sex, the spring breeze would still remain to quicken the pulses of men and women.

No one has ever summed up the futility of sex censorship more succinctly.

HALF A LOAF

If attempts to repeal the existing obscenity laws have met with rebuffs—the sponsor of the repealing statute being in some cases made the victim of political reprisal—some solace may be found in the fact that no new sex-censorship laws have been passed, and that attempts to tighten the old ones have been consistently defeated.

The Patman Bill to purify the movies has gone down to defeat a number of times. A similar fate has met the equally unconscionable Post Office Bill which has periodically bobbed up in Congress. Under the postal law as it now stands a person accused of sending obscene or contraceptive matter through the mails can be prosecuted only in the federal district where the mailing occurs. The postal authorities have for years complained that the bulk of the "objectionable" matter distributed in this country flows from New York City, and that it is extremely difficult to secure convictions there. The last part of their complaint is undoubtedly true. But they have themselves to thank. Had the government not made itself ridiculous by prosecuting Mrs Dennett and condemning *Married Love* and *Ulysses,* it would have been in a much better position to proceed against outright pornography, and the New York courts would not have been compelled to lay down liberal rules which hamper convictions in less deserving cases.

The proposed Post Office Bill would give the federal authorities the choice of trying a defendant either in the district of mailing or in the district of *receiving.* In other words, the government could arbitrarily select the most benighted and bigoted section of the country (where a conviction would be a virtual certainty), send a decoy order from there to New York and place the sender on trial in the district so chosen. A New York publisher could be tried in Kentucky or Utah or California. What a simple way to convert the intermeddling of the postmaster into a dictatorship!

WORDS, WORDS, WORDS

It is not hard to catalogue the sins of censorship. To suggest a solution is quite another matter.

Free speech and a free press, we say, are the inalienable attributes of democracy. But liberty, we are warned, is not license. It doesn't mean (as the late Mr Justice Holmes pointed out) that one may get up and shout *fire!* in a crowded theater. There are limits to what a man can say or print; if he oversteps the line he can be brought to justice. His rights as an individual must not be so exercised as to infringe the equal rights of others or the general good. These generalities are mere words; they're planks in a platform not signposts.

A riot is bad for the community; a man maligned in his trade or profession is bound to have trouble earning a living; a corrupt society is doomed. So the law says: "You may speak your mind freely, but if you incite to violence we'll jail you; if you utter a libel we'll make you pay damages, and if you offend decency we'll muzzle you." To be sure, the law doesn't define these ifs; they are enunciated in loose general terms, and their enforcement is left to officialdom. So we have words again: words which law-enforcement agencies may twist any way they wish to serve their particular notions of expediency, or to please pressure groups, or to express their spite or prejudice or wrongheadedness.

Some Axioms

Much of the confusion that plagues discussions of this kind could be cleared up if a few basic points were recognized.

(1) For the first hundred years of our national existence we had no obscenity laws. We got along without them. There is nothing to indicate that we were headed for perdition.

(2) Nor is there any evidence that after 1873 our morality improved, or if it did improve, that the Comstock laws were responsible.

(3) The code of decency of an age springs directly from the people of that age; it represents a consensus; it cannot be dictated by saints or sinners. If the majority of people at any time and place want something which is objectionable to those in power, they will get it no matter how rigorous

the interdict. Prohibition didn't stop drinking, any more than the cropping of ears stopped the unlicensed use of the printing press in Queen Elizabeth's day.

(4) The rallying cry of the uplifters resounds with such good old stand-bys as "the shielding of the young and impressionable" and "the protection of society from sex filth." The movement has the aura of embattled respectability; everyone on the other side is an abettor of evil, a champion of corruption, an accomplice of the devil.

(5) Morality statutes are easy to acquire and hard to get rid of.

(6) The law, always behind the times, is especially a laggard when it comes to matters of decency.

(7) Social customs do not wait for the law to catch up; people simply ignore the law and, by ignoring it, make it a dead letter.

It is in these truisms that we must seek clues to a practical approach. Three broad lines of procedure suggest themselves: legislative change, education of the public and court fights.

As to the first, we must bear in mind that the Comstock laws have been with us for more than three generations. It's folly to expect to wipe them out overnight. A common-sense legislative program must be specific, workable and moderate; it must be tempered with patience. The most that can be hoped for by way of immediate result is the elimination of the worst statutes and a revision of the rest.

However active the fight for modification or repeal, too much faith shouldn't be pinned to either. Nullification must go on. Its processes must be kept alive by showing up censorship for what it is, by publicizing the falsity of its premises, by dramatizing its hostility to our institutions, by exposing its blunders and futilities.

And every attempt to throttle free expression, no matter what the source or purported reason, must be stubbornly and aggressively resisted in the courts. A default to the censor is not individual surrender; it's a betrayal of the public.

As to Legislation

We have said that a legislative policy must be clean-cut and practical. What, specifically, should be done about the Comstock Law?

Should it be abolished altogether? Should it be modified so that it will be directed solely against pornography, of the *Only a Boy* and French post-card type? How about the dissemination of contraceptive literature and advice? Should nudist books and practices be banned? Should we try to correct the pernicious looseness of the statutory words—obscene, lewd, lascivious and indecent—by enacting precise and elaborate criteria of decency, like those of the Motion Picture Production Code? Or should we refrain from tampering with the law and seek to avoid its misapplication by entrusting its enforcement to better censors?

Vice crusaders have always had a twofold advantage over the liberal forces: organization and singleness of purpose. The Sumners and the Yarrows know exactly what they're after, and the groups they head back them up with unanimity. But those on the other side of the fence can agree only as to one thing: that they're on the other side. As to everything else there is dissent.

Some of them think that there should be no obscenity law at all. Public taste, they say, is a sufficient bulwark against smut; community reaction will always drive offensive material from the market place; the law is a useless nuisance. Others insist that the law is all right, and that whatever ills there are flow from its misapplication; the remedy they urge is administrative reform, with emphasis on the more scrupulous selection of censors and the elimination of politics. Middle-of-the-roaders wish to see the law amended so as to narrow its scope to pornography alone.

The spectrum of decency runs from Sunday-school stuff at one end to unmitigated filth at the other. Obscenity lies somewhere, perhaps midway, between these extremes. What of the shadowy no man's land between obscenity and smut? Where should we draw the line?

One thing is certain. Any attempt to legislate a detailed code would be disastrous. The vagueness of the statutory words is bad enough, but at least a measure of elasticity exists which enables conscientious judges to interpret the law in the light of the times. A rigid set of rules would be infinitely worse because it would hamstring the courts and destroy the "changing content" of the statute so essential to its sane administration.

A Starting Point

Here is the tentative outline of a legislative program which is moderate enough to warrant hope of success and yet sufficiently forward looking to yield real gains:

(1) Obscenity laws in all jurisdictions should be amended so as to make it indisputably clear that they are aimed solely against smut—dirt for dirt's sake—such as photographs of perverted practices and nothing else.

(2) The federal postal law should be amended so as to harmonize its procedure with that under the Tariff Act. The postmaster should not be permitted, by a mere administrative gesture, to exclude matter from the mails. Whatever material he challenges should be made subject to a jury trial.

(3) The opinions or policies of a newspaper or a periodical should never be made the basis of granting or revoking second-class mailing privileges.

(4) Motion-picture censorship should be abolished throughout the country. There are penal provisions in every state which afford ample protection against immoral exhibitions. Failing this, the law should be amended: (a) to remove the appointment of film review boards from politics, and to assure trained and competent reviewers, possibly through civil service; and (b) to compel the reviewers to make their records available to the public.

(5) The Wales Theater Padlock Law and similar statutes or ordinances should be repealed.

(6) State and federal laws against the dissemination of contraceptive advice and material should be wholly repealed. Failing this, the ban on birth control should be removed from general obscenity statutes—at the present time contraceptive advice is in the same legal category as pornography—and specific exemptions should be created in favor of physicians, nurses, hospitals, clinics and so on. These exemptions exist today by judicial interpretation, but since they are sometimes flouted by obdurate officials they should be made part of the law.

(7) The birth-control ban should be excised from the Tariff Act. Contraceptive books and supplies should be free to enter this country no matter to whom addressed, and after entry should be subject to the laws of the various jurisdictions. At the present time only "qualified persons," physicians and the like, may receive such material.

(8) Indecent-exposure laws in all jurisdictions should be revised so as to expressly exempt legitimate nudist activities. Anti-nudist laws should be repealed.

(9) The laws under which licensing authorities operate should be amended so as to obviate pre-censorship by license refusal or revocation, and to provide that licenses may be refused or revoked only upon conviction for obscenity.

(10) The rules of evidence should be changed so as to permit the introduction of expert testimony (by literary critics, pub-

lishers, authors and, in proper instances, physicians, psychologists, psychiatrists, prison and hospital officials, welfare workers and the like) in obscenity cases as to the probable effect of the material. The courts have already shown a cautious willingness to accept such proof; the law should be made clear on the subject.

(11) Wherever under state laws vice societies are recognized as quasi-public agencies, such laws should be abolished. Vice societies should be made strictly accountable for their depredations.

(12) New radio legislation should be enacted:

    (a) Requiring each station to set aside regular periods at the desirable times of the day and evening for uncensored discussion on a nonprofit basis on public, social, political and economic problems, and for educational purposes;

    (b) Making it mandatory for every station presenting a controversial issue to give a hearing to at least one opposing view.

    (c) Freeing stations, but not speakers, from legal liability for remarks on such programs.

    (d) Requiring stations to keep accurate and public records of all applications for time, indicating which were granted and which refused and why.

Root and Flower

The dominant social element in every age seeks to curb that which is hostile to its principles or existence. When the Church ruled, heresy and blasphemy were warred against. With the waning of religious dominance and the advent of Victorian morality, sex became the bugaboo. Industrial unrest precipitates sanctions against syndicalism. In times of political stress or war it is sedition that must be rooted out.

With the world as it is today, the future of censorship is not hard to foresee. Though there may be sporadic squawks from cranks outraged by this or that bit of erotica, and consequent bursts of activity on the part of officialdom, sex is no longer a real issue. The shackles of mid-Victorian morality have been cast off. The asterisk has vanished permanently from the novel; four-letter words may be frowned on as bad taste, but they're legitimate if the rationale of the story needs them. Sex-instruction books, and works dealing with the pathological and anthropological phases of sex—Krafft-Ebing, Forel, Stekel, Malinowski, Hirschfeld, Bloch, Mantegazza, Ellis—may be picked up by anyone in a bookshop or drugstore. "Free love" and "trial marriage" were fighting words a generation ago; today they sound curiously trite and dated. For all the fulminations against nudism, women's bathing suits have become more and more abbreviated; and now that the great majority of men wear only swimming trunks, it's difficult to believe that only a few years ago men were arrested for dispensing with the shirts. The Pecksniffs and the Grundys have tried to buck the tide of popular will and have been swept aside.

The clash today is not between convention and sexual freedom, but between irreconcilable political ideologies. Half the people of the world today live under the iron heel of dictators. The Second World War is on. The power and menace of the totalitarian countries, with all their trappings of propaganda, regimentation of opinion, secret police, persecution of minorities, concentration camps, purges, flouting of individual rights, are dismaying enough. But what is infinitely more disturbing is that illiberalism has made inroads on the democracies.

Even before France declared war against Germany it was governed by decrees; the General Election had been postponed for two years. In England the picture is no brighter.

In this country too there have been disquieting signs. Tinhorn Hitlers have sprung up in many places. In Jersey City "I-am-the-law" Hague makes a brazen attempt to nullify the right of public assemblage and to deport "undesirables" from his bailiwick; the case has to be carried to the Supreme Court to rescue Jersey City from the Rome-Berlin axis. Re-elected mayor of Omaha, Dan Butler, warns: "I'm not backtracking one bit," and points proudly to his record, which includes the emasculation of *Tobacco Road* and *Idiot's Delight* and *Yes, My Darling Daughter,* and the removal of Mari Sandoz' *Slogum House* from the public library shelves.

Down South the Klan rides again. Wearied by the internecine warfare between the A.F. of L. and the C.I.O., many states have enacted antiunion laws. Wisconsin, the Wisconsin of old Bob La Follette, is one of them. Vigilante groups have been formed in dozens of places to combat labor "lawlessness." In Louisiana Governor Leche has resigned, and the Long dynasty reigns again. The hatred sown by the Coughlins, the Fritz Kuhns, the Moseleys, the Campbells, the Pelleys, has infected Congress; the last session witnessed a flood of bills hatched in bigotry. One bill would jail aliens who are to be deported but cannot return to their countries; another would stop all immigration for five years; another would prescribe fingerprinting and concentration camps for aliens; still another would so broaden the application of espionage laws as to make them ready instruments for all sorts of reprisal. Senator Reynolds publicly praises the blood-and-iron regimes of Germany and Italy, and Representative Thorkelson professes to see much to justify religious persecution in

Europe. The National Labor Relations Act, labor's Magna Charta, has been viciously attacked by the die-hards.

But there are some encouraging signs also. The Supreme Court has made no bones about rapping Hague's knuckles. Out in Omaha, Methodist Bishop Osnam has applied the corrective of ridicule to Mayor Butler's purification of the stage, saying: "Every little damma must be taken from our drama." The Oppressive Labor Practices bill, the fruit of the efforts of the La Follette Committee, may yet become law; it makes the hiring of labor spies and strikebreakers a criminal offense, forbids the use of private police by big corporations and gives the government the right to cancel any government order if the contractor resorts to any of these antilabor expedients. Numerous organizations, among them the Council against Intolerance, the Congress on Education for Democracy, and the Committee of Catholics for Human Rights (formerly the Committee of Catholics to Fight Anti-Semitism), are at work counteracting the preachments of the Bunds, the Orders of the White Camellia, the liberty leagues, the Stalinists.

THE HANDWRITING ON THE WALL

Censorship is at the crossroads. It is not hard to guess which way it will go. At the outset it will not seek to curb newspapers, since the "freedom of the press" is too risky a concept to challenge. It will fasten onto the radio and the movies instead. It will use every weapon in the arsenal of intolerance: new throttling legislation, the perversion of old laws to uses never contemplated (*Spain in Flames* and *Professor Mamlock* were both attacked under censorship statutes aimed

against obscenity), intimidation, economic boycott (remember what the Legion of Decency did to *Blockade*),
burdensome taxation, licensing.

The nation's safety and welfare—a term as dan-
gerously vague and elastic as censorship—will be the
tocsin; Americanism will be the banner; "police power"
will be the battery. Hague's rout at the hand of the
Supreme Court cannot blind us to the fact that in recent
years the constitutionality of repressive laws and ordinances have been repeatedly upheld under the principle
of police power; and it cannot be doubted that the
growth of police power represents a grave menace to
constitutional liberties. During the last decade or two
the federal government has vastly extended the scope of
its surveillance over the mental fare of the people.
The old New York *World* (which had dared to defy
Theodore Roosevelt's big stick in exposing some of the
malodorous details of the Panama Canal deal) was
moved to observe in 1929: "In spite of the Constitution of the United States, which plainly intended that
such matters be left to the states, we witness a constant
effort on the part of the federal government to assume
jurisdiction over the morals of citizens. Under the
guise of regulating the management of the mails it has
set up what amounts to a censorship of what can be
printed. Under the guise of regulating interstate commerce it has set up a censorship of citizens' morals and
of the moving pictures that citizens may see. Under the
guise of levying customs it has set up a censorship of
the literature that citizens may import from abroad."

The era of economic laissez faire is over. All signs
point to a planned economy. Two things are implicit in
the notion of a planned economy: a curtailment of individual rights, at least to the extent required to prevent
a predatory few from effecting the economic enslave-
ment of millions, and the growing power of govern-

ment. All over the country the federal authorities are engaged in vast enterprises: dams, canals, tunnels, bridges. It's only a question of time before the railroads are taken over. Whenever a government gets too powerful or a business too big, abuses creep in. And free criticism, an indispensable corrective, is bound to be bitterly resented.

The principle of epidemics applies to world affairs. When a disease is quiescent the bacteria seem less virulent. When the disease reaches an epidemic stage the bacteria acquire a special malignancy. The same effect may be observed with respect to the spread of the totalitarian idea throughout the world. The ascendant potency of the idea tends to reduce the resistance of the democracies. Not only are civil liberties doomed in the bailiwicks of the dictators, but they are imperiled everywhere else.

The war to end war did nothing of the kind. Militarism has been reborn; another World War is on. The United States is rearming feverishly. Rearmament psychology is a prelude to war psychology; in either case increased intolerance is inevitable.

No one doubts that if we become involved in the war this country will be put on an authoritarian basis. There will be a fresh crop of illiberal laws. And when the war is over, whatever the outcome, the central authority will not willingly surrender its power. There are pessimists who say that a vote for war by the United States means a vote to end our democracy. That may be an exaggeration. But surely it will be an evil day for free speech and free press.

THE ROAD AHEAD

Watching the stream of world events, aware of the growing force of bigotry in this country, one finds it easy to grow alarmed. Prophets of doom are shrilling everywhere. Hate and cruelty, they say, are hurtling man to his destruction; the face of the earth is darkened by rapacity; humanity is eaten with cancer; a new Dark Age is in the offing.

So did Jeremiah cry out in the wilderness. So too did Savonarola thunder in Florence, Luther in Wittenberg, Calvin in Geneva. And yet the world has managed to survive and make a modicum of progress.

To those who think that it was not by accident that countless centuries ago man dropped from the trees and began walking upright, the counsels of despair are not too persuasive. Believers in man's destiny do not ignore reality. They realize that tolerance, however nobly it may thrive in peace and prosperity, will dwindle in times of stress. But they also know that no worth-while society can be built on a system which enslaves man and exalts the state. They refuse to admit that America faces a choice between Fascism and Communism. They cling to the democratic ideal because it is predicated upon a recognition of the basic rights of man as an individual; because, springing from the common will, its mandates are voluntarily assumed instead of being dictated by some power above; because it exists for the citizen, not the citizen for it; because its attributes are freedom of speech, freedom of the press, freedom of public assemblage, freedom of religious conviction, without which men decay.

The American Way

Two things are certain. One is that democracy must tolerate propaganda directed against itself; free trade in ideas means that even those who attack democracy must be heard. The other is that democracy cannot be preserved by making passionate appeals to maintain traditional ideas, nor by silencing the advocates of change. It must justify itself as a way of life. It must convince the people that it is better for them to live under a democracy than under a Hitler or a Stalin.

"Persecution for the expression of opinions," said the late Mr Justice Holmes in his dissenting opinion in the Schenck case, Mr Justice Brandeis concurring, "seems to me perfectly logical. If you have no doubt of your premises or your power and want a certain result with all your heart, you naturally express your wishes in law and sweep away all opposition. To allow opposition by speech seems to indicate that you think the speech impotent, as when a man says that he squared the circle, or that you do not care wholeheartedly for the result, or that you doubt either your power or your premises. But when men have realized that time has upset many fighting faiths they may come to believe, even more than they believe in the very foundations of their own conduct, that the ultimate good desired is better reached by free trade in ideas, that the best test of truth is the power of the thought to get itself accepted in the competition of the market; and that truth is the only ground upon which their wishes safely can be carried out. That, at any rate, is the theory of our Constitution. It is an experiment as all life is an experiment. Every year, if not every day, we have to wager our salvation upon some prophecy based upon imperfect knowledge. While that experiment is part of our system I think that we should be eternally vigilant against attempts to check the expression of opinions that we loathe and believe to be fraught with death, unless they so imminently threaten immediate interference with the lawful and pressing purposes of the law that an immediate check is required to save the country."

Mark Twain once observed that ours was a country where we had three unspeakably precious things: freedom of speech, freedom of conscience and the prudence never to practice either. Just as pacifism with its anemic dove could not stop war, so cynicism or despair or mild protest will not avail against prejudice, fanaticism and inhumanity. Militancy must be met with militancy. Democracy must become a fighting faith. Every attempt to undermine it or to curtail freedom in any form, however cunning the guise, must be exposed and fought.

If liberty is worth having, it's worth fighting for. It looks like a lot of fighting ahead.

APPENDIX

APPENDIX A
IMPORTANT COURT DECISIONS

MADEMOISELLE DE MAUPIN, By THEOPHILE GAUTIER

Halsey v. New York Society (1922)
234 N.Y. 1, 136 N.E. 219, affirming 194 App. Div. 961,
185 N.Y. Supp. 931 (1st Dep't 1920)

The Court of Appeals refused to disturb the jury's finding that the New York Society for the Suppression of Vice had not acted reasonably in instigating a criminal prosecution against a bookseller based on the sale of a copy of *Mademoiselle de Maupin*.

Hiscock, Ch. J., Cardozo, Pound and McLaughlin, JJ., concur with Andrews, J.; Crane, J., reads a dissenting opinion in which Hogan, J., concurs.

Prevailing Opinion by Judge Andrews:

On November 17, 1917, in the city of New York, the plaintiff sold to an agent of the defendant, one Sumner, an English translation of "Mademoiselle de Maupin." Mr. Sumner submitted the book to City Magistrate House who, however, took no action. He then on November 22d presented a marked copy to Magistrate Simms with a letter calling attention to certain pages which he thought deserved examination. On the 28th he also presented a verified complaint to this magistrate charging that the book was obscene and indecent, referring not only to the marked pages but to the entire work. Thereupon an order was issued stating that it appeared "from the within depositions and statements that the crime therein mentioned has been committed" and holding the plaintiff to answer. The plaintiff was arrested at the direction of Sumner and arraigned. He waived examination, was held for the action of the Court of Special Sessions, tried and acquitted. The record of that trial is not before us, but it was conceded that the copy of "Mademoiselle de Maupin" had been sold by the plaintiff and the acquittal was for the reason, apparently, that the book was not obscene or indecent. This action to recover damages for malicious prosecution was then begun. At the close of the evidence the case was submitted to the jury which found a verdict for the plaintiff. The Appellate Division has affirmed the judgment entered thereon.

The entire book was offered in evidence. We are asked to say from its bare perusal that probable cause existed for the belief on the part of Sumner that the plaintiff was guilty by its sale of a violation of section 1141 of the Penal Law.

In an action for malicious prosecution one of the elements of the plaintiff's case is lack of probable cause. Whether or not this fact has been established may be for the jury to determine. Or it may become a question of law for the court. It is for the jury either when the circumstances upon which the answer depends are disputed or where conflicting inferences may fairly be drawn from them. (*Burns* v. *Wilkinson,* 228 N.Y. 113; *Galley* v. *Brennan,* 216 N.Y. 118.)

Theophile Gautier is conceded to be among the greatest French writers of the nineteenth century. When some of his earlier works were submitted to Sainte-Beuve, that distinguished critic was astonished by the variety and richness of his expression. Henry James refers to him as a man of genius (North American Review, April, 1873). Arthur Symons (Studies in Prose and Verse), George Saintsbury (A Short History of French Literature), James Breck Perkins (Atlantic Monthly, March, 1887) all speak of him with admiration. They tell of his command of style, his poetical imagery, his artistic conceptions, his indescribable charm, his high and probably permanent place in French literature. They say that in many respects he resembles Thackeray.

This was the man who in 1836 published "Mademoiselle de Maupin." It is a book of over four hundred pages. The moment it was issued it excited the criticism of many, but not all of the great Frenchmen of the day. It has since become a part of French literature. No review of French writers of the last one hundred years fails to comment upon it. With the author's felicitous style, it contains passages of purity and beauty. It seems to be largely a protest against what the author, we believe mistakenly, regards as the prudery of newspaper criticism. It contains many paragraphs, however, which taken by themselves are undoubtedly vulgar and indecent.

No work may be judged from a selection of such paragraphs alone. Printed by themselves they might, as a matter of law, come within the prohibition of the statute. So might a similar selection from Aristophanes or Chaucer or Boccaccio or even from the Bible. The book, however, must be considered broadly as a whole. So considered, critical opinion is divided. Some critics, while admitting that the novel has been much admired, call it both "pornographic and dull." (The Nation, Nov. 2, 1893.) Mr. Perkins writes that "there is much in Mademoiselle de Maupin that is unpleasant, and is saved only by beauty of expression from being vulgar. Though Gautier's style reached in this novel its full perfection, it is far from his best work and it is unfortunate that it is probably the one best known." An article in the June, 1868, issue of the Atlantic Monthly says that this is Gautier's representative romance. James calls it his one disagreeable performance but "in certain lights the book is almost ludicrously innocent, and we are at a loss what to think of those critics who either hailed or denounced it as a serious profession of faith." Finally in "A Century of French Fiction," Benjamin W. Wells, professor of modern languages in the University of the South, says: "Mademoiselle de Maupin is an exquisite work of art, but it spurns the conventions of received morality with a contempt that was to close the Academy to Gautier forever. With a springboard of fact in the seventeenth century to start from, he conceives a wealthy and energetic girl of twenty, freed from domestic restraints and resolved to acquire, by mingling as man among men, more knowledge of the other sex than the conventions of social intercourse would admit. He transfers the adventures from the real world to a sort of forest of Arden, where the Rosalind of Shakspere might meet a Watteau shepherdess and a melancholy Jacques. Thus he helps us over the instinctive repulsion that we feel for the situation, and gives a purely artistic interest to the self-revelation that comes to his heroine and to Albert from their prolonged association. Various forms of love reaching out for an unattainable ideal occupy the body of the book, and when once the actors learn to know themselves and each other Gautier parts them forever. In its ethics the book is opposed to the professed morality of nearly all, and doubtless to the real morality of most, but as Sainte-Beuve said of it: 'Every physician of the soul, every moralist, should have it on some back shelf of his library,' and those who, like Mithridates, no longer react to such poisons will find in Mlle. de Maupin much food for the purest literary enjoyment."

We have quoted estimates of the book as showing the manner in which it affects different minds. The conflict among the members of this court itself points a finger at the dangers of a censorship entrusted to men of one profession, of like education and similar surroundings. Far better than we, is a jury drawn from those of varied experiences, engaged in various occupations, in close touch with the currents of public feeling, fitted to say whether the defendant had reasonable ground to believe that a book such as this was obscene or indecent.

Here is the work of a great author, written in admirable style, which has become a part of classical literature. We may take judicial notice that it has been widely sold, separately and as a part of every collection of the works of Gautier. It has excited admiration as well as opposition. We know that a book merely obscene soon dies. Many a Roman poet wrote a Metamorphoses. Ovid survives. So this book also has lived for a hundred years.

On the other hand, it does contain indecent paragraphs. We are dealing too with a translation where the charm of style may be attenuated. It is possible that the morality of New York city to-day may be on a higher plane than that of Paris of 1836—that there is less vice, less crime. We hope so. We admit freely that a book may be thoroughly indecent, no matter how great the author or how fascinating the style. It is also true that well-known writers have committed crimes, yet it is difficult to trace the connection between this fact and the question we are called upon to decide. Doctor Dodd was hanged for forgery, yet his sermons were not indecent. Oscar Wilde was convicted of personal wrongdoing and confined in Reading gaol. It does not follow that all his plays are obscene. It is also true that the work before us bears the name of no publisher. That the house which issued it was ashamed of its act is an inference not perhaps justified by any evidence before us.

Regarding all these circumstances, so far as they are at all material, we believe it is for the jury, not for us, to draw the conclusion that must be drawn. Was the book as a whole of a character to justify the reasonable belief that its sale was a violation of the Penal Law? The jury has said that it was not. We cannot say as a matter of law that they might not reach this decision. We hold that the question of probable cause was properly submitted to them.

We have examined various other questions called to our attention. The jury was told that malice was to be presumed if there were no probable cause for the prosecution. This is not an accurate statement of the law. Under such circumstances malice may be presumed. It is not an inference which the jury is required to draw. (*Stewart* v. *Sonneborn*, 98 U.S. 187, 193.) The attention of the trial judge, however, was not called to this error by any exception. Nor do other exceptions as to the exclusion of evidence and as to the refusal of various requests to charge justify a reversal of the judgment appealed from.

The judgment must, therefore, be affirmed, with costs.

Dissenting Opinion by Judge Crane:

Section 1141 of the Penal Law provides that a person who sells any obscene, lewd, lascivious, indecent or disgusting book is guilty of a misdemeanor.

On the 28th day of November, 1917, the defendant filed an information in the Magistrates Court of the city of New York charging the plaintiff with the violation of this section in having sold a book entitled "Mademoiselle de Maupin" by Theophile Gautier. The accused, having waived examination before the magistrate, was held for the Special Sessions where he was thereafter tried and found not guilty. He thereupon commenced this action charging this defendant with having maliciously prosecuted him, in that it caused his arrest without any probable cause to believe him guilty of having sold an indecent book; in other words, charging the defendant with having no reasonable grounds to believe "Mademoiselle de Maupin" an indecent publication.

There have been two trials of this action. On the first trial the judge charged the jury as a matter of law that there was no probable cause to believe this book indecent.

On appeal this was reversed on the ground that probable cause in this case was a question of fact for the jury and not for the court. (*Halsey* v. *N.Y. Society for the Suppression of Vice,* 191 App. Div. 245.)

The question of probable cause, when there is no conflict in the evidence, no disputed facts, nor any doubt upon the evidence or inferences to be drawn from it, is one of law for the court, and not of fact for the jury. (*Heyne* v. *Blair,* 62 N.Y. 19; *Hazzard* v. *Flury,* 120 N.Y. 223; *Wass* v. *Stephens,* 128 N.Y. 123.)

In *Carl* v. *Ayers* (53 N.Y. 14, 17) the court, speaking through ANDREWS, J., said: "A person making a criminal accusation may act upon appearances, and if the apparent facts are such that a discreet and prudent person would be led to the belief that a crime had been committed by the person charged, he will be justified, although it turns out that he was deceived and that the party accused was innocent. Public policy requires that a person shall be protected, who in good faith and upon reasonable grounds causes an arrest upon a criminal charge, and the law will not subject him to liability therefor. But a groundless suspicion, unwarranted by the conduct of the accused, or by facts known to the accuser, when the accusation is made, will not exempt the latter from liability to an innocent person for damages for causing his arrest."

When facts and circumstances are undisputed, probable cause is a question of law for the court which it is error to submit to the jury. (*Brown* v. *Selfridge,* 224 U.S. 189, 193; *Anderson* v. *How,* 116 N.Y. 336; *Burt* v. *Smith,* 181 N.Y. 1; *Rawson* v. *Leggett,* 184 N.Y. 504.)

In *Besson* v. *Southard* (10 N.Y. 236, 240) we find the law stated as follows: "If the facts which are adduced as proof of a want of probable cause are controverted, if conflicting testimony is to be weighed, or if the credibility of witnesses is to be passed upon, the question of probable cause should go to the jury, with proper instructions as to the law. But where there is no dispute about facts, it is the duty of the court, on the trial, to apply the law to them."

As an instance where the court found on the facts that there was probable cause and dismissed the malicious prosecution complaint see *Murray* v. *Long* (1 Wend. 140). So also, in *Burlingame* v. *Burlingame*

(8 Cowen's Rep. 141) where concededly there was a mistake in making the arrest. See *Driggs* v. *Burton* (44 Vt. 124); *Gilbertson* v. *Fuller* (40 Minn. 413); *Bell* v. *Atlantic C. R. R. Co.* (58 N.J. Law, 227); *Stone* v. *Crocker* (24 Pick. 81); *Bell* v. *Keeplers* (37 Kans. 64).

In *Blachford* v. *Dod* (2 B. & Ad. 179) the facts were these. An attorney was indicted for sending a threatening letter. Being acquitted he brought suit for malicious prosecution and was nonsuited. The court said: "Here the question of probable cause depends on a document coming from the plaintiff himself, viz., the letter sent and written by him to the defendant; and the only question is, whether we are justified in point of law in giving to that letter the construction that it contained a threat of charging the defendants with endeavoring to obtain goods under false pretenses. * * * I concur, therefore, in thinking that the letter, independently of the summons, showed a reasonable and probable cause." (See page 187.)

The construction of the letter and its meaning and whether from its contents there was probable cause was held to be a question of law for the court.

"It was for the judge to construe the written instrument."

If it were always for a jury to determine what reasonable men would do on undisputed facts, there would never be a question of law for the court—the rule would be meaningless.

It was for the trial court and it is now for us to say whether or not, as a matter of law, the defendant had probable cause to believe the plaintiff guilty of selling an obscene book.

At the very outset a marked distinction must be drawn. It cannot be too strongly emphasized that we are not determining whether "Mademoiselle de Maupin" be an indecent book. All we are called upon to determine is whether or not, recognizing the latitude afforded all works of literature and of art, and that tastes may differ, a reasonable, cautious and prudent man would be justified in believing that this publication was obscene and lewd, not in certain passages, but in its main purpose and construction.

When the plaintiff was charged with having violated section 1141 of the Penal Law, that is, charged with a misdemeanor, it necessarily became a question of fact for the triers of fact, Special Sessions or jury, to determine his guilt—to determine whether the book sold was indecent and immoral. (*People* v. *Eastman,* 188 N.Y. 478, 481.)

In a criminal case the questions of fact are always for the jury. In *People* v. *Muller* (96 N.Y. 408, 411) Judge ANDREWS said: "The test of an obscene book was stated in *Regina* v. *Hicklin* (L.R. 3 Q.B. 360), to be, whether the tendency of the matter charged as obscenity is to deprave or corrupt those whose minds are open to such immoral influences, and who might come into contact with it."

The Special Sessions, as the triers of fact, have found the plaintiff not guilty, that is, have found that "Mademoiselle de Maupin" was not such an indecent book as had the tendency spoken of in the *Muller* case. When it came, however, to the trial of this action another question was presented, and that was whether the defendant here and the complainant in the criminal case had reason to believe that the book had this tendency, that is—whether reasonable men would have been justified in believing the book lascivious—corrupting to morals, even though in the mind of a jury they were mistaken.

This reasoning clearly shows that the jury, or triers of fact, in a criminal case have a different question to pass upon than those disposing of the malicious prosecution case. In the latter case when the facts are all conceded, and no different inferences are to be drawn from them, probable cause is a question of law for the court. In this case we have the book. The inferences to be drawn from it are all one way. Vice and lewdness are treated as virtues.

The book was submitted to the magistrate a week before the issuance of the warrant for the plaintiff's arrest. The plaintiff appeared, waived examination, and was held for trial before the Special Sessions. (*Schultz* v. *Greenwood Cemetery,* 190 N.Y. 276.)

What is probable cause? We have quoted above what this Court said about it in *Carl* v. *Ayers* (*supra*) and we cannot add to it. It is such a state of facts presented to the complainant as would incline or move reasonable minded men of the present day and of this generation to believe the accused guilty of the crime charged. Would reasonable, careful, prudent men acting with caution, and environed with the conditions of life as they exist to-day, and not in some past age, be justified in believing "Mademoiselle de Maupin" a filthy and indecent book and published for no useful purpose, but simply from a desire to cater to the lowest and most sensual part of human nature?

In order to justify my conclusion that the defendant had probable cause to believe this book such an one as mentioned in section 1141 of the Penal Law, it is not necessary to spread upon our pages all the indecent and lascivious part of this work. (*People* v. *Eastman, supra,* p. 481). Some facts, however, may be mentioned to give point and direction to this inquiry. In the first place the Society for the Suppression of Vice was confronted with the fact that the publisher, whoever he was, does not put his name to the book.

The book consists of certain letters purported to be written by a young man of twenty-two as a sort of satire on virtue and in praise of the sensual passions, adultery and fornication. It counsels vice. He tells his friend of his love for certain women, describes them, and relates the scenes leading up to immoral practices and to intercourse. To have a mistress in the eyes of this young man is the first qualification of a gentleman, and adultery to him appears to be the most innocent thing in the world. He writes: "I deem it quite a simple matter that a young girl should prostitute herself."

No doubt many books of fine literature known as standard works have passages in them which may shock the moral sensibilities of some people of this day, but they appear as expressions of the times and not to my knowledge as in praise of vice and derision of virtue. Most works, wherever prostitution appears, condemn or confess it as a vice or admit its evil effects and influences. The purport of this book seems to be to impress upon the readers that vice and voluptuousness are natural to society, are not wrongs but proper practices to be indulged in by the young. (*Tyomies Pub. Co.* v. *United States,* 211 Fed. Rep. 385.)

Theophile Gautier published Mlle. De Maupin in 1835. The people of his time condemned it, and by reason of its lasciviousness and bad taste he was forever barred from the French Academy. He acquired a reputation as a writer, but it was not because of this book. The New International Encyclopedia has this to say about Gautier and his Mlle. De Maupin: "Theophile Gautier 1811–1872. Gautier's next book, Mlle. De Maupin (1835), a curious attempt at self-analysis, was a frank expression of Hedonism. Its art is fascinating, but it treats the fundamental postulates of morality with a contempt that closed the Academy to him for life."

In the Encyclopedia Britannica we read the following: "His first novel of any size, and in many respects his most remarkable work, was Mlle. De Maupin. Unfortunately this book while it establishes his literary reputation on an imperishable basis, was *unfitted* by its subject, and in parts by its treatment, for *general perusal,* and created even in France, a prejudice against its author which he was very far from really deserving." (Article by George Saintsbury.) (Italics mine.)

In the Encyclopedia Americana may be read: "Gautier's whole philosophy is a philosophy of paradox, his ideal of life hardly more than a picturesque viciousness. His besetting sin was a desire to say something clever and wicked to shock the Philistines (see Mlle. De Maupin). The Academy was forever closed to him."

When the people of France and Gautier's time condemned his book as being vicious and unfit for general perusal, are we going to say that the defendant in this case did not have probable cause to believe the same thing, when the translation was published in America by a publisher who was ashamed to put his name to it?

Many things have moved in the past century, and with the teachings of church, synagogue and college, we, at least, have the right to expect that the general tone of morality in America in 1922 is equal to that of France in 1835.

It may be true that Gautier's style is fascinating and his imagination rich, but neither style, imagination or learning can create a privileged class, or permit obscenity because it is dressed up in a fashion difficult to imitate or acquire.

American literature has been fairly clean. That the policy of this state is to keep it so is indicated by section 1141 of the Penal Law. The legislature has declared in this section that no obscene, lewd, lascivious or disgusting book shall be sold. Language could not be plainer.

If the things said by Gautier in this book of Mlle. De Maupin were stated openly and frankly in the language of the street, there would be no doubt in the minds of anybody, I take it, that the work would be lewd, vicious and indecent. The fact that the disgusting details are served up in a polished style with exquisite settings and perfumed words makes it all the more dangerous and insidious and none the less obscene and lascivious.

Gautier may have a reputation as a writer, but his reputation does not create a license for the American market.

Oscar Wilde had a great reputation for style, but went to jail just the same. Literary ability is no excuse for degeneracy.

Sufficient to say that a reading of this book convinces me that as a matter of law the Society for the Suppression of Vice had probable cause to believe the defendant, plaintiff, guilty of violating section 1141 of the Penal Law in selling this book and that the complaint in this case should have been dismissed.

ULYSSES, By JAMES JOYCE

U.S. v. One Book Entitled Ulysses
72 F. (2d) 705 (C.C.A. 2d, 1934), affirming 5 F. Supp. 182 (S.D. N.Y. 1933)

The Circuit Court of Appeals affirmed Judge Woolsey's decision in the District Court that *Ulysses* was not obscene.

Before Manton, L. Hand, and Augustus N. Hand, Circuit Judges.

Prevailing opinion by Judge Augustus N. Hand:

This appeal raises sharply the question of the proper interpretation of Section 305 (a) of the Tariff Act of 1930 (19 U.S.C.A. §1305 [a]) That section provides that "all persons are prohibited from import-ing into the United States from any foreign country * * * any obscene book, pamphlet, paper, writing, advertisement, circular, print, picture, drawing, or other representation, figure, or image on or of paper or other material, * * *" and directs that, upon the appearance of any such book or matter at any customs office, the collector shall seize it and in-form the District Attorney, who shall institute proceedings for for-feiture. In accordance with the statute, the collector seized Ulysses, a book written by James Joyce, and the United States filed a libel for for-feiture. The claimant, Random House, Inc., the publisher of the Amer-ican edition, intervened in the cause and filed its answer denying that the book was obscene and was subject to confiscation and praying that it be admitted into the United States. The case came on for trial before Woolsey, J., who found that the book, taken as a whole, "did not tend to excite sexual impulses or lustful thoughts but that its net effect * * * was only that of a somewhat tragic and very powerful commentary on the inner lives of men and women." He accordingly granted a decree adjudging that the book was "not of the character the entry of which is prohibited under the provision of Section 305 of the Tariff

Act of 1930 * * * and * * * dismissing the libel", from which this appeal has been taken.

James Joyce, the author of Ulysses, may be regarded as a pioneer among those writers who have adopted the "stream of consciousness" method of presenting fiction, which has attracted considerable attention in academic and literary circles. In this field Ulysses is rated as a book of considerable power by persons whose opinions are entitled to weight. Indeed it has become a sort of contemporary classic, dealing with a new subject-matter. It attempts to depict the thoughts and lay bare the souls of a number of people, some of them intellectuals, and some social outcasts, and nothing more, with a literalism that leaves nothing unsaid. Certain of its passages are of beauty and undoubted distinction, while others are of a vulgarity that is extreme and the book as a whole has a realism characteristic of the present age. It is supposed to portray the thoughts of the principal characters during a period of about eighteen hours.

We may discount the laudation of Ulysses by some of its admirers and reject the view that it will permanently stand among the great works of literature, but it is fair to say that it is a sincere portrayal with skilful artistry of the "streams of consciousness" of its characters. Though the depiction happily is not of the "stream of consciousness" of all men and perhaps of only those of a morbid type, it seems to be sincere, truthful, relevant to the subject, and executed with real art. Joyce, in the words of Paradise Lost has dealt with "things unattempted yet in prose or rime"—with things that very likely might better have remained "unattempted"—but his book shows originality and is a work of symmetry and excellent craftsmanship of a sort. The question before us is whether such a book of artistic merit and scientific insight should be regarded as "obscene" within Section 305 (a) of the Tariff Act.

That numerous long passages in Ulysses contain matter that is obscene under any fair definition of the word cannot be gainsaid, yet they are relevant to the purpose of depicting the thoughts of the characters and are introduced to give meaning to the whole, rather than to promote lust or portray filth for its own sake. The net effect even of portions most open to attack, such as the closing monologue of the wife of Leopold Bloom, is pitiful and tragic, rather than lustful. The book depicts the souls of men and women that are by turns bewildered and keenly apprehensive, sordid and aspiring, ugly and beautiful, hateful and loving. In the end one feels, more than anything else, pity and sorrow for the confusion, misery, and degradation of humanity. Page after page of the book is, or seems to be, incomprehensible. But many passages show the trained hand of an artist, who can at one moment adapt to perfection the style of an ancient chronicler, and at another become a veritable personification of Thomas Carlyle. In numerous places there are found originality, beauty, and distinction. The book as a whole is not pornographic, and while in not a few spots it is coarse, blasphemous and obscene, it does not, in our opinion, tend to promote lust. The erotic passages are submerged in the book as a whole and have little resultant effect. If these are to make the book subject to confiscation, by the same test Venus and Adonis, Hamlet, Romeo and Juliet, and the story told in the Eighth Book of the Odyssey by the bard Demodocus of how Ares and Aphrodite were entrapped in a net spread by the outraged Hephaestus, amid the laughter of the immortal gods, as well as many other classics, would have to be suppressed. Indeed, it may be questioned whether the obscene passages in Romeo and Juliet were as necessary to the development of the play as those in the monologue of Mrs. Bloom are to the depiction of the latter's tortured soul.

It is unnecessary to add illustrations to show that, in the administration of statutes aimed at the suppression of immoral books, standard works of literature have not been barred merely because they contained *some* obscene passages and that confiscation for such a reason would destroy much that is precious in order to benefit a few.

It is settled, at least so far as this court is concerned, that works of physiology, medicine, science, and sex instruction are not within the statute, though to some extent and among some persons they may tend to promote lustful thoughts. United States v. Dennett, 39 Fed. (2d) 564. 76 A.L.R. 1092. We think the same immunity should apply to literature as to science where the presentation, when viewed objectively, is sincere and the erotic matter is not introduced to promote lust and does not furnish the dominant note of the publication. The question in each case is whether a publication taken as a whole has a libidinous effect. The book before us has such portentous length, is written with such evident truthfulness in its depiction of certain types of humanity, and is so little erotic in its result that it does not fall within the forbidden class.

In Halsey v. New York Society for the Suppression of Vice, 234 N.Y. 1, 136 N.E. 219, 220 the New York Court of Appeals dealt with Mademoiselle de Maupin, by Théophile Gautier, for the sale of which the plaintiff had been prosecuted under a New York statute forbidding the sale of obscene books, upon the complaint of the defendant. After acquittal, the plaintiff sued for malicious prosecution, and a jury rendered a verdict in his favor. The Court of Appeals refused to disturb the judgment because the book had become a recognized French classic and its merits on the whole outweighed its objectionable qualities, though, as Judge Andrews said, it contained many paragraphs which, "taken by themselves," were "undoubtedly vulgar and indecent". In referring to the obscene passages, he remarked that: "No work may be judged from a selection of such paragraphs alone. Printed by themselves they might, as a matter of law, come within the prohibition of the statute. So might a similar selection from Aristophanes or Chaucer or Boccaccio or even from the Bible. The book, however, must be considered broadly as a whole." We think Judge Andrews was clearly right and that the effect of the book as a whole is the test.

In the New York Supreme Court, Judge Morgan J. O'Brien declined to prohibit a receiver from selling Arabian Nights, Rabelais, Ovid's Art of Love, the Decameron of Boccaccio, the Heptameron of Queen Margaret of Navarre, or the Confessions of Rousseau. He remarked that a rule which would exclude them would bar "a very large proportion of the works of fiction of the most famous writers of the English language." In re Worthington Co. (Sup.) 30 N.Y.S. 361, 362, 24 L.R.A. 110. The main difference between many standard works and Ulysses is its far more abundant use of coarse and colloquial words and presentation of dirty scenes, rather than in any excess of prurient suggestion. We do not think that Ulysses taken as a whole tends to promote lust and its criticised passages do this no more than scores of standard books that are constantly bought and sold. Indeed a book of physiology in the hands of adolescents may be more objectionable on this ground than almost anything else.

But it is argued that United States v. Bennett, Fed. Cas. No. 14,571, stands in the way of what has been said, and it certainly does. There a court, consisting of Blatchford, C.J., and Benedict and Choate, D.JJ., held that the offending paragraphs in a book could be taken from their context and the book judged by them alone, and that the test of obscenity was whether the tendency of these passages in themselves was "to deprave the minds of those open to such influences and into whose hands a publication of this character might come." The opinion was founded upon a dictum of Cockburn, C.J., in Regina v. Hicklin, L.R. 3 Q.B. 360, where half of a book written to attack the alleged practices of the confession was obscene and contained, as Mellor, J., said " a great deal * * * which there cannot be any necessity for in any legitimate argument on the confessional. * * *" It is said that in Rosen v. United States, 161 U.S. 29, 16 S.Ct. 434, 480, 40 L.Ed. 606, the Supreme Court cited and sanctioned Regina v. Hicklin, and United States v. Bennett. The subject-matter of Rosen v. United States was, however, a pictorial representation of "females, in different attitudes of indecency". The figures were partially covered "with lamp black that could be easily erased with a piece of bread." p. 31 of 161 U.S., 16 S.Ct. 434. The pictures were evidently obscene, and plainly came within the statute prohibiting their transportation. The citation of Regina v. Hicklin and United States v. Bennett, was in support of a ruling that allegations in the indictment as to an obscene publication need only be made with sufficient particularity to inform the accused of the nature of the charge against him. No approval of other features of the two decisions was expressed, nor were such features referred to. Dunlop v. United States, 165 U.S. 486, 489, 17 S.Ct. 375, 41 L.Ed 799, also seems to be relied on by the government, but the publication there was admittedly obscene and the decision in no way sanctioned the rulings in United States v. Bennett which we first mentioned. The rigorous doctrines laid down in that case are inconsistent with our own decision in United States v. Dennett, (C.C.A.) 39 F. (2d) 564, 76 A.L.R. 1092, as well as with Konda v. United States, (C.C.A.) 166 F. 91, 92, 22 L.R.A. (N.S.) 304; Clark v. United States, (C.C.A.) 211

F. 916, 922; Halsey v. New York Society for the Suppression of Vice, 234 N.Y. 1, 4, 136 N.E. 219; and St. Hubert Guild v. Quinn, 64 Misc. 336, 339, 118 N.Y.S. 582, and in our opinion, do not represent the law. They would exclude much of the great works of literature and involve an impracticability that cannot be imputed to Congress and would in the case of many books containing obscene passages inevitably require the court that uttered them to restrict their applicability.

It is true that the motive of an author to promote good morals is not the test of whether a book is obscene and it may also be true that the applicability of the statute does not depend on the persons to whom a publication is likely to be distributed. The importation of obscene books is prohibited generally and no provision is made permitting such importation because of the character of those to whom they are sold. While any construction of the statute that will fit all cases is difficult, we believe that the proper test of whether a given book is obscene is its dominant effect. In applying this test, relevancy of the objectionable parts to the theme, the established reputation of the work in the estimation of approved critics, if the book is modern, and the verdict of the past, if it is ancient, are persuasive pieces of evidence; for works of art are not likely to sustain a high position with no better warrant for their existence than their obscene content.

It may be that Ulysses will not last as a substantial contribution to literature and it is certainly easy to believe, that in spite of the opinion of Joyce's laudators, the immortals will still reign, but the same thing may be said of current works of art and music and of many other serious efforts of the mind. Art certainly cannot advance under compulsion to traditional forms and nothing in such a field is more stifling to progress than limitation of the right to experiment with a new technique. The foolish judgments of Lord Eldon about one hundred years ago, proscribing the words of Byron and Southey, and the findings by the jury under a charge by Lord Denman that the publication of Shelley's "Queen Mab" was an indictable offense are a warning to all who have to determine the limits of the field within which authors may exercise themselves. We think that Ulysses is a book of originality and sincerity of treatment and that it has not the effect of promoting lust. Accordingly it does not fall within the statute, even though it justly may offend many.

Decree affirmed.

Dissenting opinion by Judge Manton:

I dissent. This libel, filed against the book Ulysses prays for a decree of forfeiture, and it is based upon the claim that the book's entry into the United States is prohibited by section 305 (a) of the Tariff Act of 1930 (19 USCA 1305 (a). On motion of appellee the court below entered an order dismissing the libel, and the collector of customs was ordered to release the book. The motion was considered on the pleadings and a stipulation entered into by the parties.

The sole question presented is whether or not the book is obscene within section 305 (a) which provides:

"All persons are prohibited from importing into the United States from any foreign country * * * any obscene book, pamphlet, paper, writing, advertisement, circular, print, picture, drawing, or other representation, figure, or image on or of paper or other material. * * *

"Upon the appearance of any such book or matter at any customs office, the same shall be seized and held by the collector to await the judgment of the district court as hereinafter provided. * * * Upon the seizure of such book or matter the collector shall transmit information thereof to the district attorney of the district in which is situated the office at which such seizure has taken place, who shall institute proceedings in the district court for the forfeiture, confiscation, and destruction of the book or matter seized. * * *

"In any such proceeding any party in interest may upon demand have the facts at issue determined by a jury and any party may have an appeal or the right of review as in the case of ordinary actions or suits."

The parties agreed as to the facts in the stipulation. There is no conflicting evidence; the decision to be made is dependent entirely upon the reading matter found on the objectionable pages of the book (pages 173, 213, 214, 359, 361, 423, 424, 434, 467, 488, 498, 500, 509, 522, 526, 528, 551, 719, 724–727, 731, 738, 739, 745, 746, 754–756, 761, 762, 765, Random House Edition). The book itself was the only evidence offered.

In a suit of this kind upon stipulation, the ultimate finding based solely on stipulated facts is reviewable on appeal to determine whether the facts support the finding. Lumbermen's Trust Co. v. Town of Ryegate, 61 F. (2d) 14 (C.C.A. 9); Order of United Commercial Travelers of America v. Shane, 64 F. (2d) 55 (C.C.A. 8). Moreover, the procedure in this suit in rem conforms to that obtaining in suits in admiralty (Coffey v. United States, 117 U.S. 233, 6 S. Ct. 717, 29 L. Ed. 890) where the appellate courts may review the facts. The Africa Maru, 54 F. (2d) 265 (C.C.A. 2); the Perry Setzer, 299 F. 586 (C.C.A. 2).

Who can doubt the obscenity of this book after a reading of the pages referred to, which are too indecent to add as a footnote to this opinion? Its characterization as obscene should be quite unanimous by all who read it.

In the year 1868 in Regina v. Hicklin L.R., 3 Q.B. 359, at page 369, Cockburn C. J., stated that "the test of obscenity is this, whether the tendency of the matter charged as obscenity is to deprave and corrupt those whose minds are open to such immoral influences, and into whose hands a publication of this sort may fall."

In 1879, in United States v. Bennett, Fed. Cas. No. 14,571, Judge Blatchford, later a justice of the Supreme Court, in this circuit, sitting with Judges Choate and Benedict, approved the rule of the Hicklin Case and held a charge to a jury proper which embodied the test of that case. The Bennett Case clearly holds the test of obscenity, within the meaning of the statute, is "whether the tendency of the matter is to deprave and corrupt the morals of those whose minds are open to such influences, and into whose hands a publication of this sort may fall." The court held that the object of the use of the obscene words was not a subject for consideration.

Judge Blatchford's decision met with approval in Rosen v. United States, 151 U.S. 29, 16 S. Ct. 434, 438, 480, 40 L. Ed. 606. The court had under consideration an indictment charging the accused with depositing obscene literature in the mails. Their instructions to the jury requested that conviction could not be had although the defendant may have had knowledge or notice of the contents of the letter "unless he knew or believed that such paper could be properly or justly characterized as obscene, lewd, and lascivious." The court said the statute was not to be so interpreted. "The inquiry under the statute is whether the paper charged to have been obscene, lewd, and lascivious was in fact of that character; and if it was of that character, and was deposited in the mail by one who knew or had notice at the time of its contents, the offense is complete, although the defendant himself did not regard the paper as one that the statute forbade to be carried in the mails. Congress did not intend that the question as to the character of the paper should depend upon the opinion or belief of the person who, with knowledge or notice of its contents, assumed the responsibility of putting it in the mails of the United States. The evils that congress sought to remedy would continue and increase in volume if the belief of the accused as to what was obscene, lewd, and lascivious were recognized as the test for determining whether the statute has been violated. Every one who uses the mails of the United States for carrying papers or publications must take notice of what, in this enlightened age, is meant by decency, purity, and chastity in social life, and what must be deemed obscene, lewd, and lascivious."

Further the Supreme Court approved the test of the Hicklin Case. On page 43 of 151 U.S., 16 S. Ct. 434, 439, the court states: "That was what the court did when it charged the jury that 'the test of obscenity is whether the tendency of the matter is to deprave and corrupt the morals of those whose minds are open to such influence, and into whose hands a publication of this sort may fall.' 'Would it,' the court said, 'suggest or convey lewd thoughts and lascivious thoughts to the young and inexperienced?' In view of the character of the paper, as an inspection of it will instantly disclose, the test prescribed for the jury was quite as liberal as the defendant had any right to demand."

Again the Supreme Court in Dunlop v. United States, 165 U.S. 486, 17 S. Ct. 375, 380, 41 L. Ed. 799, reviewed a charge in a criminal case upon the subject of obscene publications as follows: "Now, what is (are) obscene, lascivious, lewd, or indecent publications is largely a question of your own conscience and your own opinion; but it must come—before it can be said of such literature or publication—it must come up to this point: that it must be calculated with the ordinary reader to deprave him, deprave his morals, or lead to impure purposes. * * * It is your duty to ascertain, in the first place, if they are calculated to deprave the morals; if they are calculated to lower that standard which we regard as essential to civilization; if they are calculated to excite those feelings which, in their proper field, are all right, but which, transcending the limits of that proper field, play most of the mischief in the world."

In approving the charge, the court said: "The alleged obscene and indecent matter consisted of advertisements by women, soliciting or offering inducements for the visits of men, usually 'refined gentlemen,' to their rooms, sometimes under the disguise of 'Baths' and 'Massage,' and oftener for the mere purpose of acquaintance. It was in this connection that the court charged the jury that, if the publications were such as were calculated to deprave the morals, they were within the statute. There could have been no possible misapprehension on their part as to what was meant. There was no question as to depraving the morals in any other direction than that of impure sexual relations. The words were used by the court in their ordinary signification, and were made more definite by the context and by the character of the publications which have been put in evidence. The court left to the jury to say whether it was within the statute, and whether persons of ordinary intelligence would have any difficulty of divining the intention of the advertiser."

Thus the court sustained a charge having a test as to whether or no the publications depraved the morals of the ordinary reader or tended to lower the standards of civilization. The tendency of the matter to deprave and corrupt the morals of those whose minds are open to such influence and into whose hands the publication of this sort may fall, has become the test thoroughly entrenched in the federal courts. United States v. Bebout (D.C.) 28 F. 522; United States v. Wightman (D.C.) 29 F. 636; United States v. Clarke (D.C.) 38 F. 732; United States v. Smith (D.C.) 45 F. 476; Burton v. United States, 142 F. 57 (C.C.A. 8); United States v. Dennett, 39 F. (2d) 564, 76 A.L.R. 1092 (C.C.A. 2). What is the probable effect on the sense of decency of society, extending to the family made up of men, women, young boys, and girls, was said to be the test in United States v. Harmon (D.C.) 45 F. 414, 417.

Ulysses is a work of fiction. It may not be compared with books involving medical subjects or description of certain physical or biological facts. It is written for alleged amusement of the reader only. The characters described in the thoughts of the author may in some instances be true, but, be it truthful or otherwise, a book that is obscene is not rendered less so by the statement of truthful fact. Burton v. United States, supra. It cannot be said that the test above has been rejected by United States v. Dennett (C.C.A.) 39 F. (2d) 564, 76 A.L.R. 1092, nor can that case be taken to mean that the book is to be judged as a whole. If anything, the case clearly recognizes that the book may be obscene because portions thereof are so, for pains are taken to justify and show not to be obscene portions to which objection is made. The gist of the holding is that a book is not to be declared obscene if it is "an accurate exposition of the relevant facts of the sex side of life in decent language and in manifestly serious and disinterested spirit." A work of obvious benefit to the community was never intended to be within the purview of the statute. No matter what may be said on the side of letters, the effect on the community can and must be the sole determining factor. "Laws of this character are made for society in the aggregate, and not in particular. So, while there may be individuals and societies of men and women of peculiar notions or idiosyncrasies, whose moral sense would neither be depraved nor offended, * * * yet the exceptional sensibility, or want of sensibility, of such cannot be allowed as a standard." United States v. Harmon, supra.

In United States v. Kennerley (D.C.) 209 F. 119, the Bennett Case was followed despite the dictum objecting to a test which protected the "salacious" few. By the very argument used, to destroy a test which protects those most easily influenced, we can discard a test which would protect only the interests of the other comparatively small groups of society. If we disregard the protection of the morals of the susceptible, are we to consider merely the benefits and pleasures derived from letters by those who pose as the more highly developed and intelligent? To do so would show an utter disregard for the standards of decency of the community as a whole and an utter disregard for the effect of a book upon the average less sophisticated member of society, not to mention the adolescent. The court cannot indulge any instinct it may have to foster letters. The statute is designed to protect society at large, of that there can be no dispute; notwithstanding the deprivation of benefits to a few, a work must be condemned if it has a depraving influence.

And are we to refuse to enforce the statute Congress has enacted because of the argument that "obscenity is only the superstition of the day—the modern counterpart of ancient witchcraft"? Are we to be persuaded by the statement, set forth in the brief, made by the judge below in an interview with the press, "Education, not law, must solve problems of taste and choice (of books)," when the statute is clear and our duty plain?

The prevailing opinion states that classics would be excluded if the application of the statute here argued for prevailed. But the statute, Tariff Act 1930, § 305 (a), 19 USCA § 1305 (a), provides as to classics that they may be introduced into the commerce of the United States provided "that the Secretary of the Treasury * * * in his discretion, admit the so-called classics or books of recognized and established literary or scientific merit, but may, in his discretion, admit such classics or books only when imported for non-commercial purposes." The right to admission under this proviso was not sought nor is it justified by reason thereof in the prevailing opinion.

Congress passed this statute against obscenity for the protection of the great mass of our people; the unusual literator can, or thinks he can, protect himself. The people do not exist for the sake of literature, to give the author fame, the publisher wealth, and the book a market. On the contrary, literature exists for the sake of the people, to refresh the weary, to console the sad, to hearten the dull and downcast, to increase man's interest in the world, his joy of living, and his sympathy in all sorts and conditions of men. Art for art's sake is heartless and soon grows artless; art for the public market is not art at all, but commerce; art for the people's service is a noble, vital, and permanent element of human life.

The public is content with the standard of salability; the prigs with the standard of preciosity. The people need and deserve a moral standard; it should be a point of honor with men of letters to maintain it. Masterpieces have never been produced by men given to obscenity or lustful thoughts—men who have no Master. Reverence for good work is the foundation of literary character. A refusal to imitate obscenity or to load a book with it is an author's professional chastity.

Good work in literature has its permanent mark; it is like all good work, noble and lasting. It requires a human aim—to cheer, console, purify, or ennoble the life of people. Without this aim, literature has never sent an arrow close to the mark. It is by good work only that men of letters can justify their right to a place in the world.

Under the authoritative decisions and considering the substance involved in this appeal, it is my opinion that the decree should be reversed.

FEMALE, By DONALD HENDERSON CLARKE

People v. Berg
(2d Dep't 1934) 241 App. Div. 543, 272 N.Y. Supp. 586, affirmed without opinion, 269 N.Y. 514, 199 N.E. 513 (1935)

Female was held to be obscene.

Before Lazansky, P. J., Young, Kapper, Tompkins and Davis, JJ.
Per Curiam Opinion

It is admitted that the defendant loaned for a consideration a certain book. He was charged in the information with the crime of having in his possession, with intent to lend, an "obscene, lewd, lascivious, filthy, indecent and disgusting book" in violation of the provisions of section 1141 of the Penal Law. On trial in Special Sessions the defendant was convicted and was sentenced to pay a fine of $100 or serve twenty days in the city prison in default of payment. It is said that defendant paid the fine.

The principal facts are not in dispute and the only issue is whether or not the book, as a mixed question of law and fact, falls within the condemnation of the statute as stated in the words of the information. Copies of the book were furnished on the argument for our examination in connection with making a judicial determination. It has been read. We can think of no reason any person of reasonably clean mind would have to read the book other than that arising by the imposition of a duty.

We have no purpose to excite the curiosity of the prurient by naming the book—as might be desired by those interested in its publication and sale. It is sufficient to say that it is fully and completely of the type that the language of the statute condemns in article 106 of the Penal Law as a result of legislative effort to forbid indecency in different forms. In addition it lacks literary merit. It teaches no lesson and points no moral. It describes no period of history and the people or characters of that time and their conduct and habits of life—such, for instance, as the "Elizabethan Age;" and no folk lore or tales of primitive people living in isolated regions. We cannot believe that the story is one even possibly true or representative of any individual or of any limited class. In our opinion it is obscene, lewd, lascivious and disgusting, and nothing more; and was so intended to be for purely mercenary purposes.

But we are told that the intent and purpose of the Legislature in enacting the statute has been whittled away by judicial interpretation; and that in these changing times former notions of propriety and decency have in many respects been discarded. All this may be true, and there is considerable practical evidence to support that view. In brief and argument certain books have been called to our attention which contain vulgarity, coarseness, free use of profanity, and details of loose moral conduct on the part of characters described therein— all expressed in what appellant's counsel calls "forthright language;" and yet the courts have held that their sale or circulation did not offend against the statute. Chiefly, judicial opinions in such cases have dealt at length with books determined not to be obscene, with no clear standard given for determining obscenity and indecency. But from those opinions where a clean certificate of character has been given to questioned books there does emerge, somewhat hazily, the rule that an obscene book is one that "tends to corrupt the morals of youth," or "to lower the standards of right and wrong specifically as to the sexual relation." To be deemed obscene it must show "sexual impurity" and result in "the exciting of lustful and lecherous thoughts and desires" or tend "to stir sex impulses or to lead to sexually impure thoughts." The application of these standards in any particular case must in large measure depend upon the enlightened and discriminating reaction of the judicial mind. Applying these tests to the book in question here, we say that in our judgment the book falls within the class outlined by these standards as well as that condemned by the more precise and definite language of the statute. Filth, however it may be bedizened or its grossness concealed, must remain plain filth in all ages.

The judgment of conviction should be affirmed.

FRANKIE AND JOHNNIE

People v. Wendling
258 N.Y. 451, 180 N.E. 169 (1932), reversing 233 App.
Div. 704, 249 N.Y. Supp. 958 (2d Dep't. 1931)

It was held that the dramatization of the song *Frankie and Johnnie* was not obscene. The mere fact that the scenes and characters represented were coarse did not make the play obscene. A history of prostitution is not in itself indecent, and the fact that the characters are not nice people does not make the play obscene.

Cardozo, Ch. J., Lehman and Kellogg, JJ., concur; Crane, O'Brien and Hubbs, JJ., dissent.

Opinion by Pound, J.:

The prosecution herein arises out of the dramatization of the ancient folk song "Frankie and Johnnie," which told the tale of the adventures of Johnnie, a country boy, in a St. Louis resort for drinking, gambling and prostitution in the middle of the last century.[1]

The language of the play is coarse, vulgar and profane; the plot cheap and tawdry. As a dramatic composition it serves to degrade the stage where vice is thought by some to lose "half its evil by losing all its grossness." "That it is 'indecent' from every consideration of propriety is entirely clear" (*People v. Eastman*, 188 N.Y., 478, 480), but the court is not a censor of plays and does not attempt to regulate manners. One may call a spade a spade without offending decency, although modesty may be shocked thereby (*People v. Muller*, 96 N.Y., 408, 411). The question is not whether the scene is laid in a low dive where refined people are not found or whether the language is that of the bar room rather than the parlor. The question is whether the tendency of the play is to excite lustful and lecherous desire (*People v. Eastman, supra; People v. Muller, supra*).

Prostitutes are not so rarely represented on the stage as to arouse the sexual propensities of the spectators whenever they appear. G. B. Shaw's play, "Mrs. Warren's Profession," deals, in the language of the polite dramatist, with what has been styled "the oldest profession in the world." The heroine of "Rain" was a seductive harlot. Scenes of "The Shanghai Gesture" are laid in a house of bad character. "Lysistrata" is frank in the discussion of sex relations but does not excite desire as might the lascivious display of female charms. The Bible talks bluntly of harlots and whores, but it does not incite to immorality. (Chapters 17 and 18 of the Book of Revelations.)

The play is said to "tend to corrupt the morals of youth." Here again the question is not whether it would tend to coarsen or vulgarize

[1]Dr. Sigmund Spaeth, "Read 'em and Weep—The Songs You Forgot to Remember," p. 34.

the youth who might witness it but whether it would tend to lower their standards of right and wrong, specifically as to the sexual relation. Unless the mere representation on the stage of prostitutes and their patrons would tend to have the effect of stimulating sexual impulses, the performance should not be barred (*United States v. Dennett*, 39 Fed. Rep., [2d], 564; *United States v. One Obscene Book Entitled "Married Love,"* 48 Fed. Rep., [2d], 821; *United States v. One Book Entitled "Contraception,"* by Marie C. Stopes, 51 Fed. Rep., [2d], 525).

Compare the seductive "studies in the etiquette of the liaison and all its nuances" with their accompanying appeal to sexual passion contained in Schnitzler's "Reigen," where it was held by a divided court that the finders of fact might pronounce the book obscene by applying local standards of propriety thereto (*People v. Pesky*, 230 App. Div., 200, 202, aff'd 254 N.Y., 373), with this uncultured depiction of a phase in the frontier life of the middle west. A coarse realism is its dramatic offense. Perhaps in an age of innocence the facts of life should be withheld from the young but a theatre goer could not give his approval to the modern stage as "spokesman of the thought and sentiment" of Broadway (*Halsey v. New York Society for Suppression of Vice*, 234 N.Y., 1), and at the same time silence this rough and profane representation of scenes which repel rather than seduce.

The production of such a play may be repulsive to puritanical ideas of propriety as would "Camille" and may be offensive to the more liberal minded as lacking in taste and refinement, as would the morally unobjectionable "Abie's Irish Rose." The play may be gross and its characters wanting in moral sense. It may depict women who carry on a vicious trade and their male associates. It cannot be said to suggest, except "to a prurient imagination," unchaste or lustful ideas. It does not counsel or invite to vice or voluptuousness. It does not deride virtue. Unless we say that it is obscene to use the language of the street rather than that of the scholar, the play is not obscene under the Penal Law, although it might be so styled by the censorious.

We have repeatedly said that fine language does not excuse the expression of filthy thoughts. (*Halsey v. New York Society for Suppression of Vice, supra.*) Neither do coarse scenes and vulgar language in themselves create such thoughts. (*Dysart v. United States*, 272 U.S., 655.)

We do not purpose to sanction indecency on the stage by this decision or to let down the bars against immoral shows or to hold that the depiction of scenes of bawdry on the stage is to be tolerated. We hold merely that the fact that Frankie and Johnnie and their companions were not nice people does not in itself make the play obscene. A history of prostitution or of sexual life is not *per se* indecent, although such a book might easily be so written as to offend decency.

The judgment in each action should be reversed and the informations dismissed.

MOTION PICTURE CENSORSHIP

Mutual Film Corp. v. Industrial Commission of Ohio
236 U.S. 230, 59 L. ed, 552 (1915)

The Supreme Court of the United States held that motion picture censorship was constitutional.

The opinion of Mr. Justice McKenna:

Complainant directs its argument to three propositions: (1) The statute in controversy imposes an unlawful burden on interstate commerce; (2) it violates the freedom of speech and publication guaranteed by § 11, article 1, of the Constitution of the state of Ohio;[2] and (3) it attempts to delegate legislative power to censors and to other boards to determine whether the statute offends in the particulars designated.

It is necessary to consider only §§ 3, 4, and 5. Section 3 makes it the duty of the board to examine and censor motion picture films to be publicly exhibited and displayed in the state of Ohio. The films are required to be exhibited to the board before they are delivered to the exhibitor for exhibition, for which a fee is charged.

Section 4. "Only such films as are, in the judgment and discretion of the board of censors, of a moral, educational, or amusing and harmless character shall be passed and approved by such board." The films are required to be stamped or designated in a proper manner.

Section 5. The board may work in conjunction with censor boards of other states as a censor congress, and the action of such congress in approving or rejecting films shall be considered as the action of the state board, and all films passed, approved, stamped, and numbered by such congress, when the fees therefor are paid, shall be considered approved by the board.

By § 7 a penalty is imposed for each exhibition of films without the approval of the board, and by § 8 any person dissatisfied with the order of the board is given the same rights and remedies for hearing and reviewing, amendment or vacation of the order "as is provided in the case of persons dissatisfied with the orders of the Industrial Commission."

The censorship, therefore, is only of films intended for exhibition in Ohio, and we can immediately put to one side the contention that it imposes a burden on interstate commerce. It is true that, according to the allegations of the bill, some of the films of complainant are shipped

[2]"Section 11. Every citizen may freely speak, write, and publish his sentiments on all subjects, being responsible for the abuse of the right; and no law shall be passed to restrain or abridge the liberty of speech, or of the press. In all criminal prosecutions for libel the truth may be given in evidence to the jury, and if it shall appear to the jury that the matter charged as libelous is true and was published with good motives and for justifiable ends, the party shall be acquitted."

from Detroit, Michigan, but they are distributed to exhibitors, purchasers, renters, and lessors in Ohio, for exhibition in Ohio, and this determines the application of the statute. In other words, it is only films which are "to be publicly exhibited and displayed in the state of Ohio" which are required to be examined and censored. It would be straining the doctrine of original packages to say that the films retain that form and composition even when unrolling and exhibiting to audiences, or, being ready for renting for the purpose of exhibition within the state, could not be disclosed to the state officers. If this be so, whatever the power of the state to prevent the exhibition of films not approved,—and for the purpose of this contention we must assume the power is otherwise plenary,—films brought from another state, and only because so brought, would be exempt from the power, and films made in the state would be subject to it. There must be some time when the films are subject to the law of the state, and necessarily when they are in the hands of the exchanges, ready to be rented to exhibitors, or have passed to the latter, they are in consumption, and mingled as much as from their nature they can be with other property of the state.

It is true that the statute requires them to be submitted to the board before they are delivered to the exhibitor, but we have seen that the films are shipped to "exchanges" and by them rented to exhibitors, and the "exchanges" are described as "nothing more or less than circulating libraries or clearing houses." And one film "serves in many theaters from day to day until it is worn out."

The next contention is that the statute violates the freedom of speech and publication guaranteed by the Ohio Constitution. In its discussion counsel have gone into a very elaborate description of moving picture exhibitions and their many useful purposes as graphic expressions of opinion and sentiments, as exponents of policies, as teachers of science and history, as useful, interesting, amusing, educational, and moral. And a list of the "campaigns," as counsel call them, which may be carried on, is given. We may concede the praise. It is not questioned by the Ohio statute, and under its comprehensive description, "campaigns" of an infinite variety may be conducted. Films of a "moral, educational, or amusing and harmless character shall be passed and approved," are the words of the statute. No exhibition, therefore, or "campaign" of complainant will be prevented if its pictures have those qualities. Therefore, however missionary of opinion films are or may become, however educational or entertaining, there is no impediment to their value or effect in the Ohio statute. But they may be used for evil, and against that possibility the statute was enacted. Their power of amusement, and, it may be, education, the audiences they assemble, not of women alone nor of men alone, but together, not of adults only, but of children, make them the more insidious in corruption by a pretense of worthy purpose or if they should degenerate from worthy purpose. Indeed, we may go beyond that possibility. They take their attraction from the general interest, eager and wholesome it may be, in their subjects, but a prurient interest may be excited and appealed to. Besides, there are some things which should not have pictorial representation in public places and to all audiences. And not only the state of Ohio, but other states, have considered it to be in the interest of the public morals and welfare to supervise moving picture exhibitions. We would have to shut our eyes to the facts of the world to regard the precaution unreasonable or the legislation to effect it a mere wanton interference with personal liberty.

We do not understand that a possibility of an evil employment of films is denied, but a freedom from the censorship of the law and a precedent right of exhibition are asserted, subsequent responsibility only, it is contended, being incurred for abuse. In other words, as we have seen, the Constitution of Ohio is invoked, and an exhibition of films is assimilated to the freedom of speech, writing, and publication assured by that instrument, and for the abuse of which only is there responsibility, and, it is insisted, that as no law may be passed "to restrain the liberty of speech or of the press," no law may be passed to subject moving pictures to censorship before their exhibition.

We need not pause to dilate upon the freedom of opinion and its expression, and whether by speech, writing, or printing. They are too certain to need discussion—of such conceded value as to need no supporting praise. Nor can there be any doubt of their breadth, nor that their underlying safeguard is, to use the words of another, "that opinion is free, and that conduct alone is amenable to the law."

Are moving pictures within the principle, as it is contended they are? They, indeed, may be mediums of thought, but so are many things. So is the theater, the circus, and all other shows and spectacles, and their performances may be thus brought by the like reasoning under the same immunity from repression or supervision as the public press,—made the same agencies of civil liberty.

Counsel have not shrunk from this extension of their contention, and cite a case in this court where the title of drama was accorded to pantomime;[8] and such and other spectacles are said by counsel to be publications of ideas, satisfying the definition of the dictionaries,—that is, and we quote counsel, a means of making or announcing publicly something that otherwise might have remained private or unknown, —and this being peculiarly the purpose and effect of moving pictures, they come directly, it is contended, under the protection of the Ohio constitution.

The first impulse of the mind is to reject the contention. We immediately feel that the argument is wrong or strained which extends the guaranties of free opinion and speech to the multitudinous shows which are advertised on the billboards of our cities and towns, and which regards them as emblems of public safety, to use the words of

[8]Kalem Co. v. Harper Bros. 222 U.S. 55, 56 L. ed. 92, 32 Sup. Ct. Rep. 20, Ann. Cas. 1913A, 1285.

Lord Camden, quoted by counsel, and which seeks to bring motion pictures and other spectacles into practical and legal similitude to a free press and liberty of opinion.

The judicial sense supporting the common sense of the country is against the contention. As pointed out by the district court, the police power is familiarly exercised in granting or withholding licenses for theatrical performances as a means of their regulation. The court cited the following cases: Marmet v. State, 45 Ohio St. 63, 72, 73, 12 N.E. 463; Baker v. Cincinnati, 11 Ohio St. 534; Com. v. McGann, 213 Mass. 213, 215, 100 N.E. 355; People v. Steele, 231 Ill. 340, 344, 345, 14 L.R.A. (N.S.) 361, 121 Am. St. Rep. 321, 83 N.E. 236.

The exercise of the power upon moving picture exhibitions has been sustained. Greenberg v. Western Turf Asso., 148 Cal. 126, 113 Am. St. Rep. 216, 82 Pac. 684, 19 Am. Neg. Rep. 72; Laurelle v. Bush, 17 Cal. App. 409, 119 Pac. 953; State v. Loden, 117 Md. 373, 40 L.R.A. (N.S.) 193, 83 Atl. 564, Ann. Cas. 1913E, 1300; Block v. Chicago, 239 Ill. 251, 130 Am. St. Rep. 219, 87 N.E. 1011; Higgins v. Lacroix, 119 Minn. 145, 41 L.R.A. (N.S.) 737, 137 N.W. 417. See also State v. Morris, 1 Boyce (Del.) 330, 76 Atl. 479; People ex rel. Moses v. Gaynor, 77 Misc. 576, 137 N.Y. Supp. 196, 199; McKenzie v. McClellan, 62 Misc. 342, 116 N.Y. Supp. 645, 646.

It seems not to have occurred to anybody in the cited cases that freedom of opinion was repressed in the exertion of the power which was illustrated. The rights of property were only considered as involved. It cannot be put out of view that the exhibition of moving pictures is a business, pure and simple, originated and conducted for profit, like other spectacles, not to be regarded, nor intended to be regarded by the Ohio Constitution, we think, as part of the press of the country, or as organs of public opinion. They are mere representations of events, of ideas and sentiments published and known; vivid, useful, and entertaining, no doubt, but, as we have said, capable of evil, having power for it, the greater because of their attractiveness and manner of exhibition. It was this capability and power, and it may be in experience of them, that induced the state of Ohio, in addition to prescribing penalties for immoral exhibitions, as it does in its Criminal Code, to require censorship before exhibition, as it does by the act under review. We cannot regard this as beyond the power of government.

It does not militate against the strength of these considerations that motion pictures may be used to amuse and instruct in other places than theatres,—in churches, for instance, and in Sunday schools and public schools. Nor are we called upon to say on this record whether such exceptions would be within the provisions of the statute, nor to anticipate that it will be so declared by the state courts, or so enforced by the state officers.

The next contention of complainant is that the Ohio statute is a delegation of legislative power, and void for that if not for the other reasons charged against it, which we have discussed. While administration and legislation are quite distinct powers, the line which separates exactly their exercise is not easy to define in words. It is best recognized in illustrations. Undoubtedly the legislature must declare the policy of the law and fix the legal principles which are to control in given cases; but an administrative body may be invested with the power to ascertain the facts and conditions to which the policy and principles apply. If this could not be done there would be infinite confusion in the laws, and in an effort to detail and to particularize, they would miss sufficiency both in provision and execution.

The objection to the statute is that it furnishes no standard of what is educational, moral, amusing, or harmless, and hence leaves decision to arbitrary judgment, whim, and caprice; or, aside from those extremes, leaving it to the different views which might be entertained of the effect of the pictures, permitting the "personal equation" to enter, resulting "in unjust discrimination against some propagandist film," while others might be approved without question. But the statute by its provisions guards against such variant judgments, and its terms, like other general terms, get precision from the sense and experience of men, and become certain and useful guides in reasoning and conduct. The exact specification of the instances of their application would be as impossible as the attempt would be futile. Upon such sense and experience, therefore, the law properly relies. This has many analogies and direct examples in cases, and we may cite Gungling v. Chicago, 177 U.S. 183, 44 L. ed. 725, 20 Sup. Ct. Rep. 633; Red "C" Oil Mfg. Co. v. Board of Agriculture, 222 U.S. 380, 56 L. ed. 240, 32 Sup. Ct. Rep. 152; Monongahela Bridge Co. v. United States, 216 U.S. 177, 54 L. ed. 435, 30 Sup. Ct. Rep. 356; Buttfield v. Stranahan, 192 U.S. 470, 48 L. ed. 525, 24 Sup. Ct. Rep. 349. See also Waters-Pierce Oil Co. v. Texas, 212 U.S. 86, 53 L. ed. 417, 29 Sup. Ct. Rep. 220. If this were not so, the many administrative agencies created by the state and national governments would be denuded of their utility, and government in some of its most important exercises become impossible.

To sustain the attack upon the statute as a delegation of legislative power, complainant cites Harmon v. State, 66 Ohio St. 249, 53 L.R.A. 618, 64 N.E. 117. In that case a statute of the state committing to a certain officer the duty of issuing a license to one desiring to act as an engineer if "found trustworthy and competent" was declared invalid because, as the court said, no standard was furnished by the general assembly as to qualification, and no specification as to wherein the applicant should be truthworthy and competent, but all was "left to the opinion, finding, and caprice of the examiner." The case can be distinguished. Besides, later cases have recognized the difficulty of exact separation of the powers of government, and announced the principle that legislative power is completely exercised where the law "is perfect, final, and decisive in all of its parts, and the discretion given only relates to its execution." Cases are cited in illustration. And the principle finds further illustration in the decisions of the courts of lesser authority, but which exhibit the juridical sense of the state as to the delegation of powers.

Section 5 of the statute, which provides for a censor congress of the censor board and the boards of other states, is referred to in emphasis of complainant's objection that the statute delegates legislative power. But, as complainant says, such congress is "at present nonexistent and nebulous;" and we are, therefore, not called upon to anticipate its action, or pass upon the validity of § 5.

We may close this topic with a quotation of the very apt comment of the district court upon the statute. After remarking that the language of the statute "might have been extended by description and illustrative words," but doubting that it would have been the more intelligible, and that probably by being more restrictive might be more easily thwarted, the court said: "In view of the range of subjects which complainants claim to have already compassed, not to speak of the natural development that will ensue, it would be next to impossible to devise language that would be at once comprehensive and automatic." [215 Fed. 147.]

In conclusion we may observe that the Ohio statute gives a review by the courts of the state of the decision of the board of censors.

Decree affirmed.

SEX SIDE OF LIFE By MARY W. DENNETT

U.S. v. Dennett (1930)
39 F. (2d) 564, 76 A.L.R. 1092 (C.C.A. 2d 1930)

It was held that the pamphlet *Sex Side of Life,* giving an accurate exposition of the relevant facts of the sex side of life in decent language and in a manifestly serious and disinterested spirit, was not obscene. The conviction below was reversed, and the indictment dismissed.

Before Swan, Augustus N. Hand, and Chase, Circuit Judges.

Opinion by Judge Augustus N. Hand:

It is doubtless true that the personal motive of the defendant in distributing her pamphlet could have no bearing on the question whether she violated the law. Her own belief that a really obscene pamphlet would pay the price for its obscenity by means of intrinsic merits would leave her as much as ever under the ban of the statute. *Regina* v. *Hicklin,* L.R. 3 Q.B. 360; *United States* v. *Bennett,* Fed. Case No. 14,571; *Rosen* v. *United States,* 161 U.S. at page 41, 16 S. Ct. 434, 480, 40 L. Ed. 606.

It was perhaps proper to exclude the evidence offered by the defendant as to the persons to whom the pamphlet was sold, for the reason that such evidence, if relevant at all, was part of the government's proof. In other words, a publication might be distributed among doctors or nurses or adults in cases where the distribution among small children could not be justified.

The fact that the latter might obtain it accidentally or surreptitiously, as they might see some medical books which would not be desirable for them to read, would hardly be sufficient to bar a publication otherwise proper. Here the pamphlet appears to have been mailed to a married woman. The tract may fairly be said to be calculated to aid parents in the instruction of their children in sex matters. As the record stands, it is a reasonable inference that the pamphlet was to be given to children at the discretion of adults and to be distributed through agencies that had the real welfare of the adolescent in view. There is no reason to suppose that it was to be broadcast among children who would have no capacity to understand its general significance. Even the court in *Regina* v. *Hicklin,* L.R. 3 Q.B. at p. 367, which laid down a more strict rule than the New York Court of Appeals, was inclined to adopt in *People* v. *Eastman,* 188 N.Y. 478, 81 N.E. 459, 11 Ann. Cas. 302 said, that "the circumstances of the publication" may determine whether the statute has been violated.

But the important consideration in this case is not the correctness of the rulings of the trial judge as to the admissibility of evidence, but the meaning and scope of those words of the statute which prohibit the mailing of an *"obscene, lewd or lascivious * * * pamphlet."* It was for the trial court to determine whether the pamphlet could reasonably be thought to be of such a character before submitting any question of the violation of the statute to the jury. *Knowles* v. *United States.* (C.C.A.) 170 F. 409; *Magon* v. *United States* (C.C.A.) 248 F. 201. And the test most frequently laid down seems to have been whether it would tend to deprave the morals of those into whose hands the publication might fall by suggesting lewd thoughts and exciting sensual desires. *Dunlop* v. *United States,* 165 U.S. at page 501, 17 S. Ct. 375, 41 L. Ed. 799; *Rosen* v. *United States,* 161 U.S. 29, 16 S. Ct. 434, 480, 40 L. Ed. 606.

It may be assumed that any article dealing with the sex side of life and explaining the functions of the sex organs is capable in some circumstances of arousing lust. The sex impulses are present in every one, and without doubt cause much of the weal and woe of human kind. But it can hardly be said that, because of the risk of arousing sex impulses, there should be no instruction of the young in sex matters, and that the risk of imparting instruction outweighs the disadvantages of leaving them to grope about in mystery and morbid curiosity and of requiring them to secure such information, as they may be able to obtain, from ill-informed and often foul-minded companions, rather than from intelligent and high-minded sources. It may be argued that suggestion plays a large part in such matters, and that on the whole the less sex questions are dwelt upon the better. But it by no means follows that such a desideratum is attained by leaving adolescents in a state of inevitable curiosity, satisfied only by the casual gossip of ignorant playmates.

The old theory that information about sex matters should be left to chance has greatly changed, and, while there is still a difference of opinion as to just the kind of instruction which ought to be given, it is commonly thought in these days that much was lacking in the old mystery and reticence. This is evident from the current literature on the subject, particularly such pamphlets as "Sex Education," issued by the Treasury Department United States Public Health Service in 1927.

The statute we have to construe was never thought to bar from the mails everything which *might* stimulate sex impulses. If so, much chaste poetry and fiction, as well as many useful medical works would be under the ban. Like everything else, this law must be construed reasonably with a view to the general objects aimed at. While there can be no doubt about its constitutionality, it must not be assumed to have been designed to interfere with serious instruction regarding sex matters unless the terms in which the information is conveyed are clearly indecent.

We have been referred to no decision where a truthful exposition of the sex side of life, evidently calculated for instruction and for the explanation of relevant facts, has been held to be obscene. In *Dysart v. United States*, 272 U.S. 655, 47 S. Ct. 234, 71 L. Ed. 461, it was decided that the advertisement of a lying-in retreat to enable unmarried women to conceal their missteps, even though written in a coarse and vulgar style, did not fall within prohibition of the statute, and was not "obscene" within the meaning of the law.

The defendant's discussion of the phenomena of sex is written with sincerity of feeling and with an idealization of the marriage relation and sex emotions. We think it tends to rationalize and dignify such emotions rather than to arouse lust. While it may be thought by some that portions of the tract go into unnecessary details that would better have been omitted, it may be fairly answered that the curiosity of many adolescents would not be satisfied without full explanation, and that no more than that is really given. It also may reasonably be thought that accurate information, rather than mystery and curiosity, is better in the long run and is less likely to occasion lascivious thoughts than ignorance and anxiety. Perhaps instruction other than that which the defendant suggests would be better. That is a matter as to which there is bound to be a wide difference of opinion, but, irrespective of this, we hold that an accurate exposition of the relevant facts of the sex side of life in decent language and in manifestly serious and disinterested spirit cannot ordinarily be regarded as obscene. Any incidental tendency to arouse sex impulses which such a pamphlet may perhaps have is apart from and subordinate to its main effect. The tendency can only exist in so far as it is inherent in any sex instruction, and it would seem to be outweighed by the elimination of ignorance, curiosity, and morbid fear. The direct aim and the net result is to promote understanding and self-control.

No case was made for submission to the jury, and the judgment must therefore be reversed.

MARRIED LOVE, By DR. MARIE C. STOPES

U.S. v. One Obscene Book
Entitled "Married Love"
48 F. (2d) 821 (S.D. N.Y. 1931)

Dr. Marie C. Stopes' book entitled *Married Love* was held not obscene or immoral under the federal statute prohibiting the importation of obscene and immoral books.

Opinion by Judge Woolsey:

I dismiss the libel in this case.

I. The first point with which I shall deal is as to the contention that the section of the Tariff Act under which this libel was brought, title 19, U.S.C., § 1305 (19 USCA § 1305), is unconstitutional as impinging on the right of the freedom of the press. I think there is nothing in this contention. The section does not involve the suppression of a book before it is published, but the exclusion of an already published book which is sought to be brought into the United States.

After a book is published, its lot in the world is like that of anything else. It must conform to the law and, if it does not, must be subject to the penalties involved in its failure to do so. Laws which are thus disciplinary of publications, whether involving exclusion from the mails or from this country, do not interfere with freedom of the press.

II. Passing to the second point, I think that the matter here involved is *res adjudicata* by reason of the decision hereinafter mentioned.

This is a proceeding *in rem* against a book entitled "Married Love," written by Dr. Marie C. Stopes and sent from England by the London branch of G. P. Putnam's Sons to their New York office.

The libel was filed under the provisions of Title 19, U.S.C., § 1305, (19 USCA § 1305) which provides, so far as is here relevant, as follows:

"§ 1305. *Immoral Articles—Importation Prohibited.* (a) *Prohibition of importation.* All persons are prohibited from importing into the United States from any foreign country * * * any obscene book, pamphlet, paper, writing, advertisement, circular, print, pictures, drawing, or other representation, figure, or image on or of paper or other material, or any cast, instrument, or other article which is obscene or immoral, or any drug or medicine or any article whatever for the prevention of conception or for causing unlawful abortion. * * * No such articles, whether imported separately or contained in packages with other goods entitled to entry, shall be admitted to entry;

and all such articles * * * shall be subject to seizure and forfeiture as hereinafter provided, * * * *Provided further,* that the Secretary of the Treasury may, in his discretion, admit the so-called classics or books of recognized and established literary or scientific merit, but may, in his discretion, admit such classics or books only when imported for non-commercial purposes."

Then it goes on:

"Upon the appearance of any such book or matter at any customs office, the same shall be seized and held by the collector to await the judgment of the district court as hereinafter provided. * * * Upon the seizure of such book or matter the collector shall transmit information thereof to the district attorney of the district in which is situated the office at which such seizure has taken place, who shall institute proceedings in the district court for the forfeiture, confiscation, and destruction of the book or matter seized. Upon the adjudication that such book or matter thus seized is of the character the entry of which is by this section prohibited, it shall be ordered destroyed and shall be destroyed. Upon adjudication that such book or matter thus seized is not of the character the entry of which is by this section prohibited, it shall not be excluded from entry under the provisions of this section.

"In any such proceeding any party in interest may upon demand have the facts at issue determined by a jury and any party may have an appeal or the right of review as in the case of ordinary actions or suits."

The book before me now has had stricken from it all matters dealing with contraceptive instruction, and, hence, does not come now within the prohibition of the statute against imports for such purposes, even if a book dealing with such matters falls within the provisions of this Section—which I think it probably does not—and the case has to be dealt with entirely on the question of whether the book is obscene or immoral.

Another copy of this same book, without the excision of the passages dealing with contraceptive matters, was before Judge Kirkpatrick, United States District Judge for the Eastern District of Pennsylvania, on a forfeiture libel under the Tariff Act of 1922, and he ruled that the book was not obscene or immoral, and directed a verdict for the claimant.[4]

Although the Government took an exception to this ruling at the time of the trial, it did not mature this exception by an appeal, and the case therefore stands as a final decision of a coordinate court in a proceeding in rem involving the same book that we have here. The answer in this case is amended and pleads res adjudicata on the ground of the proceedings had before Judge Kirkpatrick which involved exactly the same question as that now before me.

[4] No opinion was filed.

The only difference between the Philadelphia case and this case, is that another copy of the same book has been here seized and libeled.

I think that the proper view of the meaning of the word "book" in Title 19, U.S.C., § 1305, (19 USCA § 1305), is not merely a few sheets of paper bound together in cloth or otherwise, but that a book means an assembly or concourse of ideas expressed in words, the subject matter which is embodied in the book, which is sought to be excluded, and not merely the physical object called a book which can be held in one's hands.

Assuming it is proper so to view the meaning of the word "book" in the statute under consideration, Judge Kirkpatrick's decision at Philadelphia in a proceeding in rem against this book is a bar to another similar proceeding such as this in this district.

I hold that Judge Kirkpatrick's decision established the book "Married Love" as having an admissible status at any point around the customs barriers of the United States. In this connection see Gelston v. Hoyt, 3 Wheat. 246, 312 to 316, 4 L. Ed. 381; Waples on Proceedings in Rem, §§ 87, 110, 111, 112, and cases therein cited.

It is perfectly obvious, I think, that, if a vessel had been libeled on a certain count for forfeiture at Philadelphia, and there acquitted of liability to forfeiture, on her coming around to New York she could not properly be libeled again on the same count. That is the real situation in the present case. Cf. United States v. 2180 Cases of Champagne, 9 F. (2d) 710, 712, 713 (C.C.A. 2).

III. However, in case the Circuit Court of Appeals, to which I presume this case will eventually be taken, should disagree with my construction of the word "book," and should consider that it was a copy of the book that was subject to exclusion, and not merely the book regarded as an embodiment of ideas, or should disagree with my application of the admiralty law to a situation of this kind, I will now deal with the case on the merits.

In Murray's Oxford English Dictionary the word "obscene" is defined as follows:

"Obscene—1. Offensive to the senses, or to taste or refinement; disgusting, repulsive, filthy, foul, abominable, loathsome. Now somewhat arch.

"2. Offensive to modesty or decency; expressing or suggesting unchaste or lustful ideas; impure, indecent, lewd."

In the same Dictionary the word "immoral" is defined as follows:

"Immoral—The opposite of moral; not moral.

"1. Not consistent with, or not conforming to, moral law or requirement; opposed to or violating morality; morally evil or impure; unprincipled, vicious, dissolute. (Of persons, things, actions, etc.)

"2. Not having a moral nature or character; non-moral."

The book "Married Love" does not, in my opinion, fall within these definitions of the words "obscene" or "immoral" in any respect.

Dr. Stopes treats quite as decently and with as much restraint of the sex relations as did Mrs. Mary Ware Dennett in "The Sex Side of Life, An Explanation for Young People," which was held not to be obscene by the Circuit Court of Appeals for this Circuit in United States v. Dennett, 39 F. (2d) 564.

The present book may fairly be said to do for adults what Mrs. Dennett's book does for adolescents.

The Dennett Case, as I read it, teaches that this Court must determine, as a matter of law in the first instance, whether the book alleged to be obscene falls in any sense within the definition of that word. If it does, liability to forfeiture becomes a question for the jury under proper instructions. If it does not, the question is one entirely for the Court.

"Married Love" is a considered attempt to explain to married people how their mutual sex life may be made happier.

To one who has read Havelock Ellis, as I have, the subject-matter of Dr. Stopes' book is not wholly new, but it emphasizes the woman's side of sex questions. It makes also some apparently justified criticisms of the inopportune exercise, by the man in the marriage relation of what are often referred to as his conjugal or marital rights, and it pleads with seriousness, and not without some eloquence, for a better understanding by husbands of the physical and emotional side of the sex life of their wives.

I do not find anything exceptionable anywhere in the book, and I cannot imagine a normal mind to which this book would seem to be obscene or immoral within the proper definition of these words or whose sex impulses would be stirred by reading it.

Whether or not the book is scientific in some of its theses is unimportant. It is informative and instructive and I think that any married folk who read it cannot fail to be benefited by its counsels of perfection and its frank discussion of the frequent difficulties which necessarily arise in the more intimate aspects of married life, for as Professor William G. Sumner used aptly to say in his lectures on the Science of Society at Yale, marriage, in its essence, is a status of antagonistic co-operation.

In such a status, necessarily, centripetal and centrifugal forces are continuously at work, and the measure of its success obviously depends on the extent to which the centripetal forces are predominant.

The book before me here has as its whole thesis the strengthening of the centripetal forces in marriage, and instead of being inhospitably received, it should, I think, be welcomed within our borders.

JAPANESE PESSARIES CASE

U.S. v. One Package
86 F. (2d) 737 (C.C.A. 2d 1936), affirming 13 F. Supp. 334 (S.D. N.Y. 1936).

Notwithstanding the fact that the customs statute prohibits the importation of contraceptive material and contains no exception in favor of physicians, it was held by the Circuit Court of Appeals that the importation by a licensed physician of a package containing rubber pessaries for the prevention of conception did not violate the statute, where the pessaries were sent for trial purposes and to obtain the physician's opinion as to their usefulness, and were prescribed to patients for whom it would not be desirable to undertake pregnancy. The Circuit Court of Appeals affirmed Judge Moscowitz's decision to the same effect in the District Court.

Before L. Hand, Swan, and August N. Hand, Circuit Judges.

Prevailing opinion by Augustus N. Hand, Circuit Judge:

The United States filed this libel against a package containing 120 vaginal pessaries more or less, alleged to be imported contrary to Section 305 (a) of the Tariff Act of 1930 (19 U.S.C.A. § 1305[a]). From the decree dismissing the libel the United States has appealed. In our opinion the decree should be affirmed.

The claimant Dr. Stone is a New York physician who has been licensed to practice for sixteen years and has specialized in gynecology. The package containing pessaries was sent to her by a physician in Japan for the purpose of trying them in her practice and giving her opinion as to their usefulness for contraceptive purposes. She testified that she prescribes the use of pessaries in cases where it would not be desirable for a patient to undertake a pregnancy. The accuracy and good faith of this testimony is not questioned. The New York Penal Law which makes it in general a misdemeanor to sell or give away or to advertise or offer for sale any articles for the prevention of conception excepts furnishing such articles to physicians who may in good faith prescribe their use for the cure or prevention of disease. People v. Sanger, 222 N.Y. 192, 118 N.E. 637. New York Penal Law (Consol. Laws, c.40) § 1145. The witnesses for both the government and the claimant testify that the use of contraceptives was in many cases necessary for the health of women and that they employed articles of the general nature of the pessaries in their practice. There was no dispute as to the truth of these statements.

Section 305 (a) of the Tariff Act of 1930 (19 U.S.C.A. § 1305[a]) provides that:

"All persons are prohibited from importing into the United States from any foreign country * * * any article whatever for the prevention of conception or for causing unlawful abortion * * * *"

The question is whether physicians who import such articles as those involved in the present case in order to use them for the health of their patients are excepted by implication from the literal terms of the statute. Certainly they are excepted in the case of an abortive which is prescribed to save life for Section 305 (a) of the Tariff Act only prohibits the importation of articles for causing "unlawful abortion". This was the very point decided in Bours v. United States, 229 F. 960 (C.C.A. 7), where a similar statute (Cr. Code, § 211 [18 U.S.C.A. § 334 and note]) declaring non-mailable "every article or thing designed, adapted, or intended for preventing conception or producing abortion or for any indecent or immoral use" was held not to cover physicians using the mails in order to say that they will operate upon a patient if an examination shows the necessity of an operation to save life. And this result was reached even though the statute in forbidding the mailing of any article "intended for * * * producing abortion" did not, as does Section 305 (a) of the Tariff Act, qualify the word "abortion" by the saving adjective "unlawful". In Youngs Rubber Corporation v. C. I. Lee & Co., 45 Fed. (2d) 103, (C.C.A. 2), Judge Swan, writing for this court, construed the mailing statute in the same way. In referring to the mailing of contraceptive articles bearing the plaintiff's trade-mark he adverted to the fact that the articles might be capable of legitimate use and said at page 108 of 45 F. (2d), when discussing the incidence of the mailing statute:

"The intention to prevent a proper medical use of drugs or other articles merely because they are capable of illegal uses is not lightly to be ascribed to Congress. Section 334 forbids also the mailing of obscene books and writings; yet it has never been thought to bar from the mails medical writings sent to or by physicians for proper purposes, though of a character which would render them highly indecent if sent broadcast to all classes of persons * * *. It would seem reasonable to give the word 'adapted' a more limited meaning than that above suggested and to construe the whole phrase 'designed, adapted or intended' as requiring an intent on the part of the sender that the article mailed * * * be used for illegal contraception or abortion or for indecent or immoral purposes."

While Judge Swan's remarks were perhaps dicta they are in full accord with the opinion of Judge Mack in Bours v. United States, (C.C.A.) 229 F. 960, which we have already mentioned, and were relied on by the Court of Appeals of the Sixth Circuit when construing the mailing statute in Davis v. United States, 62 F. (2d) 473.

Section 305 (a) of the Tariff Act of 1930, (19 U.S.C.A. § 1305[a]), as well as Title 18, Section 334, of the U.S. Code (18 U.S.C.A. § 334), prohibiting the mailing, and Title 18, Section 396 (18 U.S.C.A. § 396), of the U.S. Code prohibiting the importing or transporting in interstate commerce of articles "designed, adapted, or intended for preventing conception or producing abortion" all originated from the so-called Comstock Act of 1873, (17 Stat. 598) which was entitled "An

Act for the Suppression of Trade in and Circulation of Obscene Literature and Articles of Immoral Use."

Section 1 of the Act of 1873 made it a crime to sell, lend, or give
away, "any drug or medicine, or any article whatever, for the prevention of conception or for causing unlawful abortion". Section 2 prohibited sending through the mails "any article or thing designed or
intended for the prevention of conception or procuring of abortion".
Section 3 forbade the importation of "any of the hereinbefore mentioned articles or things, except the drugs hereinbefore mentioned when
imported in bulk, and not put up for any of the purposes before mentioned." All the statutes we have referred to were part of a continuous
scheme to suppress immoral articles and obscene literature and should
so far as possible be construed together and consistently. If this be done,
the articles here in question ought not to be forfeited when not intended for an immoral purpose. Such was the interpretation in the decisions of the Circuit Courts of Appeal of the Sixth and Seventh
Circuits and of this court in Youngs Rubber Corporation v. C. I. Lee
& Co., when construing the statute forbidding an improper use of the
mails.

It is argued that Section 305 (a) of the Tariff Act of 1930 (19
U.S.C.A. § 1305[a]) differs from the statutes prohibiting carriage by
mail and in interstate commerce of articles "intended for preventing
conception or producing abortion" because in Section 305 (a) the adjective "unlawful" is coupled with the word "abortion", but not with
the words "prevention of conception." But in the Comstock Act, from
which the others are derived, the word "unlawful" was sometimes
inserted to qualify the word "abortion", and sometimes omitted. It
seems hard to suppose that under the second and third sections articles
intended for use in procuring abortions were prohibited in all cases
while, under the first section, they were only prohibited when intended
for use in an "unlawful abortion." Nor can we see why the statute
should, at least in Section 1, except articles for producing abortions if
used to safeguard life, and bar articles for preventing conception
though employed by a physician in the practice of his profession in
order to protect the health of his patients or to save them from infection.

It is true that in 1873, when the Comstock Act was passed, information now available as to the evils resulting in many cases from conception was most limited and accordingly it is argued that the
language prohibiting the sale or mailing of contraceptives should be
taken literally and that Congress intended to bar the use of such
articles completely. While we may assume that Section 305 (a) of the
Tariff Act of 1930 (19 U.S.C.A. § 1305[a]) exempts only such articles
as the Act of 1873 excepted, yet we are satisfied that this statute, as
well as all the acts we have referred to, embraced only such articles
as Congress would have denounced as immoral if it had understood
all the conditions under which they were to be used. Its design, in our
opinion, was not to prevent the importation, sale, or carriage by mail
of things which might intelligently be employed by conscientious and

competent physicians for the purpose of saving life or promoting the
well being of their patients. The word "unlawful" would make this
clear as to articles for producing abortion and the courts have read
an exemption into the act covering such articles even where the word
"unlawful" is not used. The same exception should apply for preventing
conception. While it is true that the policy of Congress has been to forbid the use of contraceptives altogether if the only purpose of using
them be to prevent conception in cases where it would not be injurious
to the welfare of the patient or her offspring, it is going far beyond
such a policy to hold that abortions, which destroy incipient life, may
be allowed in proper cases, and yet that no measures may be taken to
prevent conception even though a likely result should be to require
the termination of pregnancy by means of an operation. It seems unreasonable to suppose that the national scheme of legislation involves
such inconsistencies and requires the complete suppression of articles,
the use of which in many cases is advocated by such a weight of
authority in the medical world.

The Comstock Bill, as originally introduced in the Senate, contained the words "except on a prescription of a physician in good
standing, given in good faith", but those words were omitted from
the bill as it was ultimately passed. The reason for amendment seems
never to have been discussed on the floor of Congress, or in Committee, and the remarks of Senator Conklin, when the bill was up for
passage in final form, indicate that the scope of the measure was not
well understood and that the language used was to be left largely for
future interpretation. We see no ground for holding that the construction placed upon similar language in the decisions we have referred to is not applicable to the articles which the government seeks
to forfeit, and common sense would seem to require a like interpretation in the case at bar.

The decree dismissing the libel is affirmed.

Concurring opinion by Learned Hand, Circuit Judge:

If the decision had been left to me alone, I should have felt more
strongly than my brothers the force of the Senate amendment in the
original act, and of the use of the word, "unlawful", as it passed.
There seems to me substantial reason for saying that contraconceptives
were meant to be forbidden, whether or not prescribed by physicians,
and that no lawful use of them was contemplated. Many people have
changed their minds about such matters in sixty years, but the act
forbids the same conduct now as then; a statute stands until public
feeling gets enough momentum to change it, which may be long after
a majority would repeal it, if a poll were taken. Nevertheless, I am
not prepared to dissent. I recognize that the course of the act
through Congress does not tell us very much, and it is of considerable
importance that the law as to importations should be the same as that
as to the mails; we ought not impute differences of intention upon

slight distinctions in expression. I am content therefore to accept my brothers' judgment, whatever might have been, and indeed still are, my doubts.

MARRIAGE HYGIENE CASE

U.S. v. Himes
U.S. v. Nicholas
97 F. (2d) 510 (C.C.A. 2d 1938), affirming 19 F. Supp. 1017 (S.D. N.Y. 1937) as to decree in Himes case and modifying the decree in Nicholas case.

In the *Himes* case it was held that *Marriage Hygiene,* a periodical containing detailed birth control information, and sent to Dr. Himes from abroad, should be released by the customs to Dr. Himes because he, as American editor of the magazine, was "qualified" to receive it, contraceptive books and pamphlets being "lawful in the hands of those who would not abuse the information they contained." Dr. Himes' right to receive such literature was not altered by the fact that material coming in at the customs ultimately had to be delivered by the Post Office, nor by the blanket prohibition against the transmission of birth control information in the mails.

It was held in the *Nicholas* case that the book entitled *Parenthood: Design or Accident* dealing with contraception, and mailed to Mr. Nicholas from abroad, should not be confiscated despite the absence of a showing that Mr. Nicholas was a "qualified" recipient, but should be sent to the Dead Letter Office, without prejudice to the sender's right to recover the book or the addressee's right to claim it upon proving his qualification.

Before L. Hand, Swan, and Chase, Circuit Judges:

Opinion by Learned Hand, Circuit Judge:

These are appeals from two decrees, dismissing libels of information against a book and certain copies of a magazine, all of which "represent" that articles described in them can be used to prevent conception, (§ 211, Criminal Code, 18 U.S.C.A. § 334), and give information "where, how or of whom" such articles "may be obtained", (§ 245, Criminal Code, 18 U.S.C.A. § 396). The publications came from abroad through the mails and were stopped at the Port of New York. The book was addressed to the claimant, Nicholas, about whom nothing appeared except that he was not a physician; the magazines were addressed to the claimant, Himes, who is the American editor of the magazine which is published in India. The Collector of the Port of New York after examination seized the publications as contraband and the District Attorney filed two libels to confiscate them under § 593 (b) of the Tariff Act of 1930, 19 U.S.C.A. § 1593 (b). When these came on for hearing the judge held that § 615, 19 U.S.C.A. § 1615, of the Tariff Act did not shift the burden of proof to the claimant, unless the publications were seized under some law "relating to the collection of duties on imports", which was not the case because no duties were payable upon them, their importation being forbidden. The libellant therefore failed, because it had not proved the scienter necessary under § 593(b).

We shall assume arguendo that that section covers any merchandise imported "contrary to law", even though the "law" is not part of the Tariff Act itself. We shall also assume arguendo, contrary to the judge below, that § 615 is not limited to cases in which the proposed forfeiture is for the violation of a law designed to protect the revenue of the United States, but that the phrase, "law relating to the collection of duties", is satisfied by any prosecution under § 593(b). We can make both these assumptions, because we think that § 593(b) does not cover contraconceptive publications for the following reasons. It does not define unlawful importation, but incorporates by reference such other statutes as do. In the case at bar only two statutes might answer—§ 211 and § 245 of the Criminal Code 18 U.S.C.A. §§ 334, 396—but we think that neither will. The Joint Regulations of the Treasury and the Post-Office govern the disposal of matter coming through the mail from abroad; Article 2(a) requires a customs officer to be present when mails are distributed, and to segregate all "printed matter". Articles whose importation is prohibited must be "taken and held by customs officers for appropriate treatment under the customs laws". Article 20(c). By § 2204(2) of the Post-Office regulations prohibited matter from abroad must be withdrawn from the mails and dealt with under § 725, which requires it to be sent to the Dead Letter Office. Second and third class mail must be so wrapped that "the contents of the package can be easily examined", Art. 581(a). Thus it appears that prohibited printed matter arriving by mail from abroad must inevitably be examined at the border and detained, and from this it seems to us to follow that it has not yet been imported or brought into the United States within § 593(b) 19 U.S.C.A. § 1593(b). If the sender has not actually invited the examination, at least he has in fact facilitated it, unlike the importer in United States v. Ritterman, 273 U.S. 261, 47 S. Ct. 371, 71 L. Ed. 636, who contrived and set in execution a plan, surreptitiously to introduce the goods, which would have succeeded if it had not been uncovered. We hold therefore that § 593(b) of the Tariff Act did not apply. This conclusion is confirmed by § 305, 19 U.S.C.A. § 1305, of the same act, which provided for the seizure among other things of contraconceptive drugs—but not of publications about them—upon their "appearance * * * at any customs office" where they shall be "held by the collector to await the judgment of the district court". Thus there are two statutes dealing with contraconceptive drugs; one which forfeits them on their "appearance" at the customs and the other when they are imported. It seems to us unlikely that § 305, 19 U.S.C.A. § 1305, should be wholly superseded, as it would be, if "appearance" and seizure were "importation"; and if

§ 593 (b), 19 U.S.C.A. § 1593 (b), does not include contraconceptive drugs stopped at the border, certainly the "appearance at a customs office" of contraconceptive books and pamphlets is not importation, for the same words cannot mean one thing as to one kind of goods and another as to another. It is probably true that the omission from § 305 was unintentional, but we are not free to supply the defect, or to twist § 593 (b) out of its meaning. Hence it seems to us that the judge was right in refusing to forfeit the res in either suit.

It does not follow that the publications should be delivered to the addressees. It is one thing to say that they may not be confiscated, and another that the Post-Office must forward them to the addressees in the teeth of §§ 211 and 245 of the Criminal Code 18 U.S.C.A. §§ 334, 396. Certainly that would have been unlawful, if the importation had been absolutely prohibited, or the mails absolutely denied to them. We have hitherto assumed that that was true, but it is not. We have twice decided that contraconceptive articles may have lawful uses and that statutes prohibiting them should be read as forbidding them only when unlawfully employed. Youngs Rubber Corp. v. C. I. Lee & Co., 2 Cir, 45 F. (2) 103; United States v. One Package, 2 Cir, 86 F. (2) 737. See also Davis v. United States, 6 Cir, 62 F. (2) 473. Contraconceptive books and pamphlets are of the same class, and those at bar were therefore lawful in the hands of those who would not abuse the information they contained. This excuses the magazines, addressed as they were to their local editor; being lawful in the hands of physicians, scientists and the like, the claimant at bar was their most appropriate distributor. True, he might misuse his privilege, but that does not cancel it; if he does, he will then be subject to punishment, but he is not so subject yet, nor can he now be deprived of his property. Hence we conclude that the decree was right as to the magazines. The same reasoning does not apply to the book, for the addressee may, or may not, be one of those in whose hands it would be lawful. The regulations, as we have seen, require prohibited matter to be detained, and while theoretically it would be possible to require the officials to prove that the addressee was not privileged in order to detain it, that would effectively frustrate the statute. Only the addressee can prove whether he is among the privileged classes; he ought at least to go forward with the evidence, even if the burden of proof is not eventually upon him. For these reasons we think that although the book may not be confiscated, it should not be delivered. It must go to the Dead Letter Office and its eventual disposition is not before us; but the decree will be without prejudice to any rights of the sender to recover his property.

Decree in United States v. Himes affirmed.

Decree in United States v. Nicholas modified to authorize disposition of the book seized in accordance with the Postal Regulations; this without prejudice to any rights of the sender.

APPENDIX B

CODE OF STANDARDS
FOR THE BROADCASTING INDUSTRY

Adopted July 11, 1939
by the
National Association of Broadcasters

Recognizing the importance of radio broadcasting in the national life and believing that broadcasters have sufficient experience with the social side of the industry to formulate basic standards for the guidance of all, the National Association of Broadcasters hereby formulates and publishes the following revised code:

CHILDREN'S PROGRAMS

Programs designed specifically for children reach impressionable minds and influence social attitudes, aptitudes and approaches and, therefore, they require the closest supervision of broadcasters in the selection and control of material, characterization and plot.

This does not mean that the vigor and vitality common to a child's imagination and love of adventure should be removed. It does mean that programs should be based upon sound social concepts and presented with a superior degree of craftsmanship; that these programs should reflect respect for parents, adult authority, law and order, clean living, high morals, fair play and honorable behavior. Such programs must not contain sequences involving horror or torture or use of the supernatural or superstitious or any other material which might reasonably be regarded as likely to over-stimulate the child listener, or be prejudicial to sound character development. No advertising appeal which would encourage activities of a dangerous social nature will be permitted.

To establish acceptable and improving standards for children's programs, the National Association of Broadcasters will continuously engage in studies and consultations with parent and child study groups. The results of these studies will be made available for application to all children's programs.

CONTROVERSIAL PUBLIC ISSUES

As part of their public service, networks and stations shall provide time for the presentation of public questions including those of controversial nature. Such time shall be allotted with due regard to all

313

the other elements of balanced program schedules and to the degree of public interest in the questions to be discussed. Broadcasters shall use their best efforts to allot such time with fairness to all elements in a given controversy.

Time for the presentation of controversial issues shall not be sold, except for political broadcasts. There are three fundamental reasons for this refusal to sell time for public discussion and, in its stead, providing time for it without charge.

First, it is a public duty of broadcasters to bring such discussion to the radio audience regardless of the willingness of others to pay for it.

Second, should time be sold for the discussion of controversial issues, it would have to be sold, in fairness, to all with the ability and desire to buy at any given time. Consequently, all possibility of regulating the amount of discussion on the air in proportion to other elements of properly balanced programing or allotting the available periods with due regard to listener interest in the topics to be discussed would be surrendered.

Third, and by far the most important, should time be sold for the discussion of controversial public issues and for the propagation of the views of individuals or groups, a powerful public forum would inevitably gravitate almost wholly into the hands of those with the greater means to buy it.

The political broadcasts excepted above are any broadcasts in connection with a political campaign in behalf of or against the candidacy of a legally qualified candidate for nomination or election to public office, or in behalf of or against a public proposal which is subject to ballot. This exception is made because at certain times the contending parties want to use and are entitled to use more time than broadcasters could possibly afford to give away.

Nothing in the prohibition against selling time for the presentation of controversial public issues shall be interpreted as barring sponsorship of the public forum type of program when such a program is regularly presented as a series of fair-sided discussions of public issues and when control of the fairness of the program rests wholly with the broadcasting station or network.

Educational Broadcasting

While all radio programs possess some educative values, broadcasters nevertheless desire to be of assistance in helping toward more specific educational efforts, and will continue to use their time and facilities to that end and, in cooperation with appropriate groups, will continue their search for improving applications of radio as an educational adjunct.

News:

News shall be presented with fairness and accuracy and the broadcasting station or network shall satisfy itself that the arrangements made for obtaining news insure this result. Since the number of broadcasting channels is limited, news broadcasts shall not be editorial. This means that news shall not be selected for the purpose of furthering or hindering either side of any controversial public issue nor shall it be colored by the opinions or desires of the station or network management, the editor or others engaged in its preparation or the person actually delivering it over the air, or, in the case of sponsored news broadcasts, the advertiser.

The fundamental purpose of news dissemination in a democracy is to enable people to know what is happening and to understand the meaning of events so that they may form their own conclusions and, therefore, nothing in the foregoing shall be understood as preventing news broadcasters from analyzing and elucidating news so long as such analysis and elucidation are free of bias.

News commentators as well as all other news casters shall be governed by these provisions.

RELIGIOUS BROADCASTS:

Radio, which reaches men of all creeds and races simultaneously, may not be used to convey attacks upon another's race or religion. Rather it should be the purpose of the religious broadcast to promote the spiritual harmony and understanding of mankind and to administer broadly to the varied religious needs of the community.

COMMERCIAL PROGRAMS AND LENGTH OF COMMERCIAL COPY

Acceptance of programs and announcements shall be limited to products and services offered by individuals and firms engaged in legitimate commerce, whose products, services, radio advertising, testimonials and other statements comply with pertinent legal requirements, fair trade practices and accepted standards of good taste.

Brief handling of commercial copy is recommended procedure at all times.

Member stations shall hold the length of commercial copy, including that devoted to contests and offers, to the following number of minutes and seconds:

Daytime

Fifteen-minute programs—3:15.
Thirty-minute programs—4:30.
Sixty-minute programs—9:00.

Nighttime

Fifteen-minute programs . . . . 2:30.
Thirty-minute programs . . . . 3:00.
Sixty-minute programs . . . . 6:00.

The above limitations do not apply to participation programs, announcement programs, "musical clocks," shoppers' guides and local programs falling within these general classifications.

Because of the varying economic and social conditions throughout the United States, members of the N.A.B. shall have the right to present to the N.A.B. for special ruling local situations which in the opinion of the member may justify exceptions to the above prescribed limitations.

Resolved, That the National Association of Broadcasters in convention assembled hereby adopts the code as presented; and

That the incoming board of directors be authorized to devise the machinery necessary to insure compliance of members with the code and to determine date of taking effect.

APPENDIX C

A CODE
TO GOVERN THE MAKING
OF MOTION AND TALKING
PICTURES
the
Reasons Supporting It
And the
Resolution for Uniform
Interpretation
by
Motion Picture Producers and Distributors of America, Inc.
JUNE 13, 1934

Motion picture producers recognize the high trust and confidence which have been placed in them by the people of the world and which have made motion pictures a universal form of entertainment.

They recognize their responsibility to the public because of this trust and because entertainment and art are important influences in the life of a nation.

Hence, though regarding motion pictures primarily as entertainment without any explicit purpose of teaching or propaganda, they know that the motion picture within its own field of entertainment may be directly responsible for spiritual or moral progress, for higher types of social life, and for much correct thinking.

During the rapid transition from silent to talking pictures they have realized the necessity and the opportunity of subscribing to a Code to govern the production of talking pictures and of reacknowledging this responsibility.

On their part, they ask from the public and from public leaders a sympathetic understanding of their purposes and problems and a spirit of cooperation that will allow them the freedom and opportunity necessary to bring the motion picture to a still higher level of wholesome entertainment for all the people.

GENERAL PRINCIPLES

1. No picture shall be produced which will lower the moral standards of those who see it. Hence the sympathy of the audience shall never be thrown to the side of crime, wrong-doing, evil or sin.

2. Correct standards of life, subject only to the requirements of drama and entertainment, shall be presented.

3. Law, natural or human, shall not be ridiculed, nor shall sympathy be created for its violation.

PARTICULAR APPLICATIONS

I. CRIMES AGAINST THE LAW

These shall never be presented in such a way as to throw sympathy with the crime as against law and justice or to inspire others with a desire for imitation.

1. Murder
   a. The technique of murder must be presented in a way that will not inspire imitation.
   b. Brutal killings are not to be presented in detail.
   c. Revenge in modern times shall not be justified.
2. Methods of Crime should not be explicitly presented.
   a. Theft, robbery, safe-cracking, and dynamiting of trains, mines, buildings, etc., should not be detailed in method.
   b. Arson must be subject to the same safeguards.
   c. The use of firearms should be restricted to essentials.
   d. Methods of smuggling should not be presented.
3. Illegal drug traffic must never be presented.
4. The use of liquor in American life, when not required by the plot or for proper characterization, will not be shown.

II. SEX

The sanctity of the institution of marriage and the home shall be upheld. Pictures shall not infer that low forms of sex relationship are the accepted or common thing.

1. Adultery, sometimes necessary plot material, must not be explicitly treated, or justified, or presented attractively.
2. Scenes of Passion.
   a. They should not be introduced when not essential to the plot.
   b. Excessive and lustful kissing, lustful embraces, suggestive postures and gestures, are not to be shown.
   c. In general passion should so be treated that these scenes do not stimulate the lower and baser element.
3. Seduction or Rape
   a. They should never be more than suggested, and only when essential for the plot, and even then never shown by explicit method.
   b. They are never the proper subject for comedy.
4. Sex perversion or any inference to it is forbidden.
5. White slavery shall not be treated.
6. Miscegenation (sex relationship between the white and black races) is forbidden.
7. Sex hygiene and venereal diseases are not subjects for motion pictures.

8. Scenes of actual childbirth, in fact or in silhouette, are never to be presented.

9. Children's sex organs are never to be exposed.

III. VULGARITY
The treatment of low, disgusting, unpleasant, though not necessarily evil, subjects should be subject always to the dictate of good taste and a regard for the sensibilities of the audience.

IV. OBSCENITY
Obscenity in word, gesture, reference, song, joke, or by suggestion (even when likely to be understood only by part of the audience) is forbidden.

V. PROFANITY
Pointed profanity (this includes the words, God, Lord, Jesus, Christ —unless used reverently—hell, S. O. B., damn, Gawd), or every other profane or vulgar expression however used, is forbidden.

VI. COSTUME
1. Complete nudity is never permitted. This includes nudity in fact or in silhouette, or any lecherous or licentious notice thereof by other characters in the picture.
2. Undressing scenes should be avoided, and never used save where essential to the plot.
3. Indecent or undue exposure is forbidden.
4. Dancing costumes intended to permit undue exposure or indecent movements in the dance are forbidden.

VII. DANCES
1. Dances suggesting or representing sexual actions or indecent passion are forbidden.
2. Dances which emphasize indecent movements are to be regarded as obscene.

VIII. RELIGION
1. No film or episode may throw ridicule on any religious faith.
2. Ministers of religion in their character as ministers of religion should not be used as comic characters or as villains.
3. Ceremonies of any definite religion should be carefully and respectfully handled.

IX. LOCATIONS
The treatment of bedrooms must be governed by good taste and delicacy.

X. NATIONAL FEELINGS
1. The use of the Flag shall be consistently respectful.
2. The history, institutions, prominent people and citizenry of other nations shall be represented fairly.

XI. TITLES

Salacious, indecent or obscene titles shall not be used.

XII. REPELLENT SUBJECTS

The following subjects must be treated within the careful limits of good taste:

1. Actual hangings or electrocutions as legal punishments for crime.
2. Third Degree methods.
3. Brutality and possible gruesomeness.
4. Branding of people or animals.
5. Apparent cruelty to children or animals.
6. The sale of women, or a woman selling her virtue.
7. Surgical operations.

REASONS SUPPORTING PREAMBLE OF CODE

1. Theatrical motion pictures, that is, pictures intended for the theatre as distinct from pictures intended for churches, schools, lecture halls, educational movements, social reform movements, etc., are primarily to be regarded as ENTERTAINMENT.

   Mankind has always recognized the importance of entertainment and its value in rebuilding the bodies and souls of human beings.

   But it has always recognized that entertainment can be of a character either HELPFUL or HARMFUL to the human race, and in consequence has clearly distinguished between:

   a. Entertainment which tends to improve the race, or at least to re-create and rebuild human beings exhausted with the realities of life; and

   b. Entertainment which tends to degrade human beings, or to lower their standards of life and living.

   Hence the MORAL IMPORTANCE of entertainment is something which has been universally recognized. It enters intimately into the lives of men and women and affects them closely; it occupies their minds and affections during leisure hours; and ultimately touches the whole of their lives. A man may be judged by his standard of entertainment as easily as by the standard of his work.

   So correct entertainment raises the whole standard of a nation. Wrong entertainment lowers the whole living conditions and moral ideals of a race.

   Note, for example, the healthy reactions to healthful, moral sports, like baseball, golf; the unhealthy reactions to sports like cockfighting, bullfighting, bear baiting, etc.

Note, too, the effect on ancient nations of gladiatorial com-
bats, the obscene plays of Roman times, etc.

2. Motion pictures are very important as ART.
Though a new art, possibly a combination art, it has the same
object as the other arts, the presentation of human thought, emo-
tion, and experience, in terms of an appeal to the soul through the
senses.
Here, as in entertainment:
Art enters intimately into the lives of human beings.
Art can be morally good, lifting men to higher levels. This has
been done through good music, great painting, authentic fiction,
poetry, drama.
Art can be morally evil in its effects. This is the case clearly
enough with unclean art, indecent books, suggestive drama.
The effect on the lives of men and women is obvious.
Note: It has often been argued that art in itself is unmoral,
neither good nor bad. This is perhaps true of the THING
which is music, painting, poetry, etc. But the thing is the
PRODUCT of some person's mind, and the intention of that
mind was either good or bad morally when it produced the
thing. Besides, the thing has its EFFECT upon those who come
into contact with it. In both these ways, that is, as a product
of a mind and as the cause of definite effects, it has a deep
moral significance and an unmistakable moral quality.
Hence: The motion pictures, which are the most popular of
modern arts for the masses, have their moral quality from the
intention of the minds which produce them and from their
effects on the moral lives and reactions of their audiences. This
gives them a most important morality.
  1. They reproduce the morality of the men who use the pic-
     tures as a medium for the expression of their ideas and
     ideals.
  2. They affect the moral standards of those who through the
     screen take in these ideas and ideals.
In the case of the motion pictures, this effect may be particularly emphasized because no art has so quick and so widespread
an appeal to the masses. It has become in an incredibly short
period the art of the multitudes.

3. The motion picture, because of its importance as an entertainment
and because of the trust placed in it by the peoples of the world,
has special MORAL OBLIGATIONS:
A. Most arts appeal to the mature. This art appeals at once to
every class, mature, immature, developed, undeveloped, law
abiding, criminal. Music has its grades for different classes;
so has literature and drama. This art of the motion picture,
combining as it does the two fundamental appeals of looking

at a picture and listening to a story, at once reaches every class of society.

B. By reason of the mobility of a film and the ease of picture distribution, and because of the possibility of duplicating positives in large quantities, this art reaches places unpenetrated by other forms of art.

C. Because of these two facts, it is difficult to produce films intended for only certain classes of people. The exhibitor's theatres are built for the masses, for the cultivated and the rude, the mature and the immature, the self-respecting and the criminal. Films, unlike books and music, can with difficulty be confined to certain selected groups.

D. The latitude given to film material cannot, in consequence, be as wide as the latitude given to book material. In addition:

   a. A book describes; a film vividly presents. One presents on a cold page; the other by apparently living people.

   b. A book reaches the mind through words merely; a film reaches the eyes and ears through the reproduction of actual events.

   c. The reaction of a reader to a book depends largely on the keenness of the reader's imagination; the reaction to a film depends on the vividness of presentation.

   Hence many things which might be described or suggested in a book could not possibly be presented in a film.

E. This is also true when comparing the film with the newspaper.

   a. Newspapers present by description, films by actual presentation.

   b. Newspapers are after the fact and present things as having taken place; the film gives the events in the process of enactment and with the apparent reality of life.

F. Everything possible in a play is not possible in a film.

   a. Because of the larger audience of the film, and its consequential mixed character. Psychologically, the larger the audience, the lower the moral mass resistance to suggestion.

   b. Because through light, enlargement of character, presentation, scenic emphasis, etc., the screen story is brought closer to the audience than the play.

   c. The enthusiasm for and interest in the film actors and actresses, developed beyond anything of the sort in history, makes the audience largely sympathetic toward the characters they portray and the stories in which they figure. Hence the audience is more ready to confuse actor and actress and the characters they portray, and it is most receptive of the emotions and ideals presented by their favorite stars.

G. Small communities, remote from sophistication and from the hardening process which often takes place in the ethical and moral standards of groups in larger cities, are easily and readily reached by any sort of film.

H. The grandeur of mass settings, large action, spectacular features, etc., affects and arouses more intensely the emotional side of the audience.

In general, the mobility, popularity, accessibility, emotional appeal, vividness, straightforward presentation of fact in the film make for more intimate contact with a larger audience and for greater emotional appeal.

Hence the larger moral responsibilities of the motion pictures.

Reasons Supporting the General Principles

1. No picture shall be produced which will lower the moral standards of those who see it. Hence the sympathy of the audience should never be thrown to the side of crime, wrong-doing, evil or sin.

    This is done:

    1. When evil is made to appear attractive or alluring, and good is made to appear unattractive.
    2. When the sympathy of the audience is thrown on the side of crime, wrong-doing, evil, sin. The same thing is true of a film that would throw sympathy against goodness, honor, innocence, purity or honesty.

    Note: Sympathy with a person who sins is not the same as sympathy with the sin or crime of which he is guilty. We may feel sorry for the plight of the murderer or even understand the circumstances which led him to his crime. We may not feel sympathy with the wrong which he has done.

    The presentation of evil is often essential for art or fiction or drama.

    This in itself is not wrong provided:

    a. That evil is not presented alluringly. Even if later in the film the evil is condemned or punished, it must not be allowed to appear so attractive that the audience's emotions are drawn to desire or approve so strongly that later the condemnation is forgotten and only the apparent joy of the sin remembered.
    b. That throughout, the audience feels sure that evil is wrong and good is right.

2. Correct standards of life shall, as far as possible, be presented. A wide knowledge of life and of living is made possible through the film. When right standards are consistently presented, the motion picture exercises the most powerful influences. It builds character, develops right ideals, inculcates correct principles, and all this in the attractive story form.

If motion pictures consistently hold up for admiration high types of characters and present stories that will affect lives for the better, they can become the most powerful natural force for the improvement of mankind.

3. Law, natural or human, shall not be ridiculed, nor shall sympathy be created for its violation.

By natural law is understood the law which is written in the hearts of all mankind, the great underlying principles of right and justice dictated by conscience.

By human law is understood the law written by civilized nations.

1. The presentation of crimes against the law is often necessary for the carrying out of the plot. But the presentation must not throw sympathy with the crime as against the law nor with the criminal as against those who punish him.

2. The courts of the land should not be presented as unjust. This does not mean that a single court may not be represented as unjust, much less that a single court official must not be presented this way. But the court system of the country must not suffer as a result of this presentation.

REASONS UNDERLYING PARTICULAR APPLICATIONS

Preliminary:

1. Sin and evil enter into the story of human beings and hence in themselves are dramatic material.

2. In the use of this material, it must be distinguished between sin which repels by its very nature, and sins which often attract.

a. In the first class come murder, most theft, many legal crimes, lying, hypocrisy, cruelty, etc.

b. In the second class come sex sins, sins and crimes of apparent heroism, such as banditry, daring thefts, leadership in evil, organized crime, revenge, etc.

The first class needs far less care in treatment, as sins and crimes of this class are naturally unattractive. The audience instinctively condemns and is repelled.

Hence the important objective must be to avoid the hardening of the audience, especially of those who are young and impressionable, to the thought and fact of crime. People can become accustomed even to murder, cruelty, brutality, and repellent crimes, if these are sufficiently repeated.

The second class needs real care in handling, as the response of human natures to their appeal is obvious. This is treated more fully below.

3. A careful distinction can be made between films intended for general distribution, and films intended for use in theatres re-

stricted to a limited audience. Themes and plots quite appropriate for the latter would be altogether out of place and dangerous in the former.

Note: In general the practice of using a general theatre and limiting its patronage during the showing of a certain film to "Adults Only" is not completely satisfactory and is only partially effective.

However, maturer minds may easily understand and accept without harm subject matter in plots which do younger people positive harm.

Hence: If there should be created a special type of theatre, catering exclusively to an adult audience, for plays of this character (plays with problem themes, difficult discussions and maturer treatment) it would seem to afford an outlet, which does not now exist, for pictures unsuitable for general distribution but permissible for exhibitions to a restricted audience.

I. CRIMES AGAINST THE LAW

The treatment of crimes against the law must not:

1. Teach methods of crime.
2. Inspire potential criminals with a desire for imitation.
3. Make criminals seem heroic and justified.

Revenge in modern times shall not be justified. In lands and ages of less developed civilization and moral principles, revenge may sometimes be presented. This would be the case especially in places where no law exists to cover the crime because of which revenge is committed.

Because of its evil consequences, the drug traffic should not be presented in any form. The existence of the trade should not be brought to the attention of audiences.

The use of liquor should never be excessively presented even in picturing countries where its use is legal. In scenes from American life, the necessities of plot and proper characterization alone justify its use. And in this case, it should be shown with moderation.

II. SEX

Out of regard for the sanctity of marriage and the home, the triangle, that is, the love of a third party for one already married, needs careful handling. The treatment should not throw sympathy against marriage as an institution.

Scenes of passion must be treated with an honest acknowledgment of human nature and its normal reactions. Many scenes cannot be presented without arousing dangerous emotions on the part of the immature, the young or the criminal classes.

Even within the limits of pure love, certain facts have been universally regarded by lawmakers as outside the limits of safe presentation.

In the case of impure love, the love which society has always regarded as wrong and which has been banned by divine law, the following are important:

1. Impure love must not be presented as attractive and beautiful.
2. It must not be the subject of comedy or farce, or treated as material for laughter.
3. It must not be presented in such a way as to arouse passion or morbid curiosity on the part of the audience.
4. It must not be made to seem right and permissible.
5. In general, it must not be detailed in method and manner.

III. VULGARITY; IV. OBSCENITY; V. PROFANITY, hardly need further explanation than is contained in the Code.

VI. COSTUME
General principles:

1. The effect of nudity or semi-nudity upon the normal man or woman, and much more upon the young and upon immature persons, has been honestly recognized by all lawmakers and moralists.
2. Hence the fact that the nude or semi-nude body may be beautiful does not make its use in the films moral. For, in addition to its beauty, the effect of the nude or semi-nude body on the normal individual must be taken into consideration.
3. Nudity or semi-nudity used simply to put a "punch" into a picture comes under the head of immoral actions. It is immoral in its effect on the average audience.
4. Nudity can never be permitted as being necessary for the plot. Semi-nudity must not result in undue or indecent exposures.
5. Transparent or translucent materials and silhouette are frequently more suggestive than actual exposure.

VII. DANCES
Dancing in general is recognized as an art and as a beautiful form of expressing human emotions.
But dances which suggest or represent sexual actions, whether performed solo or with two or more, dances intended to excite the emotional reaction of an audience, dances with movement of the breasts, excessive body movements while the feet are stationary, violate decency and are wrong.

VIII. RELIGION
The reason why ministers of religion may not be comic characters or villains is simply because the attitude taken toward them may easily become the attitude taken toward religion in general. Religion is low-

ered in the minds of the audience because of the lowering of the audience's respect for a minister.

IX. LOCATIONS
Certain places are so closely and thoroughly associated with sexual life or with sexual sin that their use must be carefully limited.

X. NATIONAL FEELINGS
The just rights, history, and feelings of any nation are entitled to consideration and respectful treatment.

XI. TITLES
As the title of a picture is the brand on that particular type of goods, it must conform to the ethical practices of all such honest business.

XII. REPELLENT SUBJECTS
Such subjects are occasionally necessary for the plot. Their treatment must never offend good taste nor injure the sensibilities of an audience.

RESOLUTION FOR UNIFORM INTERPRETATION as amended June 13, 1934.

1. When requested by production managers, the Motion Picture Producers & Distributors of America, Incorporated, shall secure any facts, information or suggestions concerning the probable reception of stories or the manner in which in its opinion they may best be treated.

2. That each production manager shall submit in confidence a copy of each or any script to the Production Code Administration of the Motion Picture Producers & Distributors of America, Incorporated, (and of the Association of Motion Picture Producers, Inc., California). Such Production Code Administration will give the production manager for his guidance such confidential advice and suggestions as experience, research, and information indicate, designating wherein in its judgment the script departs from the provisions of the Code, or wherein from experience or knowledge it is believed that exception will be taken to the story or treatment.

3. Each production manager of a company belonging to the Motion Picture Producers & Distributors of America, Incorporated, and any producer proposing to distribute and/or distributing his picture through the facilities of any member of the Motion Picture Producers & Distributors of America, Incorporated, shall submit to such Production Code Administration every picture he produces before the negative goes to the laboratory for printing. Said Production Code Administration, having seen the picture, shall inform the production manager in writing whether in its opinion the picture conforms or does not conform

to the Code, stating specifically wherein either by theme, treatment or incident, the picture violates the provisions of the Code. In such latter event, the picture shall not be released until the changes indicated by the Production Code Administration have been made; provided, however, that the production manager may appeal from such opinion of said Production Code Administration, so indicated in writing, to the Board of Directors of the Motion Picture Producers & Distributors of America, Incorporated, whose finding shall be final, and such production manager and company shall be governed accordingly.

I, Carl E. Milliken, Secretary of the Motion Picture Producers and Distributors of America, Inc., hereby certify that the foregoing is a true and correct copy of the Production Code, Reasons Supporting the Code, and Resolution For Uniform Interpretation, as amended, of the Motion Picture Producers and Distributors of America, Inc.

IN WITNESS WHEREOF I have hereunto set my hand and affixed the seal of the said Association this 10th day of December, 1934.

CARL E. MILLIKEN
Secretary.

INDEX

INDEX